EARLY WORD LEARNING

Early Word Learning explores the processes leading to a young child learning words and their meanings. Word learning is here understood as the outcome of overlapping and interacting processes, starting with an infant's learning of native speech sounds to segmenting proto-words from fluent speech, mapping individual words to meanings in the face of natural variability and uncertainty, and developing a structured mental lexicon.

Experts in the field review the development of early lexical acquisition from empirical, computational and theoretical perspectives to examine the development of skilled word learning as the outcome of a process that begins even before birth and spans the first two years of life. Drawing on cutting-edge research in infant eye-tracking, neuroimaging techniques and computational modeling, this book surveys the field covering both established results and the most recent advances in word learning research.

Featuring chapters from international experts whose research approaches the topic from these diverse perspectives using different methodologies, this book provides a comprehensive yet coherent and unified representation of early word learning. It will be invaluable for both undergraduate and postgraduate courses in early language development as well as being of interest to researchers interested in lexical development.

Gert Westermann is Professor of Psychology at Lancaster University. He is the Director of the Leverhulme Doctoral Scholarship Programme in Interdisciplinary Research on Infant Development and currently holds a British Academy/Leverhulme Trust Senior Research Fellowship.

Nivedita Mani is Professor of Psychology at Georg-August-Universität Göttingen in Germany. In 2014 she won the Fritz-Behrens Stiftung's Science Prize and became a Member of the Göttingen Academy of Sciences and Humanities in 2017.

Current Issues in Developmental Psychology
Series Editor: Margaret Harris
Professor of Psychology, Oxford Brookes University, UK

Current Issues in Developmental Psychology is a series of edited books that reflect the state-of-the-art areas of current and emerging interest in the psychological study of human development. Each volume is tightly focused on a particular topic and consists of seven to ten chapters contributed by international experts. The editors of individual volumes are leading figures in their areas and provide an introductory overview. Example topics include: developmental disorders, implicit knowledge, gender development, word learning and categorization.

Published titles in the series
Gender and Development
Edited by Patrick Leman and Harriet Tenenbaum

Trust and Skepticism
Children's Selective Learning from Testimony
Edited by Elizabeth J. Robinson and Shiri Einav

Current Issues in Developmental Disorders
Edited by Chloë R. Marshall

New Perspectives on Moral Development
Edited by Charles C. Helwig

Early Word Learning
Edited by Gert Westermann and Nivedita Mani

Understanding Motor Behaviour in Developmental Coordination Disorder
Edited by Anna Barnett and Elisabeth Hill

EARLY WORD LEARNING

*Edited by Gert Westermann
and Nivedita Mani*

Routledge
Taylor & Francis Group
LONDON AND NEW YORK

First published 2018
by Routledge
2 Park Square, Milton Park, Abingdon, Oxon OX14 4RN

and by Routledge
711 Third Avenue, New York, NY 10017

Routledge is an imprint of the Taylor & Francis Group, an informa business

© 2018 selection and editorial matter, Gert Westermann and Nivedita Mani; individual chapters, the contributors

The right of Gert Westermann and Nivedita Mani to be identified as the authors of the editorial material, and of the authors for their individual chapters, has been asserted in accordance with sections 77 and 78 of the Copyright, Designs and Patents Act 1988.

All rights reserved. No part of this book may be reprinted or reproduced or utilized in any form or by any electronic, mechanical, or other means, now known or hereafter invented, including photocopying and recording, or in any information storage or retrieval system, without permission in writing from the publishers.

Trademark notice: Product or corporate names may be trademarks or registered trademarks, and are used only for identification and explanation without intent to infringe.

British Library Cataloguing-in-Publication Data
A catalogue record for this book is available from the British Library

Library of Congress Cataloging-in-Publication Data
Names: Westermann, Gert, 1966- editor. | Mani, Nivedita, 1980- editor.
Title: Early word learning / edited by Gert Westermann & Nivedita Mani.
Description: Milton Park, Abingdon, Oxon ; New York, NY : Routledge, [2017]
Identifiers: LCCN 2017026347| ISBN 9781138843516 (hardback : alk. paper) |
ISBN 9781138843523 (pbk. : alk. paper) | ISBN 9781315730974 (ebk.)
Subjects: LCSH: Vocabulary—Study and teaching (Early childhood) | Children—Language. | Lexicology—Psychological aspects | Language awareness in children. | Psycholinguistics.
Classification: LCC PE1449 .E24 2017 | DDC 401/.93—dc23
LC record available at https://lccn.loc.gov/2017026347

ISBN: 978-1-138-84351-6 (hbk)
ISBN: 978-1-138-84352-3 (pbk)
ISBN: 978-1-315-73097-4 (ebk)

Typeset in Bembo
by Keystroke, Neville Lodge, Tettenhall, Wolverhampton

To our early word learners Karl Xunguang and Elise Yuanting (GW), and Mark Siddharth and Mayur Theodor (NM).

CONTENTS

List of contributors ix
Preface xi

1 Before the word: Acquiring a phoneme inventory 1
  Titia Benders and Nicole Altvater-Mackensen

2 The proto-lexicon: Segmenting word-like units from the
  speech stream 15
  Caroline Junge

3 Intrinsic and extrinsic cues to word learning 30
  Padraic Monaghan, Marina Kalashnikova, and Karen Mattock

4 Mapping words to objects 44
  Jessica S. Horst

5 Building a lexical network 57
  Nivedita Mani and Arielle Borovsky

6 Verbs: Learning how speakers use words to refer to actions 70
  Jane B. Childers, Angeline Bottera, and Tyler Howard

7 Listening to (and listening through) variability during
  word learning 83
  Katherine S. White

8	Individual differences in early word learning *Meredith L. Rowe and Kathryn A. Leech*	96
9	Early bilingual word learning *Christopher Fennell and Casey Lew-Williams*	110
10	ERP indices of word learning: What do they reflect and what do they tell us about the neural representations of early words? *Manuela Friedrich*	123
11	Computational models of word learning *Gert Westermann and Katherine Twomey*	138
Index		*155*

CONTRIBUTORS

Nicole Altvater-Mackensen, Department of Psychology, Johannes-Gutenberg-University Mainz, Germany

Titia Benders, Department of Linguistics, Macquarie University, Australia

Arielle Borovsky, Speech, Language and Hearing Sciences, Purdue University, West Lafayette, Indiana, USA

Angeline Bottera, Department of Psychology, Trinity University, USA

Jane B. Childers, Department of Psychology, Trinity University, USA

Christopher Fennell, University of Ottawa, Canada

Manuela Friedrich, Humboldt-University Berlin, Institute of Psychology, Germany, and the Max Planck Institute for Human Cognitive and Brain Sciences, Department of Neuropsychology, Leipzig, Germany

Jessica S. Horst, University of Sussex, School of Psychology, Brighton, UK

Tyler Howard, Department of Psychology, Trinity University, USA

Caroline Junge, Departments of Experimental and Developmental Psychology, Utrecht University, the Netherlands

Marina Kalashnikova, The MARCS Institute, University of Western Sydney, Australia

Kathryn A. Leech, Harvard Graduate School of Education, USA

Casey Lew-Williams, Princeton University, USA

Nivedita Mani, Psychology of Language Research Group, Georg-August-Universität Göttingen, Germany

Karen Mattock, School of Social Sciences & Psychology and The MARCS Institute, University of Western Sydney, Australia

Padraic Monaghan, Department of Psychology, Lancaster University, UK

Meredith L. Rowe, Harvard Graduate School of Education, USA

Katherine Twomey, Department of Psychology, Lancaster University, UK

Gert Westermann, Department of Psychology, Lancaster University, UK

Katherine S. White, Department of Psychology, University of Waterloo, Canada

PREFACE

One of the core challenges in early language development is for infants and toddlers to learn about the words in their language and the concepts to which these words refer. As a consequence, the study of early word learning has long been a vibrant domain of research at the junction of developmental psychology and language development.

At first glance, word learning may seem like a relatively simple task, at least when compared to the demands of learning grammar: here is a word, there, an object, and all that the child needs to do is to learn the link between the two. However, closer enquiry quickly shows that this view is too simplistic and that mapping words to objects or concepts is just one step in a complex process. Early word learners must first learn the sounds of their language, that is, they must learn which sounds belong to their native language and learn to recognize when two sounds are merely different tokens of the same sound category and when two sounds belong to two different categories. Then, they must become able to group sequences of sounds to form meaningful word-like units and to extract these units from fluent speech, often without prior familiarity with the phonological form of these word-like units. Furthermore, in mapping words to objects, they must deal with ambiguity and uncertainty as well as variation in the language they hear. That is, among other things they must learn, on the one hand, which of the many unfamiliar objects in their immediate environment is referred to by a word and, on the other hand, that two tokens of the same word, spoken by different people with different accents in different settings, refer to the same object. Once a sufficient mass of words has been learnt, it probably makes intuitive sense for the child to start noting the commonalities between words so that the words can be organized in a systematic way. Thus, children must build a mental lexicon that reflects the semantic, phonological and other perceptual relations between words. This word learning task is further complicated when the child must learn the meanings of words that refer to abstract concepts (e.g., adjectives) and actions (e.g., verbs) where a particular word is presented across a variety of objects and situations, or when the bilingual child must learn to associate two words from two different languages to the same object or concept. Finally, learned lexical representations must be refined such that words can be recognized with ease even in the face of speaker and accent variability, and even in the absence of specific referents for these words.

In this book we aim to reflect these aspects of early word learning and consider word learning as a continuous learning process, going from the early stages of children learning the speech sounds of their language(s) and extracting word-like units from a fluent speech stream to associating words with meaning, and to refining lexical representations such that they are recognized in the face of natural variability and uncertainty. This perspective stands in contrast to previous approaches to early word learning that typically focus on how children initially map meaning onto words. Word learning, for us, begins well before the child maps meanings onto word-forms and continues across development even after the child has learnt to associate a specific word with a specific object. We believe, therefore, that this book presents the reader with a novel and integrated perspective on word learning that highlights the continuity of the word learning process throughout early development.

The chapters in this book can be roughly grouped into three sections. Chapters 1–5 traverse the different aspects of early word learning described above. In Chapter 1, Benders and Altvater-Mackensen review the main experimental findings and theoretical positions on infants' acquisition of their native phoneme system both in perception and production, and they discuss how speech perception shows continuity with later word learning. In Chapter 2, Junge describes the main theories of how infants can find possible word candidates in continuous speech, and she reviews experimental work on when and how infants achieve this ability while highlighting how infants' speech segmentation skills predict later vocabulary knowledge. In Chapter 3, Monaghan, Kalashnikova and Mattock discuss the learning biases and linguistic and environmental cues that help young word learners to identify the referents for words. Here the focus is on extrinsic cues that involve the structure of heard utterances, prosody and gestures. Chapter 4 by Horst asks how children become able to map words onto objects from the age of six months, how knowledge of objects' names influences knowledge of these objects and how learned object names become consolidated. Finally, Mani and Borovsky in Chapter 5 discuss the early development of lexical structure; that is, how learned words are organized in memory, and how this developing structure affects the learning of further words.

Chapters 6–9 then consider more specialist aspects of early word learning. In Chapter 6, Childers, Bottera and Howard describe empirical research on the learning and generalization of verb meanings and discuss two influential theories of this ability. Both Chapters 7 and 8 deal with variability in word learning but from very different perspectives. Chapter 7 by White asks how children cope with variability in their input due to speakers' accents and speaker variability in general, and how this flexibility to process variability is balanced with the need for representations that are detailed enough to distinguish similar-sounding words such as *bear* and *pear*. Rowe and Leech in Chapter 8 discuss individual differences in early word learners and the potential factors affecting these differences such as gender, temperament, family socioeconomic status, and quantity and quality of speech input. In Chapter 9, Fennell and Lew-Williams review the literature on early word learning in bilingual children and discuss how bilingual word learning differs (or not) from that in monolinguals.

Chapters 10 and 11 are based around methodologies that are used in the study of early word learning. While the majority of research in this field employs behavioral paradigms and measures children's choices, responses and looking behavior, Friedrich in Chapter 10 extends these approaches by describing the contribution made by event-related potentials (ERP) as a measure of the neural processes associated with word learning in infants. After providing a background in this technique and describing the known markers associated with word learning and processing, this chapter discusses the additional insights into early word learning gained by complementing behavioral with neurophysiological studies. Finally, in Chapter 11, Westermann and Twomey address the role of computational modeling as a method to develop and test specific theories of the mechanism underlying word learning. This chapter provides an introduction into the principles of computational, and specifically, neural network models of cognitive development and then discusses a range of models that have addressed the various aspects of early word learning treated in the other chapters.

We hope that this book will be useful for a wide readership. Advanced undergraduate and (post)graduate students can use it to gain a comprehensive overview of the many facets of word learning in infants and toddlers. Experienced researchers can find a cutting-edge treatment of the different aspects of early word learning written by experts in their field.

The original idea for this book was developed while Gert Westermann was a fellow at the Lichtenberg Kolleg at Georg-August-Universität Göttingen hosted by Nivedita Mani, and funding for this fellowship is gratefully acknowledged. The completion of this book was supported by the ESRC International Centre for Language and Communicative Development (LuCiD; [ES/L008955/1]) and by a British Academy/Leverhulme Trust Senior Research Fellowship (SF150163) to Gert Westermann, and funding from the German Research Foundation (FOR 2253, GRK 2070) and the Fritz-Behrens Stiftung to Nivedita Mani as well as the Excellence Initiative of the German Research Foundation (Institutional Strategy) to Georg-August-Universität Göttingen.

Gert Westermann
Nivedita Mani
May 2017

1

BEFORE THE WORD

Acquiring a phoneme inventory

Titia Benders
DEPARTMENT OF LINGUISTICS, MACQUARIE UNIVERSITY, AUSTRALIA

Nicole Altvater-Mackensen
DEPARTMENT OF PSYCHOLOGY, JOHANNES-GUTENBERG-
UNIVERSITY MAINZ, GERMANY

Introduction

One of the benchmark questions parents are asked about their child's language development is 'Does she already say some words?'. While the first word is very tangible proof that a child's language development has taken off, that first word is part of a developmental trajectory including babbling, word comprehension and— one of infants' very first accomplishments on the way to the first word—the acquisition of language-specific sound perception. The current chapter reviews the main experimental findings and theoretical positions on infants' acquisition of the native phoneme system. In particular, we will discuss how speech perception and production evolve in the early stages of language development and how speech perception shows continuity with later word learning. We first introduce general developments in speech perception and production in the first year of life and present the main theoretical views on the developmental relationship between perception, production and word learning. The second and third parts examine the acquisition of particular contrasts in speech perception, speech production and word learning, highlighting the parallels in development across domains and discussing their potential interplay. The chapter will conclude with avenues for future research.

Speech perception and production in the first year of life: The main developmental patterns

In one of the first studies investigating infant speech perception, Eimas et al. (1971) found that infants as young as 1 month of age perceive speech sounds categorically, i.e., they perceive acoustic differences that cross a category boundary better than within-category differences. This categorical perception of speech allows listeners to attend more to acoustic differences that are meaningful in the ambient language. Interestingly, monkeys and birds also perceive speech categorically (Dooling et al., 1989; Kuhl & Miller, 1975), suggesting a cognitive mechanism that partially results from the structure of the auditory system. Follow-up studies showed that infants are initially sensitive to both native and non-native sound contrasts but lose sensitivity to the latter between 6 and 12 months of age (Werker & Tees, 1984). The resulting view was that infants are born as "universal" listeners who categorically perceive all sound contrasts from the languages of the world, and then become "native" listeners in the first year of life who are only sensitive to the phonemic sound contrasts of their native language (Werker & Tees, 1999). Yet, not all sound contrasts follow this developmental path. Infants and adults retain their ability to discriminate non-native sound contrasts if the contrasting sounds are assimilated into distinct native phoneme categories or are very different from any native sound (Best et al., 2001; Best et al., 1995). In addition, some native contrasts are initially not discriminated optimally and infants' sensitivity to these contrasts improves in the first year of life (Kuhl et al., 2006). Specifically contrasts that are acoustically less salient initially pose problems for younger infants. For instance, the discrimination of the (native) fricatives /f/, /ʃ/ and /θ/ is difficult for English babies (Eilers et al., 1977), and they have more difficulty discriminating differences in voicing for negative than positive voice onset times (Aslin et al., 1981). Changes in perception are further influenced by phoneme frequency, as sensitivity to sound contrasts that are initially difficult to perceive improves earlier for more frequent than less frequent sound contrasts (Anderson et al., 2003). This maintenance, facilitation and loss of sound contrasts in perception as a result of early experience with the native language is often referred to as perceptual attunement (Aslin & Pisoni, 1980).

In contrast to their elaborate perception capacities, infants are born with very limited speech production abilities. Their earliest vocalizations are vegetative sounds and crying, soon followed by an increasing use of vowel- and consonant-like sounds during cooing (Stark, 1980). This cumulates in canonical babbling, i.e., in the production of speech-like consonant-vowel syllables, starting around 6 months of age (Oller, 2000). Early babbles are repetitions of the same consonant-vowel syllables (e.g., *bababa*) and then evolve into variegated babbles with different syllables in one vocalization (e.g., *wubade*). Even though the prosody of pre-speech vocalizations is influenced by the native language (De Boysson-Bardies et al., 1984; Mampe et al., 2009), the segmental content and structure of early babbles are highly similar across languages (Wermke et al., 2013). The productive segmental repertoire is initially mainly restricted to labials, coronals and stops, and gradually expands along the lines of the native phonological system that is used in the production of early word forms (De Boysson-Bardies & Vihman, 1991, and references therein). The initial state is shaped by early speech motor control, and subsequent development is thought to be driven by the maturation of speech motor control (Davis & MacNeilage, 2000) and native language input (De Boysson-Bardies et al., 1984).

Speech perception and production thus appear to develop in opposite directions, in that infants are born with sophisticated perceptual but limited productive abilities and both are tuned to just the abilities that are required for their native language.

Yet, infants' babbling starts to show native-language characteristics around the same time that their speech perception attunes to the native language. This parallel development across domains has led to the proposal that productive and perceptive abilities develop in concert, as we will discuss next.

The interplay between speech perception and production in native language attunement

Many theories addressing the development of speech sound categories focus on perception rather than production (cf. Werker et al., 2012). The implicit assumption appears to be that speech production follows perception, as is often the case in language acquisition (Fenson et al., 1994). This assumption is explicit in Kuhl et al.'s (2008) Native Language Magnet Theory-expanded, which states that infants imitate the sounds they hear and in doing so create links between their perceptual and motor representations. Best's (1991) Perceptual Assimilation Model envisions a more direct role for production, as it assumes that perception and production refer to the same gestural categories and are thus interdependent (see also motor theory of speech perception, Liberman et al., 1967, and direct realism, Fowler, 1986). Despite these theoretical stances about the relation between perception and production in phoneme acquisition, only a few studies so far provide experimental evidence that perception and production are related in development.

In a series of studies, Vihman and colleagues found that infants' babbling patterns are related to their speech preferences (Majorano et al., 2014, and references therein). When infants initially produce word-like babbles, they prefer to listen to sound sequences that they master themselves; when their repertoire expands, their preference in perception shifts to sound sequences outside of their abilities. These findings comply with Vihman's (1996) Articulatory Filter Hypothesis, which states that infants' speech perception is influenced by motoric recall, i.e., that patterns from the infant's own babbling stand out in the perceived speech stream.

Motoric experience also directly influences audio-visual speech perception in younger infants. Concurrently performed lip movements influence 4.5-month-olds' ability to match auditory and visual speech cues (Yeung & Werker, 2013), and 8-month-olds are better able to map (non-native) sounds to the corresponding mouth gesture if these sounds occur often rather than rarely in infants' early babbling (Mugitani et al., 2008). These results might merely reflect the impact of non-linguistic motoric experience on perception, but could also be indicative of a connection in development between the sound representations for production and perception. Such a link is, for example, suggested by Westermann and Miranda's (2004) model that couples motoric (and visual) patterns with their auditory consequences during the babbling period. The resulting cross-modal sound representations are shaped by self-generated babbles as well as by ambient speech sounds. The constant coupling of auditory, visual and motoric patterns leads to a tight perception–production link in development.

Recent neurobiological evidence confirms that infants learn to recruit articulatory information during speech perception. Infants between 6 and 12 months of age increasingly activate motor areas in the brain during speech sound discrimination, whereas such activation is absent in newborns (Imada et al., 2006). And while 7-month-olds show similar activation in auditory and motor areas for native and non-native speech sounds, 11- to 12-month-olds show distinct activation patterns depending on the type of speech they hear (Kuhl et al., 2014). These results suggest that the perception of speech triggers activation of the motor system, but only after substantial (native) language experience.

The link between speech perception and early word learning

The literature agrees that the main factor driving native language attunement in perception and production is the ambient language input, but accounts largely differ when it comes to the role of words. Theories of phoneme acquisition originally entertained the idea that a lexicon is necessary to acquire which sounds contrast meaningfully in a language. According to this view, children represent their first words in a holistic, unsegmented fashion. The system of phonemic contrast results from the demand to learn and unambiguously represent similar-sounding words, and phoneme acquisition is a slow process relying on a crucial mass in the lexicon (Walley, 2005, for perception; Waterson, 1971, for production). The idea of roughly represented words was challenged by the finding that infants are sensitive to subtle phonological changes to words from early on (Swingley & Aslin, 2000, and subsequent studies). The findings discussed before showing that infants undergo native language attunement within the first year of life further suggests that at least some aspects of phoneme learning take place before the child has acquired a reasonably large lexicon. Theories now had to explain how phoneme acquisition takes place in the absence of a (large) lexicon.

One widely-accepted answer to this conundrum was statistical learning. Every realization of a phoneme sounds slightly different. The resulting phonetic variation reveals the underlying phoneme structure, as the distribution of speech sounds along a (relevant) phonetic continuum has one local maximum per phoneme (Allen & Miller, 1999). Such distributions of exemplars indeed modulate infants' discrimination of speech sounds (Maye et al., 2002). The idea of distributional learning as the primary mechanism underlying infants' early acquisition of language-specific phoneme perception has been embraced across theories of early speech perception (Werker & Curtin, 2005; Kuhl et al., 2008). However, computational modeling of phoneme acquisition suggests that sound categories can only be learned successfully when the word context of the phonemes is considered (Feldman et al., 2013). Behavioral evidence supports the modeling results, as familiarity with two different word forms that each contain a specific sound, such as /d/ in *dog* and /t/ in *teddy*, enhances infants' perception of this sound contrast (Thiessen, 2011; Thiessen & Yee, 2010). Similarly, consistently pairing minimal pair syllables with visual objects or facial information fosters the perception of the phonological contrast involved (Mani & Schneider, 2013; Teinonen et al., 2008; Yeung & Werker, 2009). Since infants have basic knowledge about some word forms and their referents by

6 to 9 months of age (Bergelson & Swingley, 2012; Parise & Csibra, 2012; Tincoff & Jusczyk, 2012), the lexicon may indeed support native language attunement. This stance is reflected in interactive views on the development of speech perception and word learning (e.g., Werker & Curtin, 2005; Swingley, 2009). Note, however, that these accounts so far do not cover processes of speech production.

Vowels versus consonants

The perception of different sound contrasts is attuned to the native language at different rates, with the trajectories of attunement to vowels and consonants being the most obvious example. While the perception of vowels becomes language-specific around 5 to 6 months of age (Polka & Werker, 1994; Kuhl et al., 1992), the development of language-specific consonant perception takes place around 8 to 10 months of age (Werker & Tees, 1984). This section discusses potential sources of this vowel primacy in speech perception, its parallels with speech production and the transition from a vowel primacy in speech perception to a consonant bias in word recognition.

Vowels versus consonants in speech perception and production

The observation that vowels are acquired at a faster rate than consonants in perception can be explained in terms of auditory salience as well as infants' developing auditory system. Vowels are longer, louder and thus acoustically more salient than consonants (Repp, 1984). This makes them better perceivable than consonants already in-utero (Gerhardt & Abrams, 2000). Vowels may also be attractive, as they carry the pitch characteristics of infant-directed speech (Fernald & Kuhl, 1987). In contrast, early speech perception disadvantages consonants: accurate consonant perception requires sensitivity to fast changes, but infants' auditory temporal resolution still improves over the first year of life (Werner et al., 1992). The perceptual primacy of vowels, with their fast attunement, is mirrored in early production, as vowels appear before consonants in vocal play (Stark, 1980). Vowels may be produced earlier because they are articulatorily simple: opening the vocal tract and activating the vocal folds suffices. Consonant production, on the other hand, requires a measured opening of the vocal tract, movement of the articulators, and possibly coordination between the articulators and vocal folds.

If the vowel primacy is due to auditory factors in perception and articulatory factors in production, the perception-production parallel is accidental. Alternatively, the vowel primacy in both domains could be attributed to the interplay between perception and production. Perception-before-production accounts would argue that vowels, which are acoustically salient and to which perception becomes quickly attuned, are attractive production targets (Kuhl et al., 2008). Alternatively, the articulation-driven early production of vowel-like sounds improves first the perception-production mapping of vowels and consequently the early perceptual attunement to vowels, rendering the production component primary (Best, 1991; Westermann & Miranda, 2004).

However, does the vowel primacy imply that vowels are more important in early language development? Perceptual attunement entails different processes for vowel than for consonant perception. Vowel attunement entails an increased sensitivity to native contrasts (Tsuji & Cristia, 2014), whereas consonant attunement often involves the loss of sensitivity to non-native contrasts. While the development of language-specific perception may start with vowels, consonant perception is ultimately more tuned to the native language as listeners are less sensitive to non-phonemic consonant than vowel differences. And while infants may produce vowels first, consonants keep up with vowels in terms of language-specific effects in babbling: vowels have language-specific acoustics at ten months (De Boysson-Bardies et al., 1989), and the distribution of consonants is language specific around the same age (De Boysson-Bardies & Vihman, 1991). Upon a closer look, the vowel primacy is primarily temporal. It is short-lived in production, as consonants quickly catch up and may even be outweighed by lower specificity in perception.

Vowels versus consonants in speech perception and word learning

The vowel primacy in early speech perception cascades into early word recognition. Five-month-old French infants note a change in their name's initial vowel ("Elix" is not "Alix"), while they accept consonant mispronunciations ("Zictor" is accepted for "Victor"; Bouchon et al., 2014). Young infants thus rely more on the match between the correct and heard vowel than on a consonant match, a phenomenon called "vowel bias" in word recognition. Adults have the reversed "consonant bias" in word recognition (e.g., Cutler et al., 2000). This consonant bias reflects a seemingly language-universal division of labor that consonants are more relevant for the lexicon, whereas vowels carry prosodic information (Nespor et al., 2003). The rate at which infants gravitate towards the consonant bias in word recognition is language dependent. Italian infants have a consonant bias around their first birthday (Hochmann et al., 2011) as do French infants from 14 months onwards (Nazzi, 2005; Havy et al., 2014). English infants can learn some vowel minimal pairs at 15 months (Curtin et al., 2009) when consonant minimal pairs still appear difficult (Stager & Werker, 1997). Across languages, a clear consonant bias only emerges around 30 months (Floccia et al., 2014; Nazzi et al., 2009).

Given the vowel bias in first word recognition, the consonant bias is probably not innately specified (Bonatti et al., 2007). Accounts of the transition from the vowel to consonant bias have focused on the different acoustic-phonetic properties of vowels and consonants (Floccia et al., 2014) or their different distribution or function in the lexicon (Keidel et al., 2007; Mayor & Plunkett, 2014). The "acoustic-phonetic" account states that the emerging consonant bias is a continuation of the categorical nature of consonant perception (Floccia et al., 2014). The "lexical" explanation strongly resonates with recent findings that infants start building a lexicon well before their first birthday (Keidel et al., 2007; cf. references above). In keeping with theories that ascribe a large role to the interaction between speech sounds and the lexicon (Feldman et al., 2013), one could also integrate the "acoustic-phonetic" and "lexical" accounts: infants without categorical perception for vowels (as pinpointed by the "acoustic-phonetic" account) and with some lexical knowledge (a stronghold of the "lexical" account) will discover that not all vowel differences they perceive signal a lexical contrast and these infants will consequently redirect their attention to the perceptually more reliable consonants. One could even speculate that the onset of perceptual attunement for consonants around 10 months of age is a consequence of the acquisition of the first words, a speculation that differs from Walley's (1993) lexical account of phoneme acquisition in that (a) it states that primarily consonants become more defined as a result of lexical acquisition, and (b) it takes the first words rather than the vocabulary spurt as the restructuring force.

Easy and difficult sound contrasts

Although the time course of the acquisition of speech sound categories differs between vowels and consonants in general, not all vowels, nor all consonants, are equal. We first present the case of vowel height and backness to discuss that infants use some cues before others. We then continue with labial and coronal consonants to address asymmetries within a contrast. Both parts address the role of salience and frequency, synchronic parallels between speech perception and production, and the (dis)continuities from speech perception to word recognition.

Early versus late contrasts: The case of vowel height and backness

Infants across their first year detect vowel height contrasts (e.g., from mid /ɛ/ to low /æ/) better than vowel place contrasts (e.g., from front /ɛ/ to back /ɔ/; Lacerda, 1993, 1994). Vowel height is signalled by lower, louder formant frequencies than vowel place. Moreover, most languages have more height than place contrasts (Crothers, 1978). Infants' sensitivity to vowel height could thus be due to the acoustic salience of its phonetic correlates as well as to the number of vowel height contrasts in the phoneme system of the ambient language and the frequency of their occurrence. If these factors contribute to perceptual attunement as well, we should expect that infants' ability to detect changes in vowel height is further strengthened over their first year.

Infants' earliest production is the birth cry, which resembles a mid-low schwa or /a/ (Vorperian & Kent, 2007). Vocalizations then become differentiated, first along the height and then the backness dimension (Rvachew et al., 1996). Infants' early use of the height dimension could be a result of their tendency to start speech production with biomechanically simple jaw movements, which can vary vowel height (MacNeilage & Davis, 2000).

The vowel height dimension is thus favoured over vowel backness across both perception and production. Note that such parallels are not specific to vowels, but also are observed in consonants. For instance, plosive contrasts are more salient than fricative contrasts (Eilers et al., 1977) and enter production earlier (Gildersleeve-Neumann et al., 2000).

Parallel perception/production trends are coincidental if salience and frequency determine perception while articulatory factors explain production, but they might also arise from an intrinsic perception-production connection. In the height-before-backness development, infants' perceptual sensitivity to height contrasts may trigger them to mimic and frequently produce these contrasts, resulting in strong perception-production representations for vowel height (e.g., Kuhl et al., 2008). Alternatively, infants' articulatory control over vowel height paired with self-monitoring of the resulting babbles may link perception and production representations, which then guide the perceptual attention to vowel height (e.g., Vihman, 1996; Westermann & Miranda, 2004). If perception takes place through production representations, auditory vowel height differences will be easily mapped onto the practiced vowel height gestures, resulting in even more differentiated production along this dimension (e.g., Best, 1991).

After children's early perception and production of vowel height, the height-before-backness trend may continue into the word-recognition phase. Fifteen-month-olds are more sensitive to height than to place contrasts in word learning (Curtin et al., 2009), and potentially also in word recognition (Mani et al., 2008). Given that the perception and production of vowel height in infants' first year precedes word learning, this pattern suggests that early acquired speech sound categories continue to play a prominent role for later-acquired words by influencing children's sensitivity to phonetic detail in words (Werker & Curtin, 2005; Kuhl et al., 2008).

Asymmetric contrasts: The case of labial and coronal consonants

Some phonemic changes are detected more easily in one direction than the other. Such asymmetric perception can be explained by salience, as infants may initially be better at detecting changes from non-salient to salient speech sounds (e.g., Polka & Bohn, 2011). This salience-driven initial state may then be modulated by frequency as infants become better at detecting changes from low-frequency to high-frequency speech sounds (e.g., Pons et al., 2012).

Possibly the most frequently observed asymmetry in consonant perception occurs for labial (e.g., /b/, /m/) versus coronal (e.g., /d/, /n/) places of articulation: infants are better at noticing the labial-to-coronal than the coronal-to-labial change (Tsuji et al., 2015; Dijkstra & Fikkert, 2011; for other asymmetries see Polka & Bohn, 2011). Possible explanations for this bias are that coronal sounds have more focused and louder energy than labials, rendering them acoustically more salient, and that coronals are more frequent in most languages (Paradis & Prunet, 1991). The labial-coronal asymmetry is thus another case of better discrimination from non-salient, low-frequency to salient, high-frequency speech sounds.

While coronals are more salient and more frequent than labials, and potentially function as a default category in early perception, coronals are equal to labials in early production, at least in terms of the timing of their occurrence (De Boysson-Bardies & Vihman, 1991, and references therein). The early production of labials, despite their low acoustic salience and lower frequency, may be due to the fact that labial-/a/ sequences can be produced without a change in the location of the tongue, which makes labial consonants articulatorily easy (MacNeilage & Davis, 2000). Another potentially important factor is the high visibility of the labial (lip) closure, which could inspire infants to imitate labials.

The early production of labials could strengthen the linked perception-production representations of these sounds (e.g., Kuhl et al., 2008). And these labial perception-production representations could in turn be enhanced through self-monitoring (Vihman, 1996; Westermann & Miranda, 2004). The early motor experience with labials may also improve children's mapping of perceived labials onto gestural representations (Best, 1991) and guide their uptake of labial sounds from the input (Vihman, 1996). All these accounts predict that the early production of labials results in well-specified representations, despite their lower salience and frequency.

The labial-coronal asymmetry from early speech perception spills over to word recognition. Infants up to 24 months of age more easily detect a coronal mispronunciation of a labial than vice versa (Fikkert, 2010; Altvater-Mackensen et al., 2014). These asymmetries in word recognition were first explained as a result of lexicon-specific representations that are fairly independent of speech perception (Fikkert, 2010). Note that this account is different from the claim that the lexicon influences perceptual attunement (Feldman et al., 2013). Counter to both accounts, the early occurrence of perceptual asymmetries suggests that at least some characteristics of early perception continue to influence later word recognition.

Discussions and conclusions

Infants' acquisition of the native language phoneme system is generally researched independently with respect to speech perception, speech production or word recognition. The present chapter attempted to break through the barriers between these domains by outlining parallels and (apparent) discontinuities across domains. We focused on the differences between vowels and consonants, on the acquisition of vowel height before vowel backness and on the asymmetries between labial and coronal consonants. Discussing the parallels between the domains in such detail highlights the potential to explain development from the interplays between perception, production and word learning

Speech perception development can often be explained by acoustic salience and frequency; speech production development is well understood from articulatory development. A challenge in disentangling salience, frequency, and articulatory ease is that these effects often go in the same direction. Such overlap is expected, as both salience and articulatory ease may contribute to phoneme frequencies (e.g., Liljencrants & Lindblom, 1972). The typical solution to this challenge is cross-linguistic research. Salience and articulatory ease are supposedly language universal, but phoneme frequencies can differ between languages.

Pinpointing the interaction between domains is even more difficult. Correlations between speech perception and production have been identified e.g., for specific word patterns (Majorano et al., 2014), but do not establish the direction of influence. The influence of word learning on speech perception has been established experimentally (Thiessen, 2011), but identifying a learning mechanism infants *can* use is different from determining what mechanism they *do* use in actual acquisition. An interesting venue for future research would be for models that implement the links between domains of learning, such as Feldman et al. (2013) and Westermann and Miranda (2004), to go beyond a general level of perception, production or lexical acquisition and be targeted at specific contrasts, such as those outlined in the present chapter.

References

Allen, J.S., & Miller, J.L. (1999). Effects of syllable-initial voicing and speaking rate on the temporal characteristics of monosyllabic words. *Journal of the Acoustical Society of America*, 106, 2031–2039.

Altvater-Mackensen, N., Van der Feest, S.V.H., & Fikkert, P. (2014). Asymmetries in early word recognition: The case of stops and fricatives. *Language Learning and Development*, 10, 149–178.

Anderson, J.L., Morgan, J.L., & White, K.S. (2003). A statistical basis for speech sound discrimination. *Language and Speech*, 46, 155–182.

Aslin, R.N., & Pisoni, D.B. (1980). Some developmental processes in speech perception. In G.H. Yeni-Komshian, J.F. Kavanagh, & C.A. Ferguson (Eds.), *Child Phonology, Vol. 2, Perception* (pp. 67–96). New York: Academic.

Aslin, R.N., Pisoni, D.B., Henessy, B.L., & Perey, A.J. (1981). Discrimination of voice onset time by human infants: New findings and implications for the effect of early experience. *Child Development*, 52, 1135–1145.

Bergelson, E., & Swingley, D. (2012). At 6–9 months, human infants know the meanings of many common nouns. *Proceedings of the National Academy of Sciences*, 109, 3253–3258.

Best, C. (1991). The emergence of native-language phonological influences in infants: A perceptual assimilation model. *Haskins Laboratories Status Report on Speech Research*, SR-107/108, 1–30.

Best, C.T., McRoberts, G.W., & Goodell, E. (2001). Discrimination of non-native consonant contrasts varying in perceptual assimilation to the listener's native phonological system. *Journal of the Acoustical Society of America*, 109, 775–794.

Best, C.T., McRoberts, G.W., LaFleur, R., & Silver-Isenstadt, J. (1995). Divergent developmental patterns for infants' perception of two nonnative consonant contrasts. *Infant Behavior and Development*, 18, 339–350.

Bonatti, L.L., Peña, M., Nespor, M., & Mehler, J. (2007). On consonants, vowels, chickens, and eggs. *Psychological Science*, 18, 924–925.

Bouchon, C., Floccia, C., Fux, T., Adda-Decker, M., and Nazzi, T. (2014). Call me Alix, not Elix: Vowels are more important than consonants in own-name recognition at 5 months. *Developmental Science, Early Edition*, 18(4), 587–598.

Crothers, J. (1978). Typology and universals of vowel systems. In J.H. Greenberg, C.A. Ferguson, & E.A. Moravcsik (Eds.), *Universals of human language. Vol 2: Phonology* (pp. 93–152). Stanford: Stanford University Press.

Curtin, S., Fennell, C., & Escudero, P. (2009). Weighting of vowel cues explains patterns of word-object associative learning. *Developmental Science*, 12, 725–731.

Cutler, A., Sebastian-Galles, N., Soler-Vilageliu, O., & Van Ooijen, B. (2000). Constraints of vowels and consonants on lexical selection: Cross-linguistic comparisons. *Memory & Cognition, 28*, 746–755.

Davis, B.L., & MacNeilage, P.F. (2000). An embodiment perspective on the acquisition of speech perception. *Phonetica, 57*, 229–241.

De Boysson-Bardies, B., Halle, P., Sagart, L., & Durand, C. (1989). A crosslinguistic investigation of vowel formants in babbling. *Journal of Child Language, 1*, 1–17.

De Boysson-Bardies, B., Sagart, L., & Durand, C. (1984). Discernible differences in the babbling of infants according to target language. *Journal of Child Language, 11*, 1–15.

De Boysson-Bardies, B., & Vihman, M.M. (1991). Adaptation to language: Evidence from babbling and first words in four languages. *Language, 67*, 297–319.

Dijkstra, N., & Fikkert, P. (2011). Universal constraints on the discrimination of place of articulation? Asymmetries in the discrimination of 'paan' and 'taan' by 6-month-old Dutch infants. In N. Danis, K. Mesh, & H. Sung (Eds.), *Proceedings of the 35th Annual Boston University Conference on Language Development* (pp. 170–182). Boston: Cascadilla Press.

Dooling, R.J., Okanoya, K., & Brown, S.D. (1989). Speech perception by budgerigars (melopsittacus undulatus): The voiced-voiceless distinction. *Perception & Psychophysics, 46*, 65–71.

Eilers, R.E., Wilson, W.R., & Moore, J.M. (1977). Developmental changes in speech discrimination in infants. *Journal of Speech and Hearing Research, 20*, 766–780.

Eimas, P.D., Siqueland, E.R., Jusczyk, P.W., & Vigorito, J. (1971). Speech perception in infants. *Science, 209*, 1140–1141.

Feldman, N.H., Goldwater, S., Griffiths, T., & Morgan, J.L. (2013). A role for the developing lexicon in phonetic category acquisition. *Psychological Review, 120*, 751–778.

Fenson, L., Dale, P.S., Reznick, J.S., Bates, E., Thal, D.J., & Pethick, S.J. (1994). Variability in early communicative development. *Monographs of the Society for Research in Child Development, 59*(5, Serial No. 242).

Fernald, A., & Kuhl, P. (1987). Acoustic determinants of infant preference for motherese speech. *Infant Behavior and Development, 10*, 279–293.

Fikkert, P. (2010). Developing representations and the emergence of phonology: Evidence from perception and production. In C. Fougeron, B. Kühnert, M. d'Imperio, & N. Vallée (Eds.), *Laboratory Phonology 10: Variation, Phonetic Detail and Phonological Representation* (Phonology & Phonetics 4-4, pp. 227–258). Berlin: Mouton.

Floccia, C., Nazzi, T., Delle Luche, C., Poltrock, S., & Goslin, J. (2014). English-learning one- to two-year-olds do not show a consonant bias in word learning. *Journal of Child Language, 41*, 1085–1114.

Fowler, C.A. (1986). An event approach to the study of speech perception from a direct-realist perspective. *Journal of Phonetics, 15*, 3–28.

Gerhardt, K.J., & Abrams, R.M. (2000). Fetal exposures to sound and vibroacoustic stimulation. *Journal of Perinatology, 20*, S21.

Gildersleeve-Neumann, C.E., Davis, B.L., & MacNeilage, P.F. (2000). Contingencies governing the production of fricatives, affricates and liquids in babbling. *Applied Psycholinguistics, 21*, 341–363.

Havy, M., Serres, J., & Nazzi, T. (2014). A consonant/vowel asymmetry in word-form processing: Eye-tracking evidence in childhood and in adulthood. *Language and Speech, 57*, 254–281.

Hochmann, J.-R., Benavides-Varela, S., Nespor, M., & Mehler, J. (2011). Consonants and vowels: Different roles in early language acquisition. *Developmental Science, 14*, 1445–1458.

Imada, T., Zhang, Y., Cheour, M., Taulu, S., Ahonen, A., & Kuhl, P.K. (2006). Infant speech perception activates Broca's area: A developmental magnetoencehalography study. *NeuroReport, 17,* 957–962.

Keidel, J.L., Jenison, R.L., Kluender, K.R., & Seidenberg, M.S. (2007). Does grammar constrain statistical learning? Commentary on Bonatti, Peña, Nespor, and Mehler (2005). *Psychological Science, 18,* 922–923.

Kuhl, P.K., Conboy, B., Coffey-Corina, S., Padden, D., Riera-Gaxiola, M., & Nelson, T. (2008). Phonetic learning as a pathway to language: New data and native language magnet theory expanded (NLM-e). *Philosophical Transactions of the Royal Society B, 363,* 979–1000.

Kuhl, P.K., & Miller, J.D. (1975). Speech perception by the chinchilla: voiced – voiceless distinction in alveolar plosive consonants. *Science, 190,* 69–72.

Kuhl, P.K., Ramirez, R.R., Bosseler, A., Lotus Lin, J.-F., & Imada, T. (2014). Infants' brain responses to speech suggest analysis by synthesis. *Proceedings of the National Academy of Sciences, Early Edition, 111(31),* 11238–11245.

Kuhl, P.K., Stevens, E., Hayashi, A., Deguchi, T., Kiritani, S., & Iverson, P. (2006). Infants show a facilitation effect for native language phonetic perception between 6 and 12 months. *Developmental Science, 9,* F13–F21.

Kuhl, P.K., Williams, K.A., Lacerda, F., Stevens, K.N., & Lindblom, B. (1992). Linguistic experience alters phonetic perception in infants by 6 months of age. *Science, 255,* 606–608.

Lacerda, F. (1993). Sonority contrasts dominate young infants' vowel perception. *Journal of the Acoustical Society of America, 93,* 2372.

Lacerda, F. (1994). The asymmetric structure of the infant's perceptual vowel space. *Journal of the Acoustical Society of America, 95,* 3016.

Liberman, A.M., Cooper, F.S., Shankweiler, D.P., & Studdert-Kennedy, M. (1967). Perception of the speech code. *Psychological Review, 74,* 431–461.

Liljencrants, J., & Lindblom, B. (1972). Numerical simulation of vowel quality: The role of perceptual contrast. *Language, 48,* 839–862.

MacNeilage, P.F., & Davis, B. (2000). Deriving speech from nonspeech: A view from ontogeny. *Phonetica, 57,* 284–296.

Majorano, M., Vihman, M.M., & DePaolis, R.A. (2014). The relationship between infants' production experience and their processing of speech. *Language Learning and Development, 10,* 179–204.

Mampe, B., Friederici, A.D., Christophe, A., & Wermke, K. (2009). Newborns' cry melody is shaped by their native language. *Current Biology, 19,* 1994–1997.

Mani, N., Coleman, J., & Plunkett., K. (2008). Phonological specific of vowel contrasts at 18-months. *Language and Speech, 51,* 3–21.

Mani, N., & Schneider, S. (2013). Speaker identity supports phonetic category learning. *Journal of Experimental Psychology: Human Perception and Performance, 39,* 623–629.

Maye, J., Werker, J.F., & Gerken, L. (2002). Infant sensitivity to distributional information can affect phonetic discrimination. *Cognition, 82,* B101–B111.

Mayor, J., & Plunkett, K. (2014). Infant word recognition: Insights from TRACE simulations. *Journal of memory and Language, 71,* 89–123.

Mugitani, R., Kobayashi, T., & Hiraki, K. (2008). Audio-visual matching of lips and non-canonical sounds in 8-month-old infants. *Infant Behavior & Development, 31,* 307–310.

Nazzi, T. (2005). Use of phonetic specificity during the acquisition of new words: Differences between consonants and vowels. *Cognition, 98,* 13–30.

Nazzi, T., Floccia, C., Moquet, B., & Butler, J. (2009). Bias for consonantal over vocalic information in French- and English-learning 30-month-olds: Crosslinguistic evidence in early word learning. *Journal of Experimental Child Psychology, 102,* 522–537.

Nespor, M., Peña, M., & Mehler, J. (2003). On the different roles of vowels and consonants in speech processing and language acquisition. *Lingue e Linguaggio, ii*, 221–247.

Oller, D.K. (2000). *The Emergence of the Speech Capacity*. Mahwah, NJ: Lawrence Erlbaum.

Paradis, C., & Prunet, J.-F. (1991). Introduction: Asymmetry and visibility in consonant articulations. In C. Paradis & J.-F. Prunet (Eds.), *The Special Status of Coronals: Internal and External Evidence (Phonetics and Phonology 2*, pp. 1–26), San Diego: Academic Press.

Parise, E., & Csibra, G. (2012). Electrophysiological evidence for the understanding of maternal speech by 9-month-old infants. *Psychological Science, 23*, 728–733.

Polka, L., & Bohn, O.-S. (2011). Natural referent vowel (NRV) framework: An emerging view of early phonetic development. *Journal of Phonetics, 39*, 467–478.

Polka, L., & Werker, J.F. (1994). Developmental changes in the perception on non-native vowel contrasts. *Journal of Experimental Psychology: Human Perception and Performance, 20*, 421–435.

Pons, F., Albareda-Castellot, B., & Sebastián-Gallés, N. (2012). The interplay between input and initial biases: Asymmetries in vowel perception during the first year of life. *Child Development, 83*, 965–976.

Repp, B.H. (1984). Categorical perception: issues, methods, findings. In N.J. Lass (Ed.), *Speech and Language: Advances in Basic Research and Practice*, Vol. 10, 243–335. New York: Academic Press.

Rvachew, S., Slawinski, E.B., Williams, M., & Green, C.L. (1996). Formant frequencies of vowels produced by infants with and without early onset otitis media. *Canadian Acoustics / Acoustique Canadienne, 24*, 19–28.

Stager, C.L., & Werker, J.F. (1997). Infants listen for more phonetic detail in speech perception than in word-learning tasks. *Nature, 388*, 381–382.

Stark, R.E. (1980). Stages of speech development in the first year of life. In G. Yeni-Komshian, J. Kavanaugh, & C. Ferguson. (Eds.), *Child Phonology*, Vol. 1, 73–90. New York: Academic Press.

Swingley, D. (2009). Contributions of infant word learning to language development. *Philosophical Transactions of the Royal Society B, 364*, 3617–3632.

Swingley, D., & Aslin, R.N. (2000). Spoken word recognition and lexical representation in very young children. *Cognition, 76*, 147–166.

Teinonen, T., Aslin, R.N., Alku, P., & Csibra, G. (2008). Visual speech contributes to phonetic learning in 6-month-old infants. *Cognition, 108*, 850–855.

Thiessen, E.D. (2011). When variability matters more than meaning: the effect of lexical forms on use of phonemic contrasts. *Developmental Psychology, 47*, 1448–1458.

Thiessen, E.D., & Yee, M.N. (2010). Dogs, bogs, labs and lads: What phonemic generalizations indicate about the nature of children's early word-form representations. *Child Development, 81*, 1287–1303.

Tincoff, R., & Jusczyk, P.W. (2012). Six-month-olds comprehend words that refer to parts of the body. *Infancy, 17*, 432–444.

Tsuji, S., & Cristia, A. (2014). Perceptual attunement in vowels: A meta-analysis. *Developmental Psychobiology, 56*, 179–91.

Tsuji, S., Mazuka, R., Cristia, A., & Fikkert, P. (2015). Even at 4 months, a labial is a good enough coronal, but not vice versa. *Cognition, 134*, 252–256.

Vihman, M.M. (1996). *Phonological Development. The Origins of Language in the Child*. Oxford: Blackwell.

Vorperian, H.K., & Kent, R.D. (2007). Vowel acoustic space development in children: A synthesis of acoustic and anatomic data. *Journal of Speech, Language, and Hearing Research, 50*, 1510–1545.

Walley, A. (1993). The role of vocabulary development in children's spoken word recognition and segmentation ability. *Developmental Review, 12,* 286–350.

Walley, A. (2005). Speech perception in childhood. In D. Pisoni & R. Remez (Eds.), *Handbook of Speech Perception* (pp. 449–468). Oxford: Blackwell.

Waterson, N. (1971). Child phonology: A prosodic view. *Journal of Linguistics, 7,* 179–211.

Werker, J.F., & Curtin, S. (2005). PRIMIR – A developmental framework of infant speech processing. *Language Learning and Development, 1,* 197–234.

Werker, J.F., & Tees, R.C. (1984). Developmental changes across childhood in the perception of nonnative speech sounds. *Canadian Journal of Psychology, 37,* 278–286.

Werker, J.F., & Tees, R.C. (1999). Experiential influences on infant speech processing. *Annual Review of Psychology, 50,* 509–535.

Werker, J.F., Yeung, H.H., & Yoshida, K.A. (2012). How do infants become experts at native-speech perception? *Current Directions in Psychological Science, 21,* 221–226.

Wermke, K., Practhner, S., Lamm, B., Volt, V., Hain, J., Kärtner, J., & Keller, H. (2013). Acoustic properties of comfort sounds of 3-month-old Cameroonian (Nso) and German infants. *Speech, Language and Hearing, 16,* 149–162.

Werner, L.A., Marean, G.C., Halpin, C.F., Spetner, N.B., & Gillenwater, J.M. (1992). Infant auditory temporal acuity: Gap detection. *Child Development, 63,* 260–272.

Westermann, G., & Miranda, E.R. (2004). A new model of sensorimotor coupling in the development of speech. *Brain and Language, 89,* 393–400.

Yeung, H., & Werker, J.F. (2009). Learning words' sounds before learning how words sound: 9-month-olds use distinct objects as cues to categorize speech information. *Cognition, 113,* 234–243.

Yeung, H., & Werker, J.F. (2013). Lip movements affect infants' audiovisual speech perception. *Psychological Science, 24,* 603–612.

2

THE PROTO-LEXICON

Segmenting word-like units
from the speech stream

Caroline Junge

DEPARTMENTS OF EXPERIMENTAL AND DEVELOPMENTAL PSYCHOLOGY
UTRECHT UNIVERSITY, THE NETHERLANDS

There is growing evidence from experimental studies that infants start acquiring a vocabulary already when they are between 6 to 9 months old (Bergelson & Swingley, 2012; Parise & Csibra, 2012; Tincoff & Jusczyk, 1999). Clearly, infants must have learned what these words mean prior to their lab visit, that is, learned them in their natural environment. However, as infant speech corpora reveal, there are surprisingly few one-word utterances directed to 6- to 12-month-olds in maternal speech (excluding exclamations, fillers and social expressions that typically do not combine into phrases): ranging from 2% (Morgan, 1996) to 9% (Brent & Siskind, 2001). Even when parents are explicitly instructed to teach their child certain words, they present these words predominantly in multi-word utterances (Aslin et al., 1996; Johnson et al., 2013). It appears that, for most children, most of the words they hear are presented in continuous speech. As Figure 2.1 demonstrates for a typical infant-directed example from Dutch, words are generally glued together without clear pauses between them to signal word onset and offset (unlike written text, in which words are conveniently separated by spaces). While it is debated whether or not isolated words alone can function as a starting point for vocabulary acquisition (Brent & Siskind, 2001; Depaolis et al., 2014; Lew-Williams et al., 2011; Yang, 2004), it is undeniably true that in order to learn from the input, infants are required to segment the speech stream into separate word-like units from very early on. From adult research we know that the speech signal contains several cues that assist successful word extraction from speech, but these cues are probabilistic rather than deterministic; no single cue appears sufficient to signal word boundaries (Cutler, 2012). Fortunately, the past two decades have provided us with two experimental methods that allow us to examine when and under what conditions infants can segment words from speech. In what follows next, we will first discuss the main methods (Section 2.1) before we focus on the cues that infants can use to detect words from speech (Section 2.2). Section 2.3 underscores how vital early speech

16 Junge

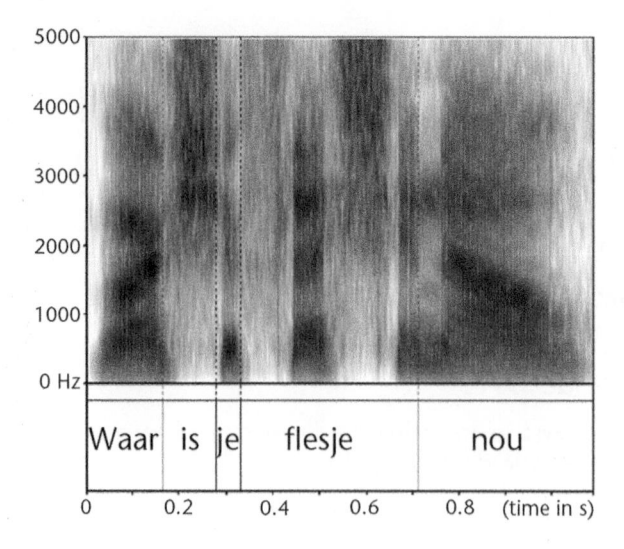

FIGURE 2.1 A spectrogram of an utterance that Dutch infants will frequently hear *waar is je flesje nou?* "where is your bottle then?" This utterance contains no silences (otherwise there would have been moments where there was no signal); there is speech from beginning to end. The dotted lines correspond to word boundaries—demonstrating that words are not demarcated by silences.

segmentation skill is for subsequent language development, while Section 2.4 ends with future directions.

2.1 Methods to test infants' ability to segment words from speech

Infants' ability to segment words from speech has predominantly been tested via one of two methods: behaviorally with the head-turn preference procedure (HPP; Fernald, 1985) and electrophysiologically with an event-related potential (ERP) paradigm. Both methods first familiarize infants with a set of words (familiarization phase) and then compare infants' responses to these familiar words against a control condition which presents infants with novel, unfamiliar words (test phase). Either the familiarization or test phase consists of multi-word utterances; thus, a recognition response at test indicates that infants must have segmented the familiar words from speech. Figure 2.2 illustrates the setup and typical results from both methods, explained in more detail below.

The HPP paradigm exploits infants' tendency to look at interesting visual stimuli (Fernald, 1985; see also Jusczyk, 2000; Bergmann et al., 2013). In a typical HPP setup, infants sit in a three-sided booth with lamps in front of and to each side of the infant, all of which can be made to blink in order to attract the infant's attention (see top left panel of Figure 2.2 for a schematic representation). When one of the side lamps starts to blink, the typical behavior of a child is to turn her head to fixate this light. As soon as the child has turned her head, an auditory stimulus begins to

Main methods

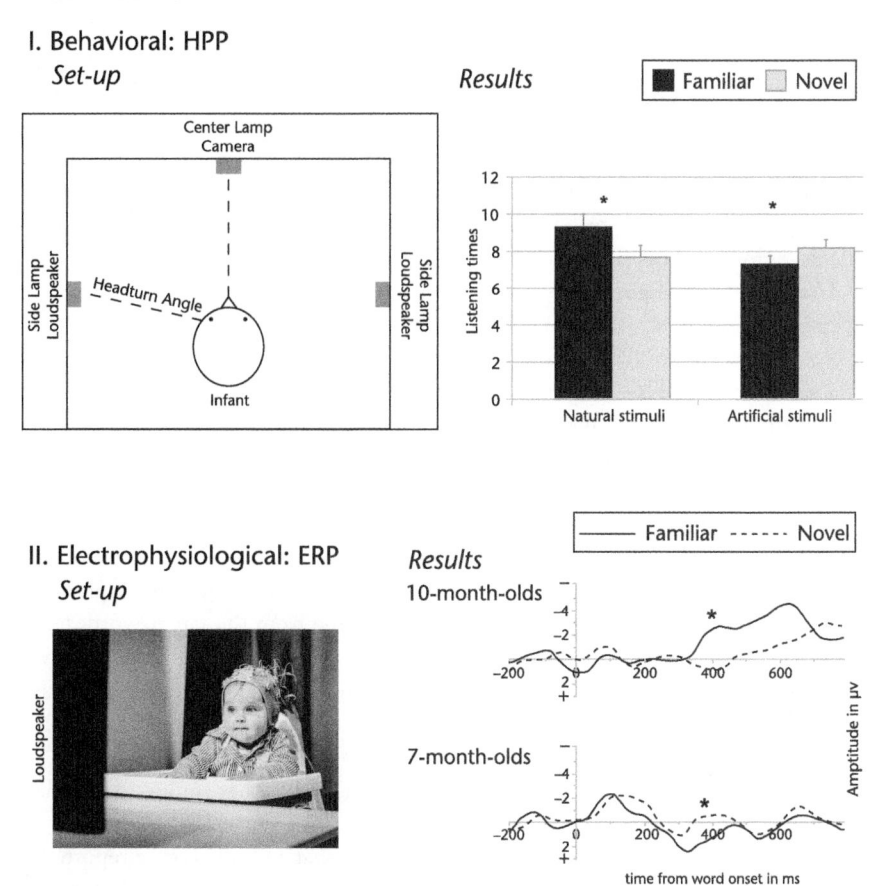

I. Behavioral: HPP

Set-up

Results

FIGURE 2.2 The current setups and main findings of the two methods to test infant segmentation skill. I—the Headturn Preference procedure (HPP): *left*, a schematic representation of how testing in lab setting occurs (adapted from Bergmann et al., 2013); *right*, the two dominant infant responses at the test phase: mean listening times to familiar (black) vs. novel words (grey) are typically larger for studies with native language stimuli (here, Jusczyk & Aslin, 1995) but shorter for studies with artificial language stimuli (here, Saffran et al., 1996). II—the event-related potential (ERP) procedure: *left*, a typical setup in which a 10-month-old is presented with auditory stimuli while she is watching a screensaver; *right*, the two dominant infant responses at the test phase: ERP results for familiar words (solid line) vs. novel words (dotted line) are more negative-going for 10-month-olds (Kooijman et al., 2005) whereas they are positive-going for 7-month-olds (Kooijman et al., 2013). Note that negativity is plotted upwards, and that time is 0, which denotes critical word onset.

play and continues until completion or when the child looks away. In this way, we can take visual attention as a proxy for auditory attention, first by examining how long the infant looks at the blinking light while listening to a particular audio recording, and then by comparing whether infants prefer one type of audio recording over another. When infants display a preference for one type of auditory stimuli—by looking longer at the blinking light while listening to this stimulus—it is typically interpreted as their having discriminated between the two types of stimuli. Next we illustrate how this paradigm can be used to examine whether infants segment words from fluent speech.

Using this paradigm, Jusczyk and Aslin (1995) were the first to test whether infants could segment words from speech. They presented infants first with multiple tokens of two monosyllabic words in isolation (either *cup* and *dog* or *bike* and *feet*; around 12 tokens per word). At test, infants listened to four six-sentence passages. Half of the passages contained familiarized target words, and the other passages the unfamiliar novel target words. Infants who were 7.5 months old (but not 6-month-olds) listened longer to passages containing familiarized words ("familiarity preference"; see Figure 2.2). This familiarity preference holds when infants were familiarized with words embedded in passages and tested with isolated words. Infants further appear to store words in phonetic detail; at test, they did not display any preference for words that differ in only one phoneme from the target words (e.g., familiarized with *tup* and tested with *cup*-passages). To summarize, this study was the first to show that infants can match words presented in isolation with those embedded in a speech stream, thus demonstrating that infants can segment words from speech.

The seminal study of Jusczyk and Aslin (1995) ignited other studies to examine when, and under which circumstances, infants can detect words embedded in a speech stream (discussed in next section). Note that not all studies reported a preference for familiar words, however. As the top right panel in Figure 2.2 shows, the direction of the preference seems to hinge on the type of the stimuli used. While most studies using natural language stimuli report a familiarity preference, studies using artificial languages typically report a novelty preference (i.e., infants prefer the novel stimuli over the familiar words; see e.g., Saffran et al., 1996). Artificial languages usually contain no real words from the child's language and are created in such a way that there is only one cue in continuous speech that signals word onset (see further Section 2.2). It is possible that the direction of the preference is driven by the type of stimuli or by the perceived difficulty of the task (Pelucchi et al., 2009a; Thiessen et al., 2005). Nevertheless, while the stimulus characteristics on which infants base their preference remain unclear (e.g., Houston-Price & Nakai, 2004), any preference—regardless of a novelty or a familiarity preference—signals infants' ability to detect recurrent word-like units in speech. Note that HPP is not the only possible paradigm to measure infants' listening preferences; to investigate infants' speech segmentation ability, one could also use a central-fixation procedure (Altvater-Mackensen & Mani, 2013; Ngon et al., 2013), which allows the possibility for future eye-tracker compatible designs.

Another method to test speech segmentation skill is to measure ERPs while infants are listening to speech. Unlike HPP, this method requires infants only to recognize familiarized words while they are passively listening to input; it does not require any behavioral change or preference. While children listen to speech and their electroencephalogram (EEG) is recorded, they can be simultaneously entertained by showing interesting silent visual stimuli not time-locked to the auditory signal, such as a silent video, a puppet theatre or toys (see lower left panel in Figure 2.2). Offline, one can derive the ERPs—reflecting the brain responses shared across similar events by averaging over multiple EEG-epochs, all of which are time-locked to the same kind of event, which is in this case the onset of familiarized vs. matched control words. Note that ERP studies need to present more test trials than is typical in behavioral research; to obtain meaningful ERPs it is common that infants contribute at least ten artifact-free epochs (trials) per condition. In fact, infant ERP experiments usually comprise 3–4 times as many trials as are minimally required; the majority of trials will be discarded because they contain movement artifacts, which obscure event-related potentials associated with cognitive events such as recognition.

The ERP paradigm offers the advantage that it allows for an online index of word recognition. By comparing the time course of ERPs time-locked to onset of familiarized words versus novel words one can observe whether and when in time the infant brain recognizes familiar words. The first study to create an electrophysiological analogue of the familiarization-and-test HPP was Kooijman, Hagoort and Cutler (2005). They presented Dutch 10-month-old infants with blocks of ten isolated word tokens (familiarization phase) followed by eight sentences, half containing the familiarized word, and half containing matched novel words. There were up to 20 familiarization-and-test blocks, each contrasting different familiarized and unfamiliar words. In this way, the authors could include more test trials in the experiment while maintaining the amount of familiarization per word comparable to HPP studies. By comparing ERPs time-locked to familiar words with those time-locked to novel words—both embedded in speech—we see that they diverge around 350 ms up to 500 ms from word onset, with ERPs to familiar words being more negative in amplitude than novel words (see Figure 2.2). The timing of this word repetition effect, also known as the N200–500, shows that infants are swift in initiating a recognition response even before the word has ended.

However, as with the HPP, we see differences across studies. Compare the two ERP figures in Figure 2.2 (note that negative voltage is here plotted upwards). Relative to unfamiliar words, familiar words elicited a negativity in 10-month-olds, while it elicited a positivity in 7-month-olds with exactly the same paradigm (Kooijman et al., 2013). Indeed, most studies report a negativity as a word recognition effect in infants of 9 months old or older (French infants: Goyet et al., 2010; German infants: Männel & Friederici, 2013), while other studies testing younger infants with a similar set-up report a positivity, i.e., familiar words are more positive than unfamiliar words (German 6-month-olds: Männel & Friederici, 2013). Although it is likely that this polarity change signals age-related changes, brain maturation alone cannot explain this shift. Some infants within the same recording session show negative word recognition effects during familiarization of single words, yet they show a less-mature positive word recognition effect when words are embedded in speech (Kooijman et al., 2013). What does such a shift then imply? One possibility is that a shift in polarity from positive to negative amplitude reflects a change from immature acoustic processing to more mature linguistic processing of the speech signal, and is thus indicative of how words are recognized (Kooijman et al., 2013). Similar explanations for shifts in polarity have also been reported in infants' phoneme processing (Garcia-Sierra et al., 2011). Another possibility stems from contrasting the ERP paradigm with the HPP paradigm. Recall that the word recognition effect with negative amplitude is present in infants from around 9 months—which is around the same age that behavioral studies on speech segmentation report familiarity preferences, i.e., that infants prefer listening to familiar words relative to novel control words. It is therefore also possible that the more mature word recognition effect (increased negativity to familiar words) not only reflects infants' ability to recognize words, but simultaneously also their preference for these words.

To summarize, the literature presents both behavioral and electrophysiological evidence that infants can segment words from speech. Both paradigms require infants to give a differential response to familiar and unfamiliar words. In both paradigms, it is interesting to see that there are two distinct types of responses (i.e. HPP: familiarity vs. novelty preference, and ERP: negative vs. positive recognition components around 200–500 ms). Of course, any differential response, regardless of its direction, shows that infants can segment speech in this experiment. Although the interpretation of each switch in one direction is far from clear, comparison across studies shows that the direction of the responses is generally consistent across studies when grouped by age or stimulus type, allowing us to sketch a developmental picture of how speech segmentation ability matures, which is the focus of the next section.

2.2 How can infants extract words from speech?

Although recognition of a word is obviously facilitated when (one of its) boundaries are clearly demarcated with silence, as is the case with isolated words (e.g., Brent & Siskind, 2001; Junge, Kooijman et al., 2012) or with words at phrase boundaries (Seidl & Johnson, 2006), infants still need to segment a large proportion of words from continuous speech. Natural languages generally contain a variety of cues to mark word onset in speech, with multiple cues often (but not always) signaling the same word boundary. However, no single cue appears to be foolproof (Cutler, 2012). For instance, one possible cue would be to use the offset of a known word as an anchor to predict the onset of the next word (Bortfeld et al., 2005), but sometimes this known word is part of a larger word (e.g., "bed" in "embedded"), which could lead to this cue misleading infants to wrongly segment the speech stream. Adult listeners can draw from a full array of cues, but they value these including cues hierarchically, favouring top-down (i.e., lexical and semantic-contextual) cues over bottom-up cues like co-articulation, phonotactic and prosodic cues (Mattys et al., 2005).

How do infants learn which cues are useful in extracting word-like units from speech? And how do they derive what word-like units are in the first place? Arguably, words in isolation provide infants with a basis for learning what word-like units are like (Altvater-Mackensen & Mani, 2013; Lew-Williams et al., 2011). Furthermore, infants can use lexical cues to segment words from speech, e.g., using the offset of a known word as an anchor to predict the onset of the next word (Bortfeld et al., 2005; Shi & Lepage, 2008). However, their lexicon is too small to make this cue very viable. Hence, it appears that, in contrast to adults, infants must predominantly rely on bottom-up cues.

One of the bottom-up cues that infants can use is tracking the probability of one syllable following another in the child's language input (Saffran et al., 1996; Thiessen & Erickson, 2012). If the transitional probability (TP) between syllables is high, this would suggest that they tend to co-occur and form a cluster (i.e., a word). In contrast, when the TP is low, this would suggest that these syllables do not belong together, i.e., are (parts of) different words. Saffran, Aslin and Newport (1996) were the first to demonstrate that 8-month-olds can use this statistical cue to extract word-like units from an artificial two-minute language stream made up of concatenations of four trisyllabic words. Each syllable was distinct, and the only cue to signal word boundaries was the TP between syllables. For consecutive syllables within a word the TP was always 1, whereas for consecutive syllables across words it was 0.33. Following familiarization with this 2-minute language stream, infants listened longer to part-words presented in isolation (consisting of novel concatenations of the syllables) relative to words, which suggests that 8-month-olds were able to use the transitional probabilities of the syllables in the stream to distinguish the "words" they had been presented with from the novel concatenations.

Arguably, such an artificial language stream poorly reflects the rich natural input that infants hear in the real world (Johnson & Tyler, 2010), but other studies provide evidence that this learning mechanism is sufficiently robust to support word segmentation in daily life. First, infants readily treat such words from an artificial stream as possible words (Saffran, 2001; Graf Estes et al., 2007). Second, when TP is the only possible cue in passages taken from a natural unfamiliar language (that has more syllable variation than the artificial language stream), infants also extract words from such familiarization (Pelucchi et al., 2009a; Pelucchi et al., 2009b). Crucially, infants can distinguish between frequent and infrequent syllable combinations in their native language (Ngon et al., 2013). Electrophysiological evidence suggests that even neonates can already recognize words based on their TPs (Kudo et al., 2011). Taken together, these results suggest that infants are able to pull out word-like units from fluent speech by relying on the TPs between syllables in the speech stream. In fact, Thiessen and colleagues note that tracking regularities, such as TPs between syllables, can be useful in two ways: first, it yields extra information about possible words in addition to the isolated words in a child's input ('conditional statistics'); and second, from this set of words one can extract language-specific regularities, such as phonotactics and prosodic regularities ('distributional statistics'), which in turn form additional cues to segment words from speech (Thiessen & Erickson, 2012; Thiessen et al., 2013).

Indeed, infants appear to use language-specific bottom-up cues to word onset at a later age than domain-general cues, with different cues following different trajectories. For (American-English) infants, word stress is the first language-specific cue to which infants show sensitivity (Curtin et al., 2005; Jusczyk et al., 1999). That is, infants can use the stressed syllable to signal the onset of a word in stress-based languages like English (but not in syllable-based languages like French), where most words receive stress on their first syllable (Cutler & Carter, 1987). When American-English infants are 7.5 months old, they correctly segment strong-weak words like *hamlet* and *doctor* from speech but only segment the strong syllable (*tar*) of a weak-strong word such as *guitar* (Jusczyk et al., 1999; see also Kooijman et al., 2009, for Dutch). In contrast, infants acquiring a language without lexical stress do not readily use such a strategy (Nazzi et al., 2006, 2014; Polka & Sundara, 2012). Furthermore, cross-linguistic differences even emerge for infants acquiring similar languages; Dutch infants are delayed in extracting strong-weak words from speech compared to American infants, presumably because the difference between stressed and unstressed syllables is less transparent in Dutch (Houston et al., 2000).

Albeit at a slightly older age (from 9 months onwards), infants further show sensitivity to the segmental properties of their native language to segment speech, for example: phonotactics (Gonzalez-Gomez & Nazzi, 2013; Johnson et al., 2003; Mattys & Jusczyk, 2001a); coarticulations (Curtin et al., 2001; Johnson & Jusczyk, 2001); and allophones (Mattys & Jusczyk, 2001b). Although this evidence usually comes from studies demonstrating that older infants can use these cues to segment speech (and not that younger infants cannot use these cues), the pattern of results reported suggests that infants learn to use suprasegmental cues to the service of speech segmentation before segmental cues. However, most of what we know comes from American-English infants listening to stimuli in their native language. It is unclear whether similar trajectories also hold for other languages, or whether this is due to suprasegmental markers such as stress being more transparent relative to other segmental cues in English (but not in other languages; for a related discussion see Johnson, 2012). The limited evidence available suggests that languages do, indeed, differ in the developmental timeline of such language-specific speech segmentation cues (e.g., Van Kampen et al., 2008).

Clearly, infants gradually learn which cues are advantageous to the segmentation of fluent speech in their language. When these cues work in concord, speech segmentation is facilitated (e.g., Mersad & Nazzi, 2012; Thiessen et al., 2005). What happens, however, when these cues conflict with one another? Do infants weigh each of these cues equally, or do they rely on some cues more than others? The limited studies on conflicting cues in word segmentation suggest that infants, like adults, weigh cues hierarchically, but across development they vary the cues they increasingly rely on. Initially, infants rely more on transitional probability cues (Thiessen & Saffran, 2003), but when infants are 8 months old, they weigh language-specific cues more heavily (Hay & Saffran, 2012; Johnson & Jusczyk, 2001; Thiessen & Saffran, 2003). Note that this shift emerges around the same time as when infants are said to be tuning into their native language (that is, show decreased sensitivity to non-native speech contrasts; Kuhl, 2004). Thus, it appears that, with increased exposure to their native language, infants become more native-like in their phonetic reorganization as well as in their ability to segment words from speech.

While most (HPP) studies examining infant speech segmentation ability manipulated the availability of speech segmentation cues, other (ERP) studies focused on how frequent infants should hear a word to elicit a recognition response. Because ERPs reflect an online manifestation of word recognition, this method allowed researchers to manipulate both the amount and type of familiarization required for word recognition. When both familiarization and test comprise continuous speech, Dutch 10-month-olds overall show a gradual recognition effect within eight tokens, i.e. the N200–500 gradually increases over repetitions (Junge et al., 2014; see also Figure 2.3). This recognition effect during familiarization developed even faster (within six repetitions) when we examined only those infants (68%) who at test continued to show the mature N200–500 for familiar words over novel words. In another study we severely reduced the familiarization to just one word embedded in an utterance: only infants with relatively large vocabularies show the mature recognition response (Junge, Kooijman et al., 2012). Thus it appears that around 10 months, some infants require fewer repetitions than others to elicit recognition.

All in all, we can conclude that by the end of their first year, infants become increasingly proficient in recognizing words from running speech because they have multiple cues to speech segmentation coupled with more mature memory skill to match words at their disposal.

2.3 Recognition of proto-words facilitates lexical acquisition

The studies summarized above show that infants gradually become more sophisticated in segmenting word-like units from speech. Jusczyk (2000) suggested that once infants recognize proto-words—word-like units without any meaning—they will start looking for concepts to match these words onto. Do infants treat these proto-words that they have segmented from speech as possible word candidates? Indeed, there is both behavioral and electrophysiological evidence that infants do so.

First, several behavioral studies demonstrate that infants learn novel mappings better when they first hear them as proto-words in fluent speech (i.e., without the matching object present; Graf Estes et al., 2007; Hay et al., 2011; Lany & Saffran, 2010; Swingley, 2007). Even when infants are confronted with ambiguous word-object pairings, they rely more on the word-form than on the object to anticipate upcoming events (Zamuner et al., 2014).

Second, we note that two electrophysiological studies reveal similar word recognition effects, regardless of whether infants were presented with accompanying visual referents or not (Junge, Cutler & Hagoort, 2012, presented infants with pictures of typical early words and their matching words, while Junge et al., 2014, presented infants with utterances in which low-frequency words were repeated, with no matching visual stimuli; cf. Figure 2.3). In both cases, the N200–500 becomes larger with repetition, which suggests that the words presented without visual context were treated like meaningful words. One might argue that this comparison merely shows that N200–500 indexes word-form repetition, but not necessarily the mapping of words to meaning. Yet, our finding that after the word-object familiarization phase the same infants notice at test whether or not specific pictures and words belonged together (as indexed by an adult-like N400; Junge, Cutler et al., 2012) suggests that infants treated the words as meaningful during the familiarization phase (see also Friedrich in Chapter 10). In short, both behavioral and electrophysiological studies highlight the likelihood that infants treat proto-words as possible words.

Other studies underscore the importance of infants' ability to find words in continuous speech by linking infant performance in speech segmentation studies to their future vocabulary development. Although infant research generally focuses on group reports, there is sufficient individual variation that reflects the infant's skill in segmenting words from speech. Several longitudinal analyses report (either via correlations or subgroup comparisons) positive linear relationships between infants' ability to detect words from fluent speech and the subsequent size of their lexicons (behavioral evidence: Newman et al., 2006, 2016; Singh et al., 2012; electrophysiological

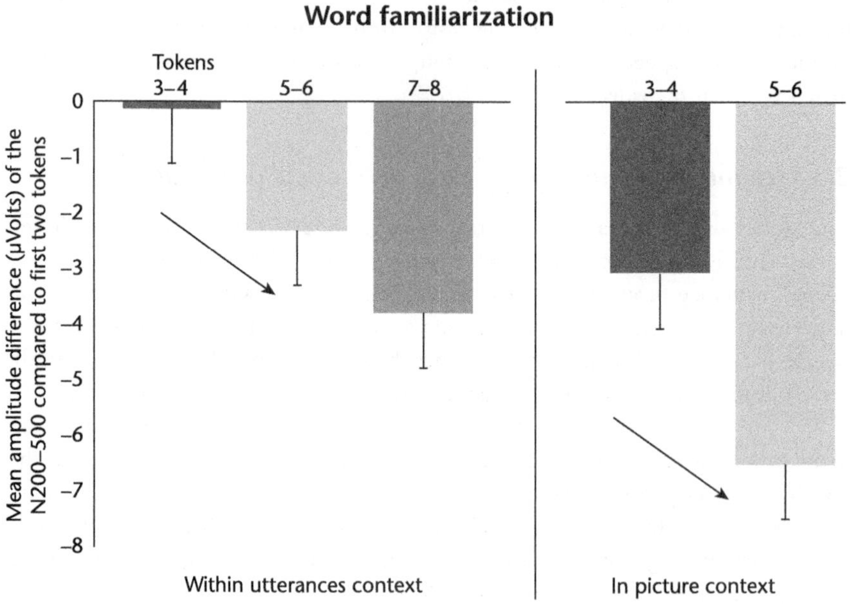

FIGURE 2.3 Results from two studies on word familiarization in 9- to 10-month-olds, differing in the context in which words are repeated: *left*, repetition of low-frequency words embedded in eight different sentences (cf. Junge et al., 2014); *right*, repetition of typical early words paired with six matching images (e.g., word *dog* paired with a picture of a dog, cf. Junge, Cutler & Hagoort, 2012). The plot shows that in both studies, the negativity corresponding to the N200–500 becomes larger for each subsequent pair of repetitions, relative to the first two tokens.

evidence: Junge, Kooijman et al., 2012; Kooijman et al., 2014; Junge & Cutler, 2014). A recent meta-analysis estimates this effect to be moderate ($r = +0.33$; 95% CIs [+0.17; +0.48]; Junge & Cutler, 2014). This further underscores how vital it is that infants can recognize word-forms from continuous speech; infants who show more advanced speech segmentation skill continue to develop larger vocabularies.

2.4 Future directions

Infants predominantly hear multi-word utterances. By the end of their first year, infants show great mastery in pulling out word-like units from speech. Most studies cited tested American-English hearing infants; only a few other (European) languages have been considered. It is therefore difficult to ascertain whether the trajectory observed in American-English infants also holds for infants in general (Fernald, 2010). Although it is likely that this development broadly generalizes to all infants, languages might differ in what they consider word-like units (i.e., compare a language like Thai, which has mainly monosyllabic words; Johnson, 2012, to a morphologically complex language like Hungarian; Gervain & Mehler, 2010). One direction for future research would be to see what kind of word-forms infants from more linguistically diverse backgrounds extract from speech, and whether their development also reflects increased reliance on language-specific cues. Notice further that even in the well-studied case of English, computational models do not agree on the units extracted from natural IDS (e.g., trigram phones; syllable or stressed syllable; e.g., Aslin et al., 1996; Bergmann et al., 2013; Curtin et al., 2005; Lignos, 2011; Yang, 2004). Future research should therefore consider the possible units into which infants decompose running speech, and whether this remains the same across development. Indeed, it is even plausible that infants show a transition in the units they segment from speech (i.e., from any type of syllable to only stressed syllable as a possible marker or word-onset; Thiessen & Saffran, 2003).

By being able to segment proto-words from speech, infants are well on their way to building a lexicon. Note that not only does a proto-lexicon enhance lexical acquisition, but it can, in turn, also affect phonological development (Martin et al., 2013), which has also been linked with later vocabulary development (see also Chapter 1). Hence, it appears that when infants are learning their first words, there are bi-directional links between different levels of spoken language acquisition (i.e., between phones, proto-words, words). This is in line with current popular models of language acquisition (e.g., PRIMIR; Werker & Curtin, 2005). Future research should examine the links between these levels more carefully to better understand differences across infants in early word learning. How do these levels of representation interact? How can we explain why some infants show more advanced speech segmentation skill than others? For instance, do infants with more advanced speech segmentation skill show earlier reliance on language-specific speech segmentation cues than others? If so, does this mirror their phonological development, or can we relate it to the number of words they already understand? The previous two decades have brought us crucial insights into how infants learn to break a speech stream into proto-words, but it remains yet unclear how this development relates to their concurrent phonological or lexical development.

To summarize, this chapter has highlighted the link between early word-form recognition (from fluent speech) and early word learning. Clearly, early word learning greatly progresses when infants are able to pull out possible words from the available input. Future research should aim to explain what drives individual differences in speech segmentation skill.

References

Altvater-Mackensen, N., & Mani, N. (2013). Word-form familiarity bootstraps infant speech segmentation. *Developmental Science*, *16*(6), 980–990.

Aslin, R.N., Woodward, J.Z., LaMendola, N.P., & Bever, T.G. (1996). Models of word segmentation in fluent maternal speech to infants. In J. Morgan & K. Demuth (Eds.), *Signal to syntax: Bootstrapping from speech to grammar in early acquisition*, 117–134. Mahwah, NJ: Lawrence Erlbaum.

Bergelson, E., & Swingley, D. (2012). At 6–9 months, human infants know the meanings of many common nouns. *PNAS*, *109*(9), 3253–3258.

Bergmann, C., Ten Bosch, L., Fikkert, P., & Boves, L. (2013). A computational model to investigate assumptions in the headturn preference procedure. *Frontiers in Psychology*, *4*.

Bortfeld, H., Morgan, J.L., Golinkoff, R.M., & Rathbun, K. (2005). Mommy and me familiar names help launch babies into speech-stream segmentation. *Psychological Science*, *16*(4), 298–304.

Brent, M.R., & Siskind, J.M. (2001). The role of exposure to isolated words in early vocabulary development. *Cognition*, *81*(2), B33–B44.

Curtin, S., Mintz, T.H., & Byrd, D. (2001). Coarticulatory cues enhance infants' recognition of syllable sequences in speech. In *Proceedings of the 25th Annual Boston University Conference on Language Development, Vol. 1*, 190. Somerville, MA: Cascadilla Press.

Curtin, S., Mintz, T.H., & Christiansen, M.H. (2005). Stress changes the representational landscape: Evidence from word segmentation. *Cognition*, *96*(3), 233–262.

Cutler, A. (2012). *Native listening: Language experience and the recognition of spoken words*. Cambridge, MA: MIT Press.

Cutler, A., & Carter, D.M. (1987). The predominance of strong initial syllables in the English vocabulary. *Computer Speech & Language*, *2*(3), 133–142.

Depaolis, R.A., Vihman, M.M., & Keren-Portnoy, T. (2014). When do infants begin recognizing familiar words in sentences? *Journal of Child Language*, *41*(01), 226–239.

Fernald, A. (1985). Four-month-old infants prefer to listen to motherese. *Infant Behavior and Development*, *8*(2), 181–195.

Fernald, A. (2010). Getting beyond the "convenience sample" in research on early cognitive development. *Behavioral and Brain Sciences*, *33*, 91–92.

Garcia-Sierra, A., Rivera-Gaxiola, M., Percaccio, C.R., Conboy, B.T., Romo, H., Klarman, L., Ortiz, S., & Kuhl, P.K. (2011). Bilingual language learning: An ERP study relating early brain responses to speech, language input, and later word production. *Journal of Phonetics*, *39*(4), 546–557.

Gervain, J., & Mehler, J. (2010). Speech perception and language acquisition in the first year of life. *Annual Review of Psychology*, *61*, 191–218.

Gonzalez-Gomez, N., & Nazzi, T. (2013). Effects of prior phonotactic knowledge on infant word segmentation: The case of nonadjacent dependencies. *Journal of Speech, Language, and Hearing Research*, *56*(3), 840–849.

Goyet, L., de Schonen, S., & Nazzi, T. (2010). Words and syllables in fluent speech segmentation by French-learning infants: An ERP study. *Brain Research*, *1332*, 75–89.

Graf Estes, K., Evans, J.L., Alibali, M.W., & Saffran, J.R. (2007). Can infants map meaning to newly segmented words? Statistical segmentation and word learning. *Psychological Science*, *18*(3), 254–260.

Hay, J.F., Pelucchi, B., Estes, K.G., & Saffran, J.R. (2011). Linking sounds to meanings: infant statistical learning in a natural language. *Cognitive Psychology*, *63*(2), 93–106.

Hay, J.F., & Saffran, J.R. (2012). Rhythmic grouping biases constrain infant statistical learning. *Infancy*, *17*(6), 610–641.

Houston, D.M., Jusczyk, P.W., Kuijpers, C., Coolen, R., & Cutler, A. (2000). Cross-language word segmentation by 9-month-olds. *Psychonomic Bulletin & Review*, *7*(3), 504–509.

Houston-Price, C., & Nakai, S. (2004). Distinguishing novelty and familiarity effects in infant preference procedures. *Infant and Child Development*, *13*(4), 341–348.

Johnson, E.K. (2012). Bootstrapping language: Are infant statisticians up to the job? In P. Rebuschat & J. Williams (Eds.), *Statistical learning and language acquisition*, 55–89. Berlin: Mouton de Gruyter.

Johnson, E.K., & Jusczyk, P.W. (2001). Word segmentation by 8-month-olds: When speech cues count more than statistics. *Journal of Memory and Language*, *44*(4), 548–567.

Johnson, E.K., Jusczyk, P.W., Cutler, A., & Norris, D. (2003). Lexical viability constraints on speech segmentation by infants. *Cognitive Psychology*, *46*(1), 65–97.

Johnson, E.K., Lahey, M., Ernestus, M., & Cutler, A. (2013). A multimodal corpus of speech to infant and adult listeners. *The Journal of the Acoustical Society of America*, *134*(6), EL534–EL540.

Johnson, E.K., & Tyler, M.D. (2010). Testing the limits of statistical learning for word segmentation. *Developmental Science*, *13*(2), 339–345.

Junge, C., & Cutler, A. (2014). Early word recognition and later language skills. *Brain Sciences*, *4*(4), 532–559.

Junge, C., Cutler, A., & Hagoort, P. (2012). Electrophysiological evidence of early word learning. *Neuropsychologia*, *50*(14), 3702–3712.

Junge, C., Cutler, A., & Hagoort, P. (2014). Successful word recognition by 10-month-olds given continuous speech both at initial exposure and test. *Infancy*, *19*(2), 179–193.

Junge, C., Kooijman, V., Hagoort, P., & Cutler, A. (2012). Rapid recognition at 10 months as a predictor of language development. *Developmental Science*, *15*(4), 463–473.

Jusczyk, P.W. (2000). *The Discovery of Spoken Language*. Cambridge, MA: MIT Press.

Jusczyk, P.W., & Aslin, R.N. (1995). Infants' detection of the sound patterns of words in fluent speech. *Cognitive Psychology*, *29*(1), 1–23.

Jusczyk, P.W., Houston, D.M., & Newsome, M. (1999). The beginnings of word segmentation in English-learning infants. *Cognitive Psychology*, *39*(3), 159–207.

Kooijman, V., Hagoort, P., & Cutler, A. (2005). Electrophysiological evidence for prelinguistic infants' word recognition in continuous speech. *Cognitive Brain Research*, *24*(1), 109–116.

Kooijman, V., Hagoort, P., & Cutler, A. (2009). Prosodic structure in early word segmentation: ERP evidence from Dutch ten-month-olds. *Infancy*, *14*(6), 591–612.

Kooijman, V., Junge, C., Johnson, E.K., Hagoort, P., & Cutler, A. (2013). Predictive brain signals of linguistic development. *Frontiers in Psychology*, *4*.

Kudo, N., Nonaka, Y., Mizuno, N., Mizuno, K., & Okanoya, K. (2011). On-line statistical segmentation of a non-speech auditory stream in neonates as demonstrated by event-related brain potentials. *Developmental Science*, *14*, 1100–1106.

Kuhl, P.K. (2004). Early language acquisition: Cracking the speech code. *Nature Reviews Neuroscience*, *5*(11), 831–843.

Lany, J., & Saffran, J.R. (2010). From statistics to meaning: Infants' acquisition of lexical categories. *Psychological Science*, *21*(2), 284–291.

Lew-Williams, C., Pelucchi, B., & Saffran, J.R. (2011). Isolated words enhance statistical language learning in infancy. *Developmental Science, 14*(6), 1323–1329.

Lignos, C. (2011). Modeling infant word segmentation. In *Proceedings of the Fifteenth Annual Conference on Computational Natural Language Learning*, 29–38. Portland, Oregon, Association for Computational Linguistics.

Männel, C., & Friederici, A.D. (2013). Accentuate or repeat? Brain signatures of developmental periods in infant word recognition. *Cortex, 49*, 2788–2798.

Martin, A., Peperkamp, S., & Dupoux, E. (2013). Learning phonemes with a proto-lexicon. *Cognitive Science, 37*(1), 103–124.

Mattys, S.L., & Jusczyk, P.W. (2001a). Phonotactic cues for segmentation of fluent speech by infants. *Cognition, 78*(2), 91–121.

Mattys, S.L., & Jusczyk, P.W. (2001b). Do infants segment words or recurring contiguous patterns? *Journal of Experimental Psychology: Human Perception and Performance, 27*(3), 644.

Mattys, S.L., White, L., & Melhorn, J.F. (2005). Integration of multiple speech segmentation cues: a hierarchical framework. *Journal of Experimental Psychology: General, 134*(4), 477.

Mersad, K., & Nazzi, T. (2012). When Mommy comes to the rescue of statistics: Infants combine top-down and bottom-up cues to segment speech. *Language Learning and Development, 8*(3), 303–315.

Morgan, J.L. (1996). Prosody and the roots of parsing. *Language and Cognitive Processes, 11*(1–2), 69–106.

Nazzi, T., Iakimova, G., Bertoncini, J., Frédonie, S., & Alcantara, C. (2006). Early segmentation of fluent speech by infants acquiring French: Emerging evidence for crosslinguistic differences. *Journal of Memory and Language, 54*(3), 283–299.

Nazzi, T., Mersad, K., Sundara, M., Iakimova, G., & Polka, L. (2014). Early word segmentation in infants acquiring Parisian French: Task-dependent and dialect-specific aspects. *Journal of Child Language, 41*(3), 600–633.

Newman, R.S., Ratner, N.B., Jusczyk, A.M., Jusczyk, P.W., & Dow, K.A. (2006). Infants' early ability to segment the conversational speech signal predicts later language development: A retrospective analysis. *Developmental Psychology, 42*(4), 643–655.

Newman, R.S., Rowe, M.L., & Ratner, N.B. (2016). Input and uptake at 7 months predicts toddler vocabulary: The role of child-directed speech and infant processing skills in language development. *Journal of Child Language, 43*(5), 1158–1173.

Ngon, C., Martin, A., Dupoux, E., Cabrol, D., Dutat, M., & Peperkamp, S. (2013). (Non) words, (non) words, (non) words: Evidence for a protolexicon during the first year of life. *Developmental Science, 16*(1), 24–34.

Parise, E., & Csibra, G. (2012). Electrophysiological evidence for the understanding of maternal speech by 9-month-old infants. *Psychological Science, 23*, 728–733.

Pelucchi, B., Hay, J.F., & Saffran, J.R. (2009a). Statistical learning in a natural language by 8-month-old infants. *Child Development, 80*, 674–685

Pelucchi, B., Hay, J.F., & Saffran, J.R. (2009b). Learning in reverse: Eight-month-old infants track backward transitional probabilities. *Cognition, 113*(2), 244–247.

Polka, L., & Sundara, M. (2012). Word segmentation in monolingual infants acquiring Canadian English and Canadian French: Native language, cross-dialect, and cross-language comparisons. *Infancy, 17*(2), 198–232.

Saffran, J.R. (2001). Words in a sea of sounds: The output of infant statistical learning. *Cognition, 81*(2), 149–169.

Saffran, J.R., Aslin, R.N., & Newport, E.L. (1996). Statistical learning by 8-month-old infants. *Science, 274*(5294), 1926–1928.

Seidl, A., & Johnson, E.K. (2006). Infant word segmentation revisited: Edge alignment facilitates target extraction. *Developmental Science, 9*(6), 565–573.

Shi, R., & Lepage, M. (2008). The effect of functional morphemes on word segmentation in preverbal infants. *Developmental Science, 11*(3), 407–413.

Singh, L., Reznick, S.J., & Xuehua, L. (2012). Infant word segmentation and childhood vocabulary development: A longitudinal analysis. *Developmental Science, 15*(4), 482–495.

Swingley, D. (2007). Lexical exposure and word-form encoding in 1.5-year-olds. *Developmental Psychology, 43*(2), 454.

Thiessen, E.D., & Erickson, L.C. (2012). Discovering words in fluent speech: The contribution of two kinds of statistical information. *Frontiers in Psychology, 3*.

Thiessen, E.D., Hill, E.A., & Saffran, J.R. (2005). Infant-directed speech facilitates word segmentation. *Infancy, 7*(1), 53–71.

Thiessen, E.D., Kronstein, A.T., & Hufnagle, D.G. (2013). The extraction and integration framework: A two-process account of statistical learning. *Psychological Bulletin, 139*(4), 792.

Thiessen, E.D., & Saffran, J.R. (2003). When cues collide: Use of stress and statistical cues to word boundaries by 7-to 9-month-old infants. *Developmental Psychology, 39*(4), 706.

Tincoff, R., & Jusczyk, P.W. (1999). Some beginnings of word comprehension in 6-month-olds. *Psychological Science, 10*(2), 172–175.

Van Kampen, A., Parmaksiz, G., van de Vijver, R., & Höhle, B. (2008). Metrical and statistical cues for word segmentation: The use of vowel harmony and word stress as cues to word boundaries by 6-and 9-month-old Turkish learners. In *Language Acquisition and Development: Proceedings of GALA, Vol. 2007*, 313–324.

Werker, J.F., & Curtin, S. (2005). PRIMIR: A developmental framework of infant speech processing. *Language Learning and Development, 1*(2), 197–234.

Yang, C.D. (2004). Universal grammar, statistics or both? *Trends in Cognitive Sciences, 8*(10), 451–456.

Zamuner, T.S., Fais, L., & Werker, J.F. (2014). Infants track word-forms in early word-object associations. *Developmental Science, 17*(4), 481–491.

3

INTRINSIC AND EXTRINSIC CUES TO WORD LEARNING

Padraic Monaghan

DEPARTMENT OF PSYCHOLOGY, LANCASTER UNIVERSITY, UK

Marina Kalashnikova

THE MARCS INSTITUTE, UNIVERSITY OF WESTERN SYDNEY, AUSTRALIA

Karen Mattock

SCHOOL OF SOCIAL SCIENCES & PSYCHOLOGY AND THE MARCS INSTITUTE, UNIVERSITY OF WESTERN SYDNEY, AUSTRALIA

Why word learning is difficult

Once the child has resolved the extremely difficult problems of figuring out the phonemes of their language (Benders & Altvater-Mackensen, this volume) and determining where word-like units begin and end in continuous speech (Junge, this volume), they are then able to map those candidate words onto objects, actions, and relations in the world around them. However, forming this link between the word and its referent in the environment is far from trivial and has been a hot topic both for developmental language researchers as well as philosophers of language over the last 60 years (Bloom, 2000).

One of the most profound issues is how children know, or learn, that words refer at all. How does the child know that (some of) the sounds emerging from the caregiver's mouth actually relate to the environment? This symbol-grounding problem may be resolved either by an innate tendency for the child to assume that meaning is carried by words (e.g., Pinker, 1984), or it may be a consequence of learning by association or by hypothesis testing, with the child noticing that certain speech sounds tend to co-occur with certain features of the environment (e.g., Siskind, 1996). A further intriguing suggestion is that symbol-grounding may piggyback upon cross-modal relations that are part of the perceptual system's structure. For instance, front versus back vowels are reliably related to a small-versus-large size distinction in language (compare the vowels in *large* versus *little*, for instance), and such sound-symbolic properties of speech may assist the child in bridging between speech sounds and aspects of the environment to which they refer (Imai et al., 2015; Spector & Maurer, 2009; Monaghan et al., 2014).

Once children understand that symbols are grounded, determining the precise mappings between words and the world is still a problem that remains to be solved. Quine (1960) articulated this issue by likening the child's word learning to the difficulty facing a field linguist trying to determine the meaning of words in an unknown language. For a native speaker emitting the utterance "Gavagai," spoken as a rabbit runs past, the problem for the field linguist is that there are infinitely many possible referents for the word. It could be the rabbit, the rabbit's fur, the rabbit's color, the running action, the manner in which the rabbit runs, the weather, the beauty of the scene, or the state of bemusement of a speaker of an alternative language. In short, there are myriad possible mappings from the word to the environment that are not disambiguated from observing a speaker describing the world.

Quine's (1960) statement of the problem focused on the size of the set of possible referents but ignores a further complication for word learning. This is that the utterance itself, "Gavagai," could comprise one or more words, each of which could refer to different aspects of the environment. Then, the child needs to be able to resolve not just a one-to-many mapping problem, but many-to-many mapping, which is combinatorially more complex to accomplish (Monaghan & Mattock, 2012). A related difficulty is to then determine the extension of the word-world mapping. Thus, if "Gavagai" does refer to the rabbit, then how does the language learner know that it is the category of rabbits, and not just this particular rabbit (Markman, 1994)?

These fundamental difficulties facing the child acquiring their first language have led to different proposals for how language-to-environment mappings are constrained. Some of these are learner-internal biases, which are perceptual, attentional, or pragmatic constraints that can limit the scope of possible referents in the environment for the spoken word. Others are learner-external, which are properties of the communicative situation itself and constraints that derive from language structure, that guide children to the word's intended referent. The remainder of the chapter reviews these two alternatives before considering current theoretical models of word learning and how these constraints may operate in tandem during language acquisition.

Intrinsic constraints for word learning

The solution to the problem of forming word-referent mappings has traditionally been discussed in terms of learner-internal biases to form constraints that limit selection of the referent from the environment and that govern the extension of the word (e.g., Markman, 1994). There are two broad categories of such constraints: biases about the word-naming process that provide information about word-world mappings that are permissible; and pragmatic constraints that derive from communicative conventions between the parent and the child (see Rowland, 2014, for a more detailed review of these constraints than presented here).

Of the word learning biases, *mutual exclusivity* refers to the assumption that the child makes in assuming that each referent in the environment has a single name (Kalashnikova et al., 2014; Markman & Wachtel, 1988). Thus, in the presence of multiple objects in the environment, if the child already knows the names for (some of) these objects, then this can assist in constraining the mapping between a novel word and its potential referent. Relatedly, the "Novel Name-Nameless Category" principle (Golinkoff et al., 1994) suggests that children are biased to link a novel word with an unnamed object, and the "Lexical Gap Filling" hypothesis (Merriman & Kutlesic, 1993) suggests that children are drawn towards trying to discover a word to attach to a novel object in their environment. Similar attentional biases also contribute to learning, with children demonstrating a preference to novelty in new label mappings (Horst et al., 2010; Mather & Plunkett, 2012).

There has been some debate about the point at which these biases begin to be applied in word learning, and whether they are therefore a prerequisite for learning, or actually emerge as a consequence of learning the way in which words seem to relate to referents (i.e., that they follow from children's observation that there is a predominantly one-to-one mapping between words and objects and actions in the environment). Halberda (2003) found that 14- and 16-month-old infants could not use mutual exclusivity, but 17-month-olds could. Bion, Borovsky, and Fernald (2013) found no evidence for 18-month-old infants using mutual exclusivity but discovered that at 24 and 30 months, mutual exclusivity use was correlated with productive vocabulary scores. However, Markman, Wasow, and Hansen (2003) did find that mutual exclusivity was present in children in early stages of language learning, with vocabularies below 50 items. Other evidence for experience driving mutual exclusivity, rather than mutual exclusivity driving learning as a bias from the outset, can be derived from infants growing up bilingually. Bilinguals, who encounter more than one label for each referent in their linguistic input, have been shown to rely on mutual exclusivity to a significantly lesser extent than monolinguals when presented with novel words (Houston-Price et al., 2010; see also Fennell, this volume).

Other learner-internal biases restrict the scope for the potential referent in the environment. Early in language acquisition, children seem to have a *whole-object bias*, where a label is not likely to be associated with an object part (such as the ears of the rabbit in the "Gavagai" example) (Macnamara, 1982). However, children also seem to be more likely to extend a word to objects that have similar shapes than other properties of the objects (such as color) (Baldwin, 1992). Other biases extend labels to objects with a similar function (Kemler Nelson, 1999) or that are determined to be of the same category, termed the *taxonomic principle* (Markman, 1994). Some of these biases can be seen to extend from general pragmatic principles of interlocution, where communication is assumed to be (maximally) informative, such that speakers will use a conventional form for the same concept and will use different words when different concepts are intended (Clark, 2009).

The role of social-pragmatic influences can be seen in the effect of contextual information about the speaker in children's learning (Tomasello, 2003), such as the reliability of an informant influencing whether the speaker's use of a word is learned by the child, and the possibility of learning multiple words for the same referent from speakers of different languages (Kalashnikova et al., 2015; Merriman & Kutlesic, 1993).

There is debate about the extent to which these learner-internal constraints are able to sufficiently constrain the learning situation for word-referent mappings (MacWhinney, 1991). Several of the constraints may also be a consequence of learning from the co-occurrences that actually occur in the environment, i.e., learner-external constraints derived from learning situations. For instance, MacWhinney (1991) argues that the example of mutual exclusivity may not be the expression of an internal bias applied to learning words but may instead be a consequence of the child learning that there is generally a one-to-one mapping between the co-occurrences of labels and their referents. Such a constraint would then be necessary for coping with a growing vocabulary and is consistent with the correlation between mutual exclusivity and vocabulary size (Bion et al., 2013).

Extrinsic cues for word learning

Alternative approaches to determining constraints on word-referent mappings, with a growing frequency (see, e.g., Smith et al., 2014), involve an empirical approach to determine what properties of the external communicative situation assist word learning. Once specified, these information sources can be simulated in models of word learning to ascertain the extent to which they guide word-referent mappings without yet requiring additional theoretical complexity of positing additional language-specific internal mechanisms for acquisition.

Statistical associative information

The problems of ambiguity in determining the referent and discovering the extension of the reference in the "Gavagai" example are mitigated to a degree by considering the child's learning experience as being across multiple instances rather than a single learning event. It is certainly true that one cannot accurately infer the referent for "Gavagai" when hearing this word just once and observing a single scene. However, over multiple experiences, the child can begin to learn the invariant property of the environment that is observed whenever "Gavagai" is heard (Siskind, 1996). Thus, if there is always a rabbit when the speaker says "Gavagai," but the color of the animal varies, and the motion of the animal changes, then the learner can begin to associate "Gavagai" with a rabbit rather than its features or the running action. Yu and Ballard (2007) showed that such associations were available in naturalistic word learning situations. Yu and Ballard encoded parent-child interactions in terms of the number of objects present in the environment and the co-occurrence of particular objects with words spoken in their presence. They found that these co-occurrences enabled mappings between particular words and objects to begin to be formed through establishing word-object associations (see also Yu and Smith, 2012, for an updated model).

Smith and Yu (2008) tested whether children in the early stages of word learning were able to use such cross-situational statistical information to acquire word-referent mappings. Eighteen-month-old infants were shown pairs of objects and heard pairs of words. From a single learning instance, the child could not know which word related to which object, but over multiple instances, words co-occurred with their referent with 100% probability, with chance co-occurrences between words and other referents reduced. The children were successful in solving the mapping. Hence, useful associative information, based on corpus-analysis studies of learning situations, was shown to be useable by children acquiring their language. However, these learning instances were idealized in that all objects that were present were named, and all words in the learning situation were nouns. Yu and Ballard (2007) showed that some disambiguation was possible from co-occurrences between words in utterances and objects and actions in the environment. Yet, as the complexity of the learning situation becomes more like that actually observed in naturalistic settings, with multi-word utterances and noisy environments, additional cues are likely to become more valuable.

Distributional constraints

As discussed in (Junge, this volume), distributional information in the form of transitional probabilities between phonemes and syllables in continuous speech proves highly useful information for determining word boundaries (e.g., Saffran et al., 1996). Such distributional information also has been shown to be important for determining the grammatical role of words in speech. Natural languages tend to follow a Zipfian distribution in terms of the relative frequencies of words. This means that a small number of words—in English, typically the function words (e.g., the, a, you, to)—occur very frequently, and they also tend to intervene between content words that refer to objects and actions in the environment (Monaghan et al., 2007). For instance, in English *the* or *a* tends to occur before nouns, and *you* and *to* tend to occur before verbs. In Yu and Ballard's (2007) analysis of word learning situations, a computational model of learning based on these data was able to better learn the mapping between nouns and objects and verbs and actions in the environment if this distributional information from function words was also available to the model to assist in categorizing the words, and consequently restricting the possible set of referents.

Monaghan and Mattock (2012) tested whether language learners could actually use this distributional information to constrain their mappings between multi-word utterances and objects in the environment. They used an artificial language of the form "a A b B" where the "a" word operated as a function word that always preceded a set of noun category words (A), and the "b" word was a function word that preceded a set of verb category words (B). Language learners viewed two objects, one of which always co-occurred with the "A" noun category word, and the other which was referred to by another "A" category word that was not heard in this learning instance. Over multiple trials, language learners were able to acquire the mapping between particular noun category words and objects, despite the additional complexity of multiple words occurring in each utterance. Furthermore, learners were able to disregard words that did not have a referent in the scene (i.e., the "B" words). Yet, when compared to a condition where the function words were not present—a language of the form "A B"—the presence of distributional information in the form of function words was found to boost learning (see also Arnon and Snider, 2010, for further evidence that greater complexity in utterances may provide assistance in language learning by increasing the constraints on structures to be acquired).

Distributional information is not restricted to just noun-object mappings, and also is prevalent in studies that have tested children's acquisition of verb-action mappings (Childers 2011). Monaghan, Mattock, Davies, and Smith (2015) tested whether cross-situational statistics, with distributional information, were sufficient for learning both noun-object and verb-action mappings. The language was again of the form "a A b B," but this time the "B" verb category word referred to the action of the object referred to by the "A" noun category word, and language learners had to select which of two moving objects were named by the utterance. Learning was successful, and follow-up tests determined that both nouns and verbs were acquired. These studies demonstrated that, even when utterances approximated more closely the complexity of naturalistic language, the inherent distributional information promoted learning by constraining which words could map to which aspects of the environment.

Phonological and prosodic constraints

Child-directed speech generally has a broader range of pitch and reaches higher frequencies than adult-directed speech (Kuhl et al., 1997; Fernald & Simon, 1984; Papousek et al., 1985), and words have longer duration (Garnica, 1977). Hence, there is substantial possible variation in prosody that could be informative for language learning. Fernald (1991), for instance, proposed that this adjustment in pitch and intonation contributed not only to maintaining the child's attention but also in helping to identify words in speech. In fact, recent evidence has shown that infants in their second year of life (17 and 21 months) are more successful at mapping novel labels to their referents when the labels are presented in infant-directed compared to adult-directed speech (Graf Estes & Hurley, 2013; Ma et al., 2011).

In stress-based languages such as English, prosodic stress provides information about word boundaries (Jusczyk et al., 1999), as words tend to have initial syllable stress. Prosodic stress also provides information about the grammatical category of the word. In English for instance, nouns are much more likely than verbs to have first syllable stress, and function words tend to have no stress at all (Kelly, 1992). A range of segmental phonological cues also correlate with grammatical category, providing further possibilities for constraints to word-referent mappings to be derived (Monaghan et al., 2007). For example, across a range of languages there is a greater prevalence of bilabials (/b/, /p/, /w/) in nouns than in verbs, and in English, nouns tend to have more syllables than verbs.

These phonological distinctions in grammatical category have been shown to influence children's decisions in word-referent mapping tasks. Cassidy and Kelly (2001) showed that the position of primary stress and word length of a new word were able to direct children to either a noun-object or a verb-action mapping. Three- to 6-year-old children viewed objects performing actions, such as a bear running, then were asked whether nonwords such as "pell" or "gebinarf" are more likely to mean "the bear" or "the running." Children reliably used the word length cue to guide their decisions about the intended referent, linking the longer word to the object and the shorter word to the action. Relatedly, Fitneva, Christiansen, and Monaghan (2009) demonstrated that segmental phonological properties were also able to guide children to correctly interpret nonwords as nouns or verbs in word-referent mapping tasks. The stimuli were constructed to be closer overall to nouns or to verbs in English and in French using a global similarity measure, termed "phonological typicality." For instance, the nonword "pralt" was more similar to nouns than to verbs, and the nonword "skik" was more similar to verbs than to nouns. Children of both language groups were more likely to accept "pralt" as an object reference than "skik," which was more likely to be paired with an action.

The general characteristics of child-directed speech, in terms of varied intonation and emphasized prosody, can facilitate learning novel word-object mappings (Fernald & Mazzie, 1991; Golinkoff & Alioto, 1995). Furthermore, Messer (1981) found that in almost 50% of utterances, the word in a sentence with the highest amplitude was the referring word, therefore a potential source of the benefit of child-directed speech for word learning being that prosody provides important cues to the speaker's intended meaning, and can thus constrain the identification of the referring word in a complex utterance. Thus, a combination of phonological information regarding grammatical category, together with prosodic information to highlight the key information in an utterance, may well combine to constrain the problems of the many-to-many mappings in word learning.

Gestural constraints

Distributional and phonological information to guide word-referent mappings are examples of constraints that emerge from the structure of the language itself. However, there are extra-linguistic cues to guide children in forming mappings that are still a key part of communicative exchanges. In particular, eye-gaze and deictic gestures are valuable information sources for drawing the child's attention to the intended referent from a potentially large array of alternatives. If the speaker of "Gavagai" accompanies the utterance with a stare toward the rabbit in the environment, then this provides some clues to the language learner about the intention of the speaker. Similarly, a pointing gesture could further constrain the possibilities in the environment. Iverson, Capirci, Longobardi, and Caselli (1999) found that approximately 15% of caregiver utterances directed toward children aged 16–20 months were accompanied by simple gestures referring to the immediate context.

Several studies have found that children's word learning is assisted by such gestural cues (Baldwin, 1991; Goodwyn et al., 2000; Houston-Price et al., 2006; Kobayashi, 1998; Moore et al., 1999) and that young infants' sensitivity to such cues can predict subsequent vocabulary development (Brooks & Meltzoff, 2008). For example, Goodwyn, Acredolo, and Brown (2000) found that 19- to 24-month-old children improved their language skills when caregivers were instructed to increase gestures and verbal information when labeling objects compared to a group asked to increase only verbal information. Similarly, Baldwin (1991) found that when an adult was naming an object that was incompatible with the child's attention to a scene, the child consulted the adult's gaze direction and gestural cues to assist in learning the referent. Such instances where the child and the adult are attending to different aspects of a scene are commonplace in parent-child interactions (Collis, 1977; Harris et al., 1983), indicating the importance of gestural cues to disambiguate a word learning situation.

Gestural information can also assist the child in distinguishing between names for whole versus part objects. Parents of children between 1 and 2 years of age tend to name the whole object before naming object parts, or attributes of the object (Ninio, 1980), and naming of whole objects is also likely to be accompanied by moving whole objects rather than parts to direct 8-month-old children's attention away from object parts as a potential referent for the word (Gogate et al., 2013). Thus, gestural information provides valuable constraints to the scope of referents, dovetailing with the constraints within the language that restrict interpretations of words.

Given that there are multiple cues that seem to provide complementary information toward resolving the problem of forming word-world mappings, the question remains—how do these multiple cues combine to assist in word learning? The next section reviews this with models of word learning.

Cue combination in models of word learning

The "Intersensory Redundancy Hypothesis" (Bahrick et al., 2004) contends that co-occurring cues increase the saliency of individual cues by drawing the learner's attention to the informative aspects of the environment. Thus, the child learns that cues are informative because those cues are correlated, which increases the child's confidence in the value of those sources. If a particular cue to word learning is just present by chance, then its co-occurrence with other information sources will not be reliable. For instance, children learn the relation between speech sounds and objects better if they have prior experience of speech sounds and motions of objects (Gogate & Bahrick, 1998), and Walker-Andrews (1997) suggested that learning social cues, such as emotion in faces, is promoted by additional sensory inputs, such as emotion present in voices.

However, the intersensory redundancy hypothesis accounts for the mutual operation of extrinsic cues to word learning but does not provide a seamless account for how intrinsic word learning heuristics or biases could align with these external cues. They may operate in tandem, but then it is not clear how use of learner-internal cues assists in increasing the saliency of the learner-external cues. Consequently, we are left without an account of how these types of cues may interpenetrate.

An alternative hypothesis for integration of information is that language learners combine cues from multiple sources, either additively (To et al., 2011), where each cue contributes to the likelihood of a mapping being formed, or hierarchically, where certain cues dominate over others (Hollich et al., 2000; Houston-Price et al., 2006; Kirkham, 2010). The Emergentist Coalition Model (ECM) (Hollich et al., 2000) proposes that both intrinsic and extrinsic constraints coalesce to assist in word learning. Thus, mutual exclusivity and the other word learning biases combine with social-pragmatic cues and gestural information, as well as statistical information from distributional and phonological sources within the language. The use of cues varies during development, with the importance of cues related to their reliability, but are modulated by the complexity of discovering the value of the cue. For instance, the ECM proposes that there is an initial dominance of attentional cues that are later refined with the child's discovery of distributional cues to constrain the grammatical category of a word's meaning. The refinement also means that disambiguation can become more and more effective as children learn. For instance, the whole-word bias may apply in initial stages of learning but then be weighted against distributional and gestural information that indicate a part is being discussed (e.g., "the penguin" versus "the penguin's feathers"). The ECM proposes that this refinement of cue combination also drives domain-general learning mechanisms to apply in the case of language. Hence, the model is based on general learning principles but becomes a language-specific model because of the way in which cues correlate within language learning situations.

Yet, using information from multiple sources is taxing, and keeping track of so many possible sources across many situations may just not be feasible, at least in the first stages of word acquisition. The child's memory and attentional limitations enable a distinction to be drawn between models of word learning that posit that children acquire words through hypothesis testing and those that learn through associative learning between words and environmental referents (see also Westermann & Twomey, this volume). A Bayesian approach to modeling children's development proposes that the child compares alternative hypotheses about her environment, and quickly responds to reject the hypothesis that is inconsistent with the data to which she is exposed. Such models result in a characterisation of the child as performing optimally to the environmental information available. Such models are extremely powerful for specifying the information that children are responding to, and they also permit different biases to be incorporated into the model to test their contribution to the task (e.g., Frank et al., 2009; Xu & Tenenbaum, 2007). An alternative is to conceive of the child as an associative learner, where multiple cues are available and used by the child in acquiring mappings between words and their meanings (Yu & Smith, 2007). Such a process is then gradual and does not require an assumption of optimal learning by the child, better reflecting the child's potential attentional and memory limitations.

In actual fact, Yu and Smith (2012) showed that the distinction between these modeling traditions is small in terms of predicting behavior when the environment is replete with information sources and the child is assumed to be able to access these sources. But in an environment where there are limitations to the available cues, associative learning reduces in accuracy and may not be so effective at simulating children's rapid word-referent mapping behavior. However, it may be that the child applies multiple systems of learning—one that applies a fast hypothesis test to the word learning situation, and the other that slowly and incrementally acquires associations between words and meanings (see Horst, this volume). Indeed, McMurray, Horst, and Samuelson (2012) demonstrated through experimental studies and a computational model that rapid learning, evident in fast mapping tasks for instance, may not result in long-term retention of a word, and that slower, associative learning may better reflect the stable acquisition of words.

A further problem with multiple cue combination is that cues are individually unreliable, and so combining multiple unreliable sources can result in worse performance than using only a single cue (referred to as the dilution effect). An intriguing study by Yurovsky, Boyer, Smith, and Yu (2013) demonstrated a possible solution to the problem of unreliability and dilution of cues. They showed that when adults observed either a reliable (70% accuracy) or a less-reliable (40% accuracy) cue, they were able to use the reliable cue, but when both cues were combined, their use of the reliable cue reduced to a level close to the average of the accuracy of the two cues. However, for infants aged 11 months, the combination of cues was better than a single cue alone. Hence, children's responses were based on optimal use of the information present in the environment, whereas adults' learning was prone to dilution from multiple, individually unreliable cues.

A final alternative is that the unreliability of individual multiple cues is exploited by the language learner in order to create a flexible and adaptable approach to changing situations in the language environment (for an analogous case in visual processing, see Nardini et al., 2008). Multiple cues vary in their presence across learning situations, thus, depending on a particular cue would be a precarious strategy for the learner. For instance, if the child began to use joint visual attention as a cue to word learning, such that the referent for a word was selected based only on this information, then when joint attention was not present (in the cases where the parent's gaze is distracted from the focus of conversation, or in cases of language production when the speaker is not directly observable), learning would be impossible. Such a brittle approach to learning would be counterproductive to language acquisition in the varied and noisy settings of natural communication and interaction. Variability in reliability of individual cues also ensures the language learner's environment is not overloaded with information—in any one word learning situation, the cues present are only a subset of the possible cues that can assist learning, and then the child's requirement to attend to all possible cues is restricted to just those that are present in the current environment. For several aspects of language learning, different types of cues are known to be co-distributed to ensure reliable learning; in situations where one cue is weak, another is stronger (Christiansen & Monaghan, 2016), and so the structure of language seems to reflect this give-and-take of multiple cue availability and usability.

Conclusion

Multiple cues, external to the learner, are prevalent in situations where children are acquiring language. These extrinsic sources of information provide an enormous number of constraints that can assist the child in learning how words map onto the world around them. These cues may be the source of some of the proposed intrinsic biases that guide children's word learning, or they may operate in concert with them. Considering the multiple information sources available from this extra-linguistic, multi-modal, interactive perspective enriches our understanding of the learning situation and also reveals the complexity and subtlety of the learning that the child applies to navigate this landscape of information.

Acknowledgements

The writing of this chapter was supported by the International Centre for Language and Communicative Development (LuCiD) at Lancaster University, funded by the Economic and Social Research Council (UK) [ES/L008955/1].

References

Arnon, I., & Snider, N. (2010). More than words: Frequency effects for multiword phrases. *Journal of Memory and Language, 62,* 67–82.

Bahrick, L.E., Lickliter, R., & Flom, R. (2004). Intersensory redundancy guides the development of selective attention, perception, and cognition in infancy. *Current Directions in Psychological Science, 13,* 99–102.

Baldwin, D.A. (1991). Infants' contribution to the achievement of joint reference. *Child Development, 62,* 875–890.

Baldwin, D.A. (1992). Clarifying the role of shape in children's taxonomic assumption. *Journal of Experimental Child Psychology, 54*(3), 392–416.

Bion, R.A.H., Borovsky, A., & Fernald, A. (2013). Fast mapping, slow learning: Disambiguation of novel word-object mappings in relation to vocabulary learning at 18, 24, and 30 months. *Cognition, 126,* 39–53.

Bloom, P. (2000). *How children learn the meanings of words.* Cambridge, MA and London: MIT Press.

Brooks, R., & Meltzoff, A.N. (2008). Infant gaze following and pointing predict accelerated vocabulary growth through two years of age: A longitudinal, growth curve modeling study. *Journal of Child Language, 35*(1), 207–220.

Cassidy, K.W., & Kelly, M.H. (2001). Children's use of phonology to infer grammatical class in vocabulary learning. *Psychonomic Bulletin and Review, 8,* 519–523.

Childers, J.B. (2011). Attention to multiple events helps two-1/2-year-olds extend new verbs. *First Language, 31,* 3–22.

Christiansen, M.H., & Monaghan, P. (2016). Division of labor in the vocabulary. *Topics in Cognitive Science, 8,* 610–624.

Clark, E.V. (2009). *First language acquisition (2nd Edition)*. Cambridge, UK: Cambridge University Press.
Collis, G. (1977). Visual co-orientation and maternal speech. In H.R. Schaffer (Ed.), *Studies in mother-infant interaction*, 355–375. London: Academic Press.
Fernald, A. (1991). Prosody in speech to children: Prelinguistic and linguistic functions. *Annals of Child Development, 8*, 43–80.
Fernald, A., & Mazzie, C. (1991). Prosody and focus in speech to infants and adults. *Developmental Psychology, 27*, 209–221.
Fernald, A., & Simon, T. (1984). Expanded intonation contours in mothers' speech to newborns. *Developmental Psychology, 20*, 104–113.
Fitneva, S., Christiansen, M.H., & Monaghan, P. (2009). From sound to syntax: Phonological constraints on children's lexical categorization of new words. *Journal of Child Language, 36*, 967–997.
Frank, M.C., Goodman, N.D., & Tenenbaum, J.B. (2009). Using speakers' referential intentions to model early cross-situational word learning. *Psychological Science, 20*, 578–585.
Garnica, O. (1977). Some prosodic and paralinguistic features of speech to young children. In C.E. Snow & C.A. Ferguson (Eds.), *Talking to children: Language input and acquisition*. Cambridge, UK: Cambridge University Press.
Gogate, L.J., & Bahrick, L.E. (1998). Intersensory redundancy facilitates learning of arbitrary relations between vowel sounds and objects in seven-month-old infants. *Journal of Experimental Child Psychology, 69*(2), 133–149.
Gogate, L.J., Maganti, M., & Laing, K.B. (2013). Maternal naming of object wholes versus parts to preverbal infants: A fine-grained analysis of scaffolding at 6–8 months. *Infant Behavior and Development, 36*(3), 470–479.
Golinkoff, R.M., & Alioto, A. (1995). Infant-directed speech facilitates lexical learning in adults hearing Chinese: Implications for language acquisition. *Journal of Child Language, 22*, 703–726.
Golinkoff, R.M., Mervis, C.B., & Hirsh-Pasek, K. (1994). Early object labels: The case for a developmental lexical principles framework. *Journal of Child Language, 21*, 125–155.
Goodwyn, S.W., Acredolo, L.P., & Brown, C.A. (2000). Impact of symbolic gesturing on early language development. *Journal of Nonverbal Behavior, 24*(2), 81–103.
Graf Estes, K., & Hurley, K. (2013). Infant-directed prosody helps infants map sounds to meanings. *Infancy, 18*(5), 797–824.
Halberda, J. (2003). The development of a word-learning strategy. *Cognition, 87*, B23–B34.
Harris, M., Jones, D., & Grant, J. (1983). The nonverbal context of mothers' speech to infants. *First Language, 4*, 21–30.
Hollich, G.J., Hirsh-Pasek, K., Golinkoff, R.M., Brand, R.J., Brown, E., Chung, H.L., Hennon, E., Rocroi, C., & Bloom, L. (2000). Breaking the language barrier: An emergentist coalition model for the origins of word learning. *Monographs of the Society for Research in Child Development, 65*, 1–135.
Horst, J.S., Scott, E.J., & Pollard, J.A. (2010). The role of competition in word learning via referent selection. *Developmental Science, 13*, 706–713.
Houston-Price, C., Caloghiris, Z., & Raviglione, E. (2010). Language experience shapes the development of the mutual exclusivity bias. *Infancy, 15*(2), 125–150.
Houston-Price, C., Plunkett, K., & Duffy, H. (2006). The use of social and salience cues in early word learning. *Journal of Experimental Child Psychology, 95*, 27–55.
Imai M., Miyazaki M., Yeung H.H., Hidaka S., Kantartzis K., Okada, H., & Kita, S. (2015) Sound symbolism facilitates word learning in 14-month-olds. *PLoS ONE, 10*, e0116494.

Iverson, J.M., Capirci, O., Longobardi, E., & Caselli, M.C. (1999). Gesturing in mother-child interactions. *Cognitive Development*, 14, 57–75.

Jusczyk, P.W., Houston, D.M., & Newsome, M. (1999). The beginnings of word segmentation in English-learning infants. *Cognitive Psychology*, 39(3), 159–207.

Kalashnikova, M., Mattock, K., & Monaghan, P. (2014). Disambiguation of novel labels and referential facts: A developmental perspective. *First Language*, 34, 125–135.

Kalashnikova, M., Mattock, K., & Monaghan, P. (2015). The effects of linguistic experience on the flexible use of mutual exclusivity in word learning. *Bilingualism: Language and Cognition*, 18(4), 626–638.

Kelly, M.H. (1992). Using sound to solve syntactic problems: The role of phonology in grammatical category assignments. *Psychological Review*, 99, 349–364.

Kemler Nelson, D.G. (1999). Attention to functional properties in toddlers' naming and problem-solving. *Cognitive Development*, 14(1), 77–100.

Kirkham, N.Z. (2010). Altogether now: Learning through multiple sources. In S.P. Johnson (Ed.), *Neoconstructivism: The new science of cognitive development*. New York: Oxford University Press.

Kobayashi, H. (1998). How 2-year-old children learn novel part names of unfamiliar objects. *Cognition* 68, B41–B51.

Kuhl, P.K., Andruski, J.E., Chistovich, I.A., Chistovich, L.A., Kozhevnikova, E.V., Ryskina, V.L., et al. (1997). Cross-language analysis of phonetic units in language addressed to infants. *Science*, 277, 684–686.

Ma, W., Golinkoff, R.M., Houston, D.M., & Hirsh-Pasek, K. (2011). Word learning in infant- and adult-directed speech. *Language Learning and Development*, 7(3), 185–201.

Macnamara, J.T. (1982). *Names for things: A study of human learning*. Cambridge, MA: MIT Press.

MacWhinney, B. (1991). A reply to Woodward and Markman. *Developmental Review*, 11, 192–194.

Markman, E.M. (1994). Constraints on word meaning in early language acquisition. *Lingua*, 92, 199–227.

Markman, E.M., & Wachtel, G.F. (1988). Children's use of mutual exclusivity to constrain the meanings of words. *Cognitive Psychology*, 20, 121–157.

Markman, E.M., Wasow, J.L., & Hansen, M.B. (2003). Use of the mutual exclusivity assumption by young word learners. *Cognitive Psychology*, 47, 241–275.

Mather, E., & Plunkett, K. (2012). The role of novelty in early word learning. *Cognitive Science*, 36(7), 1157–1177.

McMurray, B., Horst, J. S., & Samuelson, L.K. (2012). Word learning emerges from the interaction of online referent selection and slow associative learning. *Psychological Review*, 119(4), 831–877.

Merriman, W.E., & Kutlesic, V. (1993). Bilingual and monolingual children's use of two lexical acquisition heuristics. *Applied Psycholinguistics*, 14, 229–249.

Messer, D.J. (1981). The identification of names in maternal speech to infants. *Journal of Psycholinguistic Research*, 10, 69–77.

Monaghan, P., Christiansen, M.H., & Chater, N. (2007). The phonological-distributional coherence hypothesis: Cross-linguistic evidence in language acquisition. *Cognitive Psychology*, 55, 259–305.

Monaghan, P., & Mattock, K. (2012). Integrating constraints for learning word-referent mappings. *Cognition*, 123, 133–143.

Monaghan, P., Mattock, K., Davies, R.A.I., & Smith, A.C. (2015). Gavagai is as gavagai does: Learning nouns and verbs from cross-situational statistics. *Cognitive Science*, 39(5), 1099–1112.

Monaghan, P., Shillcock, R.C., Christiansen, M.H., & Kirby, S. (2014). How arbitrary is language? *Philosophical Transactions of the Royal Society B, 369*, 20130299.

Moore, C., Angelopoulos, M., & Bennett, P. (1999). Word learning in the context of referential and salience cues. *Developmental Psychology, 35*(1), 60–68.

Nardini, M., Jones, P., Bedford, R., & Braddick, O. (2008). Development of cue integration in human navigation. *Current Biology, 18*, 689–693.

Ninio, A. (1980). Ostensive definition in vocabulary teaching. *Journal of Child Language, 7*, 565–573.

Papousek, M., Papousek, H., & Bornstein, M. (1985). The naturalistic vocal environment of young infants: On the significance of homogeneity and variability in parental speech. In T.M. Field and N.A. Fox (Eds.), *Social perception in infants*. Norwood, NJ: Ablex.

Pinker, S. (1984). *Language learnability and language development*. Cambridge, MA: MIT Press.

Quine, W.V.O. (1960). *Word and object*. Cambridge, MA: MIT Press.

Rowland, C. (2014). *Understanding child language acquisition*. Abingdon, UK: Routledge.

Saffran, J.R., Aslin, R.N., & Newport, E.L. (1996). Statistical learning by 8-month-old infants. *Science, 274*, 1926–1928.

Siskind, J.M. (1996). A computational study of cross-situational techniques for learning word-to-meaning mappings. *Cognition, 61*, 39–61.

Smith, L., & Yu, C. (2008). Infants rapidly learn word-referent mappings via cross-situational statistics. *Cognition, 106*, 1558–1568.

Smith, L.B., Suanda, S.H., & Yu, C. (2014). The unrealized promise of infant statistical word–referent learning. *Trends in Cognitive Sciences, 18*(5), 251–258.

Spector, F., & Maurer, D. (2009). Synesthesia: A new approach to understanding the development of perception. *Developmental Psychology, 45*, 175–189.

To, M.P.S., Baddeley, R.J., Troscianko, T., & Tolhurst, D.J. (2011). A general rule for sensory cue summation: Evidence from photographic, musical, phonetic and cross-modal stimuli. *Proceedings of the Royal Society of London Series B, 278*, 1365–1372.

Tomasello, M. (2003). *Constructing a language: A usage-based theory of language acquisition*. Cambridge, MA: Harvard University Press.

Walker-Andrews, A.S. (1997). Infants' perception of expressive behaviors: Differentiation of multimodal information. *Psychological Bulletin, 121*, 437–456.

Xu, F., & Tenenbaum, J. B. (2007). Word learning as Bayesian inference. *Psychological Review, 114*, 245–272.

Yu, C., & Ballard, D.H. (2007). A unified model of early word learning: Integrating statistical and social cues. *Neurocomputing, 70*, 2149–2165.

Yu, C., & Smith, L. (2007). Rapid word learning under uncertainty via cross-situational statistics. *Psychological Science, 18*, 414–420.

Yu, C., & Smith, L.B. (2012). Modeling cross-situational word–referent learning: Prior questions. *Psychological Review, 119*(1), 21–39.

Yurovsky, D., Boyer, T.W., Smith, L.B., & Yu, C. (2013). Probabilistic cue combination: Less is more. *Developmental Science, 16*(2), 149–158.

4

MAPPING WORDS TO OBJECTS

Jessica S. Horst

UNIVERSITY OF SUSSEX, SCHOOL OF PSYCHOLOGY
BRIGHTON, UK

Children learn words slowly. Really slowly. Developmental psychologists like to start academic articles with flattering sentences like, "children are phenomenally effective word learners," (Namy & Gentner, 2002, p. 5) and, "children have an amazing ability to rapidly acquire novel words" (Storkel, 2001, p. 1321), but on some level we know that word learning is kind of difficult and kind of slow. This is a double-edged sword because this is what makes language research challenging—but also what makes it so rewarding.

With young children, we often consider a new word to be learned when children demonstrate reliable recall and identification of its meaning in a new context and/or after a delay. This is a good test of word learning for young children because it requires a memory representation that can be recalled in the absence of previous contextual supports and is robust enough to withstand a delay, suggesting encoding and memory consolidation have begun to take place. Indeed—unless sufficient learning supports are provided—it is difficult for children to learn new words such that they can recall and identify their referents after even a short delay (e.g., Horst & Samuelson, 2008; Munro et al., 2012). Recall and identification of word meanings may also include generalization (i.e., extending a word to a new member of the original category). In older children and adults, even stronger evidence of word learning comes from the ability to spontaneously retrieve and produce the new word to communicate with others. Importantly, however, word learning does not necessarily have a clear end point. Although our understanding of what many words mean changes very little after hundreds of exposures across developmental time, for some words it is possible to learn a partial meaning well enough to reliably recall the referents and spontaneously produce the word but still only have limited knowledge of the word's meaning—even into adulthood (Clark, 2007).

Learning names for object categories

The bulk of children's early vocabularies are nouns (Fenson et al., 1994), consequently most of the research in this area has focused on names for object categories, which I will also do in this chapter (see Childers, Bottera, and Howard, this volume, for a review of learning other word types). Although children learn other words types, e.g., adjectives and verbs, more slowly (e.g., Childers & Tomasello, 2002), they likely learn these words using the same associative learning mechanisms. In many ways it is difficult to draw a distinct line between word learning and category learning because even words that are not nouns label categories (e.g., categories of actions and spatial relationships). Critically, words and categories have a fundamentally reciprocal relationship to each other. The number of category members presented in experimental word learning tasks influences the number of words children learn (e.g., Twomey et al., 2014), and the number of words presented influences the number of categories children form (Althaus & Westermann, 2016; Plunkett et al., 2008). For example, Althaus and Westermann (2016) presented 10-month-old infants with a continuous category. Infants who heard a single novel name formed a single inclusive category, and infants who heard two consistent novel names formed two distinct categories for the same stimuli. Further, simply hearing a word can prime children's attention to other objects that share similar features that are critical for that category (e.g., Mani et al., 2013). Perhaps the clearest evidence of the reciprocal relationship between word learning and categorization comes from the shape bias literature. Only after children have acquired a large noun vocabulary do they learn to extend names on the basis of shape (e.g., cups are cup-shaped; Samuelson & Smith, 1999). Then, once they have learned that shape is critical for most object categories (Huettig, 2013; Samuelson & Smith, 1999), their vocabularies grow exponentially (Perry et al., 2010; Smith et al., 2002), and this growth is not restricted to nouns (Samuelson, 2002).

Word learning is a gradual process (Carey, 1978; Clark, 2007; McMurray et al., 2012), and slow word learning is actually a huge benefit. When children acquire word meanings slowly, their understanding will ultimately be more accurate. They minimize the risk of learning incorrect information, which could easily snowball out of control. Consider this: if a child reaches for a cup and misses, instead swiping the spoon, what's the big deal? The child can see he missed. There is immediate, undeniable feedback. Just try again. But what if the child accidentally associated the word *spoon* with the object *cup*? There could be severe cascading consequences. The child could go months mistakenly thinking that *spoon* meant *cup*, leading to instances of misunderstanding people, being misunderstood, difficulty finding a name to map onto the spoon category and struggling in other ambiguous naming situations with those objects. Given how many things could go wrong, it is in the child's best interest to take things slowly; gradually strengthening the *cup*-cup and *spoon*-spoon connections (and simultaneously pruning the *cup*-spoon, *spoon*-cup connections) across multiple occurrences until the correct connections are highly stable (McMurray et al., 2012).

Although learning a single word can be slow, most children do progress through a series of word learning milestones relatively quickly. For example, between 4 and 6 months, infants learn their own names (Mandel et al., 1995) as well as "mommy" and "daddy" (Toncoff & Jusczyk, 1999). By 6 to 9 months they recognize concrete nouns (e.g., "banana" or "spoon"; Bergelson & Swingley, 2012) and between 10 and 13 months they recognize abstract words (e.g., "hi" or "wet"; Bergelson & Swingley, 2013). Unlike 13-month-olds, 20-month-olds will no longer accept a sound as a label for an object (Woodward & Hoyne, 1999). By 2 years of age, most children can use new words in their own utterances immediately after hearing them (Clark, 2007). With increased vocabulary knowledge, hearing words can also facilitate the learning of other nonobvious object properties. For example, 2-year-old children will use shared category labels to extend non-obvious properties to new category members even if those members are perceptually more similar to a different category (Jaswal & Markman, 2007; see also Gelman & Markman, 1986). Further, hearing known object names can prime toddlers and preschoolers to look at other objects that share common features (e.g., color) with a target referent when that object is not present (Johnson & Huettig, 2011; Mani et al., 2013). By 3 to 5 years children can spontaneously produce multiple names for the same object (e.g., "dinosaur," "animal," and "crayon" for a dinosaur-shaped crayon; Deák & Maratsos, 1998; Deák et al., 2001) as well as extend names at the superordinate category level (e.g., Liu et al., 2001). Children in this age group can also use syntactic cues (e.g., the differences between *a sib*, *some sib*, and *sibbing*) to link a new word with the correct word type (e.g., Brown, 1957; see also Childers, Bottera, and Howard, this volume, for a lengthier discussion). However, because of individual differences and the high levels of variability between children, the precise ages at which these milestones are reached may not necessarily be as important as understanding the underlying social and cognitive processes that enable these changes to occur (see Horst & Simmering, 2015, for a discussion).

Narrowing the problem space

To progress through such word learning milestones, the child must associate words with objects, even if the initial associations are fragile and tentative. Making a first rough association or initial guess is commonly known as "fast mapping" (Carey, 1978), and the behavioral response of choosing one alternative meaning over others is known as "referent selection" (Horst & Samuelson, 2008). Importantly, fast mapping is just an initial step in the process and is not the same as full word learning (Carey, 1978; Clark, 2007; Horst & Samuelson, 2008; McMurray et al., 2012).

Traditionally, the difficulty of mapping words to objects has been discussed in terms of the disambiguation problem (Quine, 1960; for a longer discussion, see Monaghan, Kalashnikova, and Mattock, this volume). Imagine a child playing with a play kitchen with a parent who says "I like this *cup*." To what does that new word refer? It could refer to the entire collection of kitchen accessories, it could refer only to the red cup, or only to its handle. The possibilities are endless. ... Or are they?

First, we should acknowledge that in real life there are often several non-verbal cues children can use to determine the referent of a new word, including eye gaze (e.g., Moore et al., 1999), pointing (e.g., Meyer & Baldwin, 2013), and speakers following in on something the child is already looking at (e.g., Baldwin, 1991). Parents also scaffold their speech to match their children's developmental level (e.g., Blewitt et al., 2009). Each of these cues can help the child narrow down the number of arguably infinite possibilities—sometimes to just a single highly likely object. Combined, these cues can be even more constructive.

Non-verbal cues aside, many scholars have argued that children have at their disposal several biases that can help them narrow down the large number of possibilities to just a few likely options (for a review, see Monaghan, Kalashnikova, and Mattock, this volume). For example, the Whole Object Assumption (Markman, 1991) allows children to assume that names refer to whole objects, unless otherwise noted. Indeed, parents often label whole objects before labeling object parts (Masur, 1997). The Principle of Conventionality (Clark, 1990, 1993) dictates that, in order to effectively communicate their desires, speakers will use names familiar to everyone in the conversation. By extension, when speakers do not use familiar names, they are likely referring to something unfamiliar. Relatedly, the Principle of Contrast states that names contrast in meaning, including different forms (e.g., *cup* and *teacup*). The application of these principles can often aid children in successfully determining the referent in an ambiguous naming situation by employing mutual exclusivity (Markman & Wachtel, 1988); as if the child is reasoning, "I know that's a *spoon*, and that's a *cookie*, so *cup* must refer to the other thing." It is important to note, however, that the statistical regularities of mapping names to whole objects and the regular use of conventional names will allow something like mutual exclusivity to emerge without any top-down instruction (McMurray et al., 2012).

What is unfortunate for developing a theory of word learning that includes mapping words to objects is that each of these biases generally predicts the same behavior: children will map a new word to the most novel object present. For example, whether children are employing mutual exclusivity or applying the principle of contrast, they make the same behavioral response (i.e., choose the same object). It is also unclear whether children must use the same principle or bias across every (or most) ambiguous naming events. Given what we know about strategy use in other domains (e.g., Siegler, 2007), this is perhaps unlikely.

The recent past

Critically, what these biases fail to explicitly take into account is that word learning occurs in time. There is usually a temporal context in which words are used. It is essential that children can take time into account in word learning. Remembering what happened in the recent past is what enables children to track whether speakers are credible (Jaswal & Neely, 2006), knowledgeable (Sabbagh & Baldwin, 2001), or intended to perform some action (Carpenter et al., 1998). For example, Akhtar, Carpenter, and Tomasello (1998) presented children with sets of three unnamed novel objects. Then, the child's parent and the second experimenter left the room, and a fourth object was introduced, but not named. When the adults returned and started talking about a *gazzer*, the child could associate *gazzer* with the newest object by tracking that the adults were absent when that object was introduced. There is a debate concerning whether this association is based on an understanding of another person's point of view and speakers' intentions (Akhtar et al., 1996; Diesendruck et al., 2004) or merely understanding that the fourth object was singled out (Axelsson & Horst, 2013; Samuelson & Smith, 1998). However, both explanations require that the child recalled what had happened in the recent past. Thus, when we imagine a child playing kitchen with a parent who says "I like this *cup*," if the child remembers that the parent was just pretending to drink tea, this can serve as another cue to help the child map *cup* to cup (but, again, because the parent may have just pretended to eat a cookie, it is important to take this slowly).

Remembering what just happened also enables learning through repetition. Specifically, each time a novel name-object association is encountered, its stored memory representation is strengthened (McMurray et al., 2012; Smith & Yu, 2008), which in turn supports retrieval and recall. Using intermodal preferential looking tasks in which infants are shown two images and hear a novel name, systematic differences in looking behavior to a target novel object can be observed as early as the second repetition of a name-object pair (e.g., Mather & Plunkett, 2009). Even fairly novice word learners (e.g., 12- to 14-month-olds) can learn name-object associations through tracking the statistical regularity with which the names and objects co-occur across repeated trials (ten repetitions, Smith & Yu, 2008, note: all trials only included novel objects). When two novel objects and their names are presented on interleaved trials, 15-month-old toddlers are able to learn the correct name-object associations (12 repetitions; Schafer & Plunkett, 1998; see also Werker et al., 1998, using a habituation task). Further, 18-month-old toddlers can also learn words from repetition even when there is some variability in how often the words and objects co-occur (Vouloumanos & Werker, 2009). However, many repetitions are needed to elicit word production using novel objects (e.g., 24 repetitions; Pinkham et al., 2011).

Taking the recent past into account also enables children to map names to objects and actions that they do not experience simultaneously, such as abstract concepts that are themselves transient (e.g., it is impossible to label *kiss* at the same moment that one does the action; Bergelson & Swingley, 2013). One example emerges from a series of experiments. Samuelson, Smith, Perry, and Spencer (2011) presented toddlers with two unnamed novel objects that were presented in separate locations, i.e., on opposite ends of a table. When the experimenter cleared the table and simply pointed to one of the locations while saying a novel name, children were able to associate that name with the object seen in that location. Moreover, children retain novel object names better if the objects are consistently presented in the same locations across naming events (Benitez & Smith, 2012).

Remembering the recent past is also highly important because sometimes multiple names are introduced in quick succession. For example, the next thing the parent playing kitchen might say is, "I need a *saucer.*" Keeping the recent past in mind can help the child to exclude the cup as a possible referent of *saucer* because of the principle of mutual exclusivity or one-to-one correspondence between words and objects (that words have one meaning, so if the parent had meant the same thing as before she would have used the same word as before; Markman & Wachtel, 1988). We see this in laboratory situations in which children are presented with recently viewed objects as foils on trials with new words. For example, Wilkinson, Ross, and Diamond (2003) presented preschool children with two target novel name-object pairs to learn. On the exposure trials, one group was always presented with one novel object and three known objects (whether they were asked for Word 1 or Word 2 alternated across trials). The other group was first presented with this trial structure (one novel object and three known objects, always Word 1) and then presented with both novel targets and two known objects on the remaining exposure trials (always Word 2). All children performed well on the exposure trials (though trials with only one novel object were easier). On the critical test trials, children who needed to disambiguate which novel object was the referent on the earlier trials performed better than the children who could simply choose the most novel object present.

Mervis and Bertrand (1994) conducted a similar study with categories. They presented 16- to 20-month-old children with initial exposure trials with one novel object (e.g., a honey dipper) and four known objects. Immediately after these trials children were presented with generalization trials with a new member of the just-encountered novel category (e.g., a new honey dipper), a new novel object (e.g., soap holder), and three known objects. Children who had already begun the vocabulary spurt successfully generalized the novel name to the new category member. That is, they behaved as if they understood that a name, which was already linked to one category, could not be linked to another category. Clearly, therefore, the recent past influences children's ability to map names to objects.

The other things present

Together, Wilkinson, Ross, and Diamond (2003), and Mervis and Bertrand (1994) demonstrated systematic responses on disambiguation and test trials shortly after children heard novel objects named. However, the novel objects do not even need to be named to evoke such systematic responses. For example, my collaborators and I gave 24-month-old children novel objects to play with for two minutes but never named them during this familiarization period (Horst et al., 2011). Children then completed disambiguation trials with two of the objects they had just played with and a third "super-novel" object (a novel object that had not yet seen or played with). Children systematically chose the super-novel objects on the disambiguation trials (for a replication with 3- and 4-year-old children, see Dysart, Mather, and Riggs, 2016). Importantly, children's biases could not help them make systematic responses on these all-novel-object disambiguation trials. Because none of the objects had been associated with any names, mutual exclusivity could not be employed.

It appears that children were mapping novelty to novelty. This is not incorrect, but the situation is a bit more complicated; children were actually avoiding mapping novel names to ever-so-slightly-familiar objects. This interpretation of children's behavior is supported by additional computational simulations that demonstrate it is the pruning of spurious connections that creates a behavior resembling the mutual exclusivity bias (McMurray et al., 2012). Learning the meanings of words is not only about learning the correct associations (e.g., *cup*-cup and *spoon*-spoon) but also about pruning the incorrect associations (e.g., *cup*-spoon and *spoon*-cup; McMurray et al., 2012) of which there are many. This is yet another reason why it should be intuitive that word learning occurs along multiple timescales. Developmental time is needed to successfully prune many incorrect associations.

The fast mapping literature focuses so heavily on learning the correct name-object association that the other objects present are often overlooked, and yet these objects play a critical role in helping children learn the correct name-object association. In fact, when no other objects are present during the initial naming trials, children do not learn the target associations (Zosh et al., 2013) unless there is repetition and the objects move (Werker et al., 1998). Both the number of other objects present and how they are paired with the novel target have systematic effects on children's behavior. For example, children's ability to retain novel name-object associations decreases with the number of known competitors present during referent selection—although the number of known competitors does not influence referent selection performance itself (Horst et al., 2010; for an analogous result in a humanoid robot, see Twomey et al., 2016). In addition, children retain the novel name-object associations more when the same known competitors are always presented with the same target novel object across trials but not when the known competitors vary across trials (Axelsson & Horst, 2014, note this study provided fewer repetitions than those described above). Such findings highlight just how fragile children's initial name-object associations are. If a small change in the initial task (e.g., three rather than two competitors) can have such a dramatic influence on word learning behavior, then the initial association is clearly quite delicate.

Testing what children have learned

One question that remains, however, is whether these experiments are really testing children's memory for the word-object associations or merely children's capacity to track very recent events. It is one thing to choose the correct object in response to a new name in the moment. But is that itself word learning? No. If children could really learn words so quickly, we would not see a strong relationship between how much parents talk to their young children and the children's vocabulary scores—but we do (e.g., Hart & Risley, 1995). If children could really learn words so quickly we would never have to repeat ourselves.

There are several ways to test whether children have learned—or perhaps more accurately *have begun to learn*—new name-object associations. Production is the ultimate demonstration that the child has learned a new word, but it is very difficult to elicit in the lab (see McMurray, Horst, and Samuelson, 2012, for an explanation). However, methods such as intermodal preferential looking/looking-while-listening (e.g., Bergelson & Swingley, 2012; Mani et al., 2013), mispronunciation detection tasks (e.g., Alt & Suddarth, 2012), and the spatially-supported forced-choice recognition test (Gordon & McGregor, 2014) can help us tap into what children remember about the phonetic word forms without requiring the child to articulate the new words.

Comprehension tests may involve presenting the same objects seen earlier (retention tests) or new members of the previously encountered novel categories (generalization tests). However, it is not entirely clear whether the same cognitive processes support both behaviors because other factors such as sleep (Werchan & Gómez, 2014; Williams & Horst, 2014) and variable stimuli (Perry et al., 2010; Twomey et al., 2014) appear to differentially influence children's performance on retention and generalization tasks. Future research is needed to systematically compare retention and generalization behavior to inform understanding of how the two elements of word learning are related. Critically, tests of comprehension should present the referent in a new context, ideally without known competitors, to ensure children are replying on knowledge they have begun to store and consolidate and are not simply fast mapping again (Horst et al., 2010). Similarly, adding even a short delay between when the new word is initially presented and tested helps ensure children's behavior is the result of a stored memory representation and not merely based on short-term memory (Horst & Samuelson, 2008).

Novelty and familiarity

In some cases it may be helpful to vary the novelty of the test alternatives to investigate the errors children make when they fail to choose the target object (Horst & Samuelson, 2008; Horst et al., 2011). For example, test trials could include a new member from the target novel category, a familiar novel distractor, a "super-novel" object, and known competitor (e.g., duck; see e.g., Werchan & Gómez, 2014). However, in such cases it is unclear what baseline the children's behavior should be compared against. Is there really only a one-in-four chance of correctly choosing the target, or is one in three a more accurate estimate of what children are disambiguating? Note that whether all novel test alternatives had been presented earlier with a novel name significantly decreases the likelihood of children selecting the correct object at test (Axelsson & Horst, 2013).

In addition, familiarity can be controlled for by using unusual novel objects or presenting a pre-test. Without such control, it is unclear how much learning observed at test can be attributed to the task and how much learning had already occurred outside the lab. Several studies demonstrate the considerable influence of non-targets present during referent selection on children's ability to learn name-object associations (e.g., Axelsson & Horst, 2014; Horst et al., 2010; Zosh et al., 2013). Thus, familiarity is a serious issue if we want to understand how aspects of the present contribute to children's ability to remember newly learned name-object associations in the future. Note also that this is an issue for both the words (e.g., using *snapshot* instead of *photograph*) and for objects (e.g., using a honey dipper) that children may have encountered before coming into the lab (for a related discussion, see Ard & Beverly, 2004; Bornstein & Mash, 2010).

Conclusions

The initial memory representations of name-object associations that children form are often too fragile to support reliable recall in new contexts, especially after a delay. To enable robust learning, we as speakers must provide additional supports. Specifically, we have to provide children with the opportunity and a reason to encode the target name and object. Consider my earlier example: "I know that's a *spoon*, and that's a *cookie*, so *cup* must refer to the other thing." You may have noticed that I never said what the other thing was. I gave no details about color, size, or any other feature. "The other thing" is simply the correct answer because *spoon* and *cookie* are wrong. This kind of situation is not good enough if we want a child to later choose "the other thing" when it is presented with other equally novel things. Fortunately, there are many ways we can help children attend to the target object to encode it more deeply, including providing social pragmatic cues, ostensive naming, repetition, and exposing children to entire categories. Word learning is slow. But children do eventually learn the names of hundreds of objects. It just takes time to cultivate strong memory representations from the incremental and gradual changes in the strength of the associations children are forming.

References

Akhtar, N., Carpenter, M., & Tomasello, M. (1996). The role of discourse novelty in early word learning. *Child Development, 67*(2), 635–645. doi: 10.2307/1131837

Alt, M., & Suddarth, R. (2012). Learning novel words: Detail and vulnerability of initial representations for children with specific language impairment and typically developing peers. *Journal of Communication Disorders, 45*(2), 84–97. doi: 10.1016/j.jcomdis.2011.12.003

Althaus, N., & Westermann, G. (2016). Labels constructively shape object categories in 10-month-old infants. *Journal of Experimental Child Psychology, 151*, 5–17. doi: 10.1016/j.jecp.2015.11.013

Ard, L.M., & Beverly, B.L. (2004). Preschool word learning during joint book reading: Effect of adult questions and comments. *Communication Disorders Quarterly, 26*(1), 17–28. doi: 10.1177/15257401040260010101

Axelsson, E.L., & Horst, J.S. (2013). Testing a word is not a test of word learning. *Acta Psychologica, 144*(2), 264–268. doi: 10.1016/j.actpsy.2013.07.002

Axelsson, E.L., & Horst, J.S. (2014). Contextual repetition facilitates word learning via fast mapping. *Acta Psychologica, 152*, 95–99. doi: 10.1016/j.actpsy.2014.08.002

Baldwin, D.A. (1991). Infants' contribution to the achievement of joint reference. *Child Development, 62*(5), 875–890. doi: 10.2307/1131140

Benitez, V.L., & Smith, L.B. (2012). Predictable locations aid early object name learning. *Cognition, 125*(3), 339–352. doi: 10.1016/j.cognition.2012.08.006

Bergelson, E., & Swingley, D. (2012). At 6–9 months, human infants know the meanings of many common nouns. *PNAS Proceedings of the National Academy of Sciences of the United States of America, 109*(9), 3253–3258. doi: 10.1073/pnas.1113380109

Bergelson, E., & Swingley, D. (2013). The acquisition of abstract words by young infants. *Cognition, 127*(3), 391–397. doi: 10.1016/j.cognition.2013.02.011

Blewitt, P., Rump, K.M., Shealy, S.E., & Cook, S.A. (2009). Shared book reading: When and how questions affect young children's word learning. *Journal of Educational Psychology, 101*(2), 294–304. doi: 10.1037/a0013844

Bornstein, M.H., & Mash, C. (2010). Experience-based and on-line categorization of objects in early infancy. *Child Development, 81*(3), 881–897. doi: 10.1111/j.1467-8624.2010.01440.x

Brown, R.W. (1957). Linguistic determinism and the part of speech. *The Journal of Abnormal and Social Psychology, 55*(1), 1–5. doi: 10.1037/h0041199

Carey, S. (1978). The child as word learner. *Linguistic Theory and Psychological Reality*, 264–293.

Carpenter, M., Akhtar, N., & Tomasello, M. (1998). Fourteen- through 18-month-old infants differentially imitate intentional and accidental actions. *Infant Behavior & Development, 21*(2), 315–330. doi: 10.1016/S0163-6383(98)90009-1

Childers, J.B., & Tomasello, M. (2002). Two-year-olds learn novel nouns, verbs, and conventional actions from massed or distributed exposures. *Developmental Psychology, 38*(6), 967–978. doi: 10.1037/0012-1649.38.6.967

Clark, E.V. (1990). On the pragmatics of contrast. *Journal of Child Language, 17*(2), 417–431. doi: 10.1017/S0305000900013842

Clark, E.V. (1993). The lexicon in acquisition. *Cambridge Studies in Linguistics, 65*(12), 306. doi: 10.1017/CBO9780511554377

Clark, E.V. (2007). Young children's uptake of new words in conversation. *Language in Society, 36*(2), 157–182. doi: 10.1017/S0047404507070091

Deák, G.O., & Maratsos, M. (1998). On having complex representations of things: Preschoolers use multiple words for objects and people. *Developmental Psychology, 34*(2), 224–240. doi: 10.1037/0012-1649.34.2.224

Deák, G.O., Yen, L., & Pettit, J. (2001). By any other name: When will preschoolers produce several labels for a referent? *Journal of Child Language, 28*(3), 787–804. doi: 10.1017/S0305000901004858

Diesendruck, G., Markson, L., Akhtar, N., & Reudor, A. (2004). Two-year-olds' sensitivity to speakers' intent: An alternative account of Samuelson and Smith. *Developmental Science, 7*(1), 33–41. doi: 10.1111/j.1467-7687.2004.00320.x

Dysart, E.L., Mather, E., & Riggs, K.J. (2016). Young children's referent selection is guided by novelty for both words and actions. Journal of experimental child psychology. *Journal of Experimental Child Psychology, 146*, 231–237. doi: 10.1016/j.jecp.2016.01.003

Fenson, L., Dale, P.S., Reznick, J.S., Bates, E., Thal, D., & Pethick, S. (1994). Variability in early communicative development. *Monographs of the Society for Research in Child Development, 59*(5), v–173. doi: 10.2307/1166093

Gelman, S.A., & Markman, E.M. (1986). Categories and induction in young children. *Cognition, 23*(3), 183–209. doi: 10.1016/0010-0277(86)90034-X

Gordon, K.R., & McGregor, K.K. (2014). A spatially-supported forced-choice recognition test reveals children's long-term memory for newly learned word forms. *Frontiers in Psychology, 5*(164), 1–12. doi: 10.3389/fpsyg.2014.00164

Hart, B., & Risley, T.R. (1995). *Meaningful differences in the everyday experience of young American children*. Baltimore, MD: Paul H Brookes Publishing.

Horst, J.S., & Samuelson, L.K. (2008). Fast mapping but poor retention by 24-month-old infants. *Infancy, 13*(2), 128–157. doi: 10.1080/15250000701795598

Horst, J.S., Samuelson, L.K., Kucker, S.C., & McMurray, B. (2011). What's new? Children prefer novelty in referent selection. *Cognition*, *18*(2), 234–244. doi: 10.1016/j.cognition.2010.10.015

Horst, J.S., Scott, E.J., & Pollard, J.P. (2010). The role of competition in word learning via referent selection. *Developmental Science*, *13*(5), 706–713. doi: 10.1111/j.1467-7687.2009.00926.x

Horst, J.S., & Simmering, V.R. (2015). Category learning in a dynamic world. *Frontiers in Psychology*, *6*(46), 1–4. doi: 10.3389/fpsyg.2015.00046

Huettig, F. (2013). Young children's use of color information during language-vision mapping. In B.R. Kar (Ed.), *Cognition and brain development: Converging evidence from various methodologies*, 271–287. Washington, D.C.: American Psychological Assocation.

Jaswal, V.K., & Markman, E.M. (2007). Looks aren't everything: 24-month-olds' willingness to accept unexpected labels. *Journal of Cognition and Development*, *8*(1), 93–111. doi: 10.1207/s15327647jcd0801_5

Jaswal, V.K., & Neely, L.A. (2006). Adults don't always know best preschoolers use past reliability over age when learning new words. *Psychological Science*, *17*(9), 757–758. doi: 10.1111/j.1467-9280.2006.01778.x

Johnson, E.K., & Huettig, F. (2011). Eye movements during language-mediated visual search reveal a strong link between overt visual attention and lexical processing in 36-month-olds. *Psychological Research*, *75*(1), 35–42. doi: 10.1007/s00426-010-0285-4

Liu, J., Golinkoff, R.M., & Sak, K. (2001). One cow does not an animal make: Young children can extend novel words at the superordinate level. *Child Development*, *72*(6), 1674–1694. doi: 10.1111/1467-8624.00372

Mandel, D.R., Jusczyk, P.W., & Pisoni, D.B. (1995). Infants' recognition of the sound patterns of their own names. *Psychological Science*, *6*(5), 314–317. doi: 10.1111/j.1467-9280.1995.tb00517.x

Mani, N., Johnson, E.K., McQueen, J.M., & Huettig, F. (2013). How yellow is your banana? Toddlers' language-mediated visual search in referent-present tasks. *Developmental Psychology*, *49*(6), 1036–1044. doi: 10.1037/a0029382

Markman, E.M. (1991). The whole-object, taxonomic, and mutual exclusivity assumptions as initial constraints on word meanings. In J. P. Byrnes & S. A. Gelman (Eds.), *Perspectives on language and cognition: Interrelations in development*, 72–106. Cambridge: Cambridge University Press.

Markman, E.M., & Wachtel, G.F. (1988). Children's use of mutual exclusivity to constrain the meaning of words. *Cognitive Psychology*, *20*(2), 121–157. doi: 10.1016/0010-0285(88)90017-5

Masur, E.F. (1997). Maternal labelling of novel and familiar objects: Implications for children's development of lexical constraints. *Journal of Child Language*, *24*(2), 427–439. doi: 10.1017/S0305000997003115

Mather, E., & Plunkett, K. (2009). Learning words over time: The role of stimulus repetition in mutual exclusivity. *Infancy*, *14*(1), 60–76. doi: 10.1080/15250000802569702

McMurray, B., Horst, J.S., & Samuelson, L.K. (2012). Word learning as the interaction of online referent selection and slow associative learning. *Psychological Review*, *119*(4), 831–877. doi: 10.1037/a0029872

Mervis, C.B., & Bertrand, J. (1994). Acquisition of the novel name nameless category (N3C) principle. *Child Development*, *65*(6), 1646–1662. doi: 10.2307/1131285

Meyer, M., & Baldwin, D.A. (2013). Pointing as a socio-pragmatic cue to particular vs. generic reference. *Language Learning and Development*, *9*(3), 245–265. doi: 10.1080/15475441.2013.753802

Moore, C., Angelopoulos, M., & Bennett, P. (1999). Word learning in the context of referential and salience cues. *Developmental Psychology, 35*(1), 60–68. doi: 10.1037/0012-1649.35.1.60

Munro, N., Baker, E., McGregor, K., Docking, K., & Arciuli, J. (2012). Why word learning is not fast. *Frontiers in Psychology, 3*(41), 1–10. doi: 10.3389/fpsyg.2012.00041

Namy, L.L., & Gentner, D. (2002). Making a silk purse out of two sow's ears: Young children's use of comparison in category learning. *Journal of Experimental Psychology: General, 131*(1), 5–15. doi: 10.1037/0096-3445.131.1.5

Perry, L.K., Samuelson, L.K., Malloy, L.M., & Schiffer, R.N. (2010). Learn locally, think globally: Exemplar variability supports higher-order generalization and word learning. *Psychological Science, 21*(12), 1894–1902. doi: 10.1177/0956797610389189

Pinkham, A.M., Neuman, S.B., & Lillard, A.S. (2011). Have we underestimated repetition? Repeated exposures to promote vocabulary develpment. *Literacy Research Association Meeting*.

Plunkett, K., Hu, J.F., & Cohen, L.B. (2008). Labels can override perceptual categories in early infancy. *Cognition, 106*(2), 665–681. doi: 10.1016/j.cognition.2007.04.003

Quine, W.V.O. (1960). *Word and object: An inquiry into the linguistic mechanisms of objective reference*. Cambridge, MA: MIT Press.

Sabbagh, M.A., & Baldwin, D.A. (2001). Learning words from knowledgeable or ignorant speakers: Links between preschoolers theory of mind and semantic development. *Child Development, 72*(4), 1054–1070. doi: 10.1111/1467-8624.00334

Samuelson, L.K. (2002). Statistical regularities in vocabulary guide language acquisition in connectionist models and 15-20-month-olds. *Developmental Psychology, 38*(6), 1016–1037. doi: 10.1037/0012-1649.38.6.1016

Samuelson, L.K., & Smith, L.B. (1998). Memory and attention make smart word learning: An alternative account of Akhtar, Carpenter, and Tomasello. *Child Development, 69*(1), 94–104. doi: 10.2307/1132073

Samuelson, L.K., & Smith, L.B. (1999). Early noun vocabularies: Do ontology, category structure and syntax correspond? *Cognition, 73*(1), 1–33. doi: 10.1016/S0010-0277(99)00034-7

Samuelson, L.K., Smith, L.B., Perry, L.K., & Spencer, J.P. (2011). Grounding word learning in space. *PloS One, 6*(12), 1–13. doi: 10.1371/journal.pone.0028095

Schafer, G., & Plunkett, K. (1998). Rapid word learning by fifteen-month-olds under tightly controlled conditions. *Child Development, 69*(2), 309–320. doi: 10.2307/1132166

Siegler, R.S. (2007). Cognitive variability. *Developmental Science, 10*(1), 104–109. doi: 10.1111/j.1467-7687.2007.00571.x

Smith, L.B., Jones, S.S., Landau, B., Gershkoff-Stowe, L., & Samuelson, L.K. (2002). Object name learning provides on-the-job training for attention. *Psychological Science, 13*(1), 13–19. doi: 10.1111/1467-9280.00403

Smith, L.B., & Yu, C. (2008). Infants rapidly learn word-referent mappings via cross-situational statistics. *Cognition, 106*, 1558–1568. doi: 10.1016/j.cognition.2007.06.010

Storkel, H.L. (2001). Learning new words: Phonotactic probability in language development. *Journal of Speech, Language, and Hearing Research, 44*(6), 1321–1337. doi: 0.1044/1092-4388(2001/103

Toncoff, R., & Jusczyk, P.W. (1999). Some beginnings of word comprehension in 6-month-olds. *Psychological Science, 10*(2), 172–175. doi: 10.1111/1467-9280.00127

Twomey, K.E., Morse, A.F., Cangelosi, A., & Horst, J.S. (2016). Children's referent selection and word learning: insights from a developmental robotic system. *Interaction Studies: Social Behaviour and Communication in Biological and Artificial Systems, 17*(1), 93–119. doi: 10.1075/is.17.1.05two

Twomey, K.E., Ranson, S.L., & Horst, J.S. (2014). That's more like it: Multiple exemplars facilitate word learning. *Infant and Child Development*, *23*(2), 105–122. doi: 10.1002/icd.1824

Vouloumanos, A., & Werker, J.F. (2009). Infants' learning of novel words in a stochastic environment. *Developmental Psychology*, *45*(6), 1611–1617. doi: 10.1037/a0016134

Werchan, D.M., & Gómez, R.L. (2014). Wakefulness (not sleep) promotes generalization of word learning in 2.5-year-old children. *Child Development*, *85*(2), 429–436. doi: 10.1111/cdev.12149.

Werker, J.F., Cohen, L.B., Lloyd, V.L., Casasola, M., & Stager, C.L. (1998). Acquisition of word-object associations by 14-month-old infants. *Developmental Psychology*, *34*(6), 1289–1309. doi: 10.1037/0012-1649.34.6.1289

Wilkinson, K.M., Ross, E., & Diamond, A. (2003). Fast mapping of multiple words: Insights into when "the information provided" does and does not equal "the information perceived." *Applied Developmental Psychology*, *24*, 739–762. doi: 10.1016/j.appdev.2003.09.006

Williams, S.E., & Horst, J.S. (2014). Goodnight book: The benefit of sleep consolidation on word learning via storybooks. *Frontiers in Psychology*, *5*(184), 1–12. doi: 10.3389/fpsyg.2014.00184

Woodward, A.L., & Hoyne, K.L. (1999). Infants' learning about words and sounds in relation to objects. *Child Development*, *70*(1), 65–77. doi: 10.1111/1467-8624.00006

Zosh, J.M., Brinster, M., & Halberda, J. (2013). Optimal contrast: Competition between two referents improves word learning. *Applied Developmental Science*, *17*(1), 20–28. doi: 10.1080/10888691.2013.748420

5

BUILDING A LEXICAL NETWORK

Nivedita Mani

PSYCHOLOGY OF LANGUAGE RESEARCH GROUP,
GEORG-AUGUST-UNIVERSITÄT GÖTTINGEN, GERMANY

Arielle Borovsky

SPEECH, LANGUAGE AND HEARING SCIENCES,
PURDUE UNIVERSITY, WEST LAFAYETTE, INDIANA, USA

The adult lexicon is organized among many representational dimensions that encode phonological, semantic and perceptual links among words. Priming studies that use behavioral, eye-tracking and electrophysiological measurements highlight the interactive and dynamic nature of lexical processing and representation in the adult lexicon. These studies suggest that word recognition routinely involves simultaneous access to other words that overlap with a spoken word on phonological (Slowiaczek et al., 1987; Marslen-Wilson & Zwitserlood, 1989), semantic (Meyer & Schvaneveldt, 1971) or other perceptual dimensions (Dahan & Tanenhaus, 2005; Huettig & Altmann, 2007). While these studies provide valuable information about the mechanisms guiding lexical retrieval and the factors underlying lexical organization in the lexicons of adult college-educated individuals who know many thousands of words, it is debatable the extent to which these findings can be extended to our understanding of early lexical processing in young children. On the one hand, differences in general cognitive abilities, linguistic experience and language-related knowledge in young children and college-educated adults could imply drastic differences in the way words are linked in developing and mature lexicons. On the other hand, once a word has an entry in the mental lexicon, how many or which other words the child knows may be irrelevant, such that a) the structure of the developing lexicon is a miniature version of the adult lexicon, organized according to similar dimensions; and b) the processes guiding word recognition differ minimally across development. Adjudicating between these two proposals requires examination of the structure of the early lexicon and the processes guiding lexical processing in young children. How does this structure initially develop and change as the child's knowledge grows over time? Does the organization of the early lexicon influence subsequent word learning and word processing? Understanding these questions has the potential to inform adult theories of psycholinguistic processing and highlight important processes in early vocabulary development. This chapter will attempt to answer these questions against the background of the literature to date whilst also sketching paths for future research on the topic.

Why does structure in the lexicon matter?

Everyday language comprehension requires the listener to interpret a variety of linguistic and non-linguistic cues in real time at a rapid pace. To succeed at this task, even very young listeners efficiently and dynamically interpret the speech stream incrementally as it unfolds in real time (Swingley et al., 1999). Recognizing relational information between words can aid incremental speech processing (Borovsky et al., 2016a). For example, when hearing single words, listeners can use ongoing phonetic information to generate dynamic hypotheses about the potential referent of the spoken label. That is, when hearing a word like *dog*, young children also initially consider options like *doll* and *frog*, which overlap phonetically with the intended referent (Swingley et al., 1999; Swingley, 2009; Mani & Plunkett, 2011; Mani et al., 2012), as well as *cat*, which is semantically related to this word (Arias-Trejo & Plunkett, 2009; Mani et al., 2012; Johnson et al., 2011). While the activation of multiple competing items may seem counterintuitive for efficient speech comprehension, this information allows the listener to consider a host of potential options that are weighted with respect to the relevant contextual cues. This breadth of activation may be useful in assisting the listener to recover under adverse listening conditions when words are only partially heard, or when the discourse takes unexpected turns.

Further advantages of dynamic processing become clear when listeners leverage lexical structure to predict words that have *not yet been spoken* (Altmann & Kamide, 1999; Kamide et al., 2003). Borovsky, Elman and Fernald (2012), and Mani and Huettig (2012) published two studies showing that young children (3- to 10-year-olds and 2-year-olds, respectively) can use the syntactic and thematic constraints associated with familiar nouns (Borovsky et al., 2012) and verbs (both studies) to retrieve linguistic information associated with these stimuli and anticipate upcoming input. These studies presented children with sentences such as *The boy eats the big ... cake* as they viewed an image of a cake and a bird onscreen, and found that children fixated the image compatible with the thematic restrictions of the verb *eats*, i.e., the cake, very soon after hearing the verb *eat*, and importantly prior to hearing the word *cake*. The prior retrieval of information associated with words during lexical processing may, therefore, pre-empt and consequently speed the processing of subsequently presented information.

Lexical structure in the child's vocabulary might also promote further vocabulary acquisition by enabling a child to leverage their existing knowledge when learning new words. While we discuss the potential mechanisms underlying such leveraging in more detail below, the available evidence suggests that children who show early delays in the pace of vocabulary growth also have less coherent semantic structure in their early lexicons (Beckage, 2011). This evidence could then be taken to suggest that phonologically and semantically structured networks are not only a fundamental property of the early lexicon, but that this organization also appears to be crucial for vocabulary learning.

Populating the lexical neighborhood

While structure in the early lexicon is likely to benefit language processing and word learning, there are many questions regarding how this structure initially forms and develops. When do children begin to recognize potential connections in sound and meaning between multiple words? Is early structure beneficial to a young word learner, or does it create potential interference between lexical representations? How does this structure develop over time, and do children recognize relations between multiple dimensions simultaneously or do these links develop on staggered time scales? Below we review a growing number of studies that investigate these issues beginning with an overview of prior studies that explore phonological and semantic priming in known words.

Early phonological organization in the lexicon

Given that we have no way of directly examining the early lexicon, how can we ever make strong conclusions regarding the structure of the lexicon and the dimensions according to which words are organized therein? The most common approach has been to examine the extent to which, for instance, words or sounds that are phonologically related to a heard word influence recognition of this word. Such an influence would suggest that words or sounds overlapping in phonological structure are linked in the early lexicon such that hearing a word leads to partial or complete activation of other phonologically related words.

Indeed, recent findings suggest that children as young as 6 months of age can use the onset syllable of a word to begin lexical recognition (like /bei/ for *baby*; Becker et al., 2014). These findings indicate that young children who do not yet speak are able to recognize correspondences between words and their component sounds immediately and that word-sound priming appears to develop quite early. With regard to lexical structure, these findings suggest the emergence of links between words and their constituent sounds as early as 6 months of age.

The next step is, then, to examine when links between overlapping words in the lexicon begin to be established, similar to the adult lexicon. Swingley et al. (1999) initially asked how phonological overlap between words affects real-time lexical recognition in an eye-tracked word-object mapping task with 24-month-old children. They found that paired images of words that shared the same onset (*dog-doll*) were recognized more slowly than words that rhymed (*duck-truck*) or shared no overlap (*dog-truck*). These findings suggest that young children incrementally activate potential lexical candidates that cohere with word onsets as they are spoken and could be taken to suggest that children recognize phonological links among multiple items.

More robust evidence of phonological links among overlapping words comes from recent work examining the extent to which phonologically overlapping words influence recognition of a heard word via a picture-priming paradigm (Mani and Plunkett, 2010; 2011). This work finds that the presentation of an unnamed picture (e.g., *cat*) influences toddlers' processing of related (vs. unrelated) word-object mappings (e.g., *cup* vs. *shoe*) in 18- and 24-month-olds, though the direction of the effect differed across the two age groups. Eighteen-month-olds looked longer at targets whose onset consonants overlapped with the onset of the label for the silent picture prime; 24-month-olds showed the opposite effect by looking longer at targets whose onset consonants did not overlap with the onset of the label for the silent picture prime. Importantly, at 24 months, this result was modulated by the number of words known to children that began with the same onset consonant as the target: the more words children knew that began with the same onset consonant as the target, the less likely children were to fixate the target. Mani and Plunkett (2011) explain this result by suggesting that word recognition routinely involves retrieval of other words that sound similar to a heard word, such that in cases where there are a number of other form-overlapping words, these other words interfere with recognition of the target word. Furthermore, the influence of the number of overlapping words in the child's lexicon provides support for the suggestion that—by 24 months of age—words in the early lexicon are organized according to their phonological properties such that phonologically overlapping words are linked to one another, either through connections between words and their constituent sounds or through lexical links between overlapping words themselves. Before considering recent evidence that there is a lexical basis for these links and the implications of the developmental shift from 18 to 24 months, next we review similar evidence for semantically motivated organization of the early lexicon.

Early semantic organization in the lexicon

A number of studies that have modeled the network structure of developing lexicons suggest that they are organized according to a "small world" structure which consists of densely connected local semantic clusters which are themselves sparsely connected to other clusters of more distantly related concepts (Steyvers & Tenenbaum, 2005; Hills et al., 2009). Explorations of early lexical growth also indicate that children, in general, tend to acquire words in their vocabularies that are semantically related to existing items (Hills et al., 2009). Moreover, coherent semantic structure is positively correlated with a child's individual rate of vocabulary growth (Beckage et al., 2011). Together, these studies demonstrate the fundamental patterns of early semantic organization in the developing lexicon.

Studies examining the nature of early semantic organization via priming paradigms have used a variety of experimental methods, including electrophysiological (Torkildsen et al., 2007; Rämä et al., 2013), preferential looking/eye-tracking (Styles & Plunkett; 2009; Arias-Trejo & Plunkett, 2009; Meints et al., 1999) and head-turn preference procedures (Willits et al., 2013). This growing body of work supports modeled findings that the infant lexicon develops semantically coherent structure over time, though there may be developmental and individual differences in the kinds of semantic relationships that are initially learned. We review findings from these relevant methodologies below.

A number of studies have explored semantic priming in young children using paradigms that explored the child's recognition of words in the presence of a matching or mismatching visual reference. For instance, using a series of semantic priming experiments, Arias-Trejo & Plunkett (2009; see also Styles & Plunkett, 2009) establish the developmental time course of the influence of semantic overlap on word recognition in young toddlers. Here, 18-, 21- and 24-month-olds were presented with sentences containing familiar primes, e.g., *I saw a cat* as they viewed images of a dog and a door followed by the label for the semantically related target image, i.e., *dog*. While 18-month-olds' fixations to the target image appeared to be unaffected by the semantic relationship between the prime, *cat*, and the target, *dog*, by 21-months of age, children looked less at the target image when it was semantically related to the prime compared to when it was unrelated to the prime. Thus, it appears that it is only by 21-months of age that infants begin to develop a lexico-semantic network where words are linked to other taxonomically and associatively related words. More recently, Arias-Trejo & Plunkett (2013) report that it is only at around 24 months that word recognition is influenced by the prior presentation of either taxonomically (e.g., *rabbit-horse*) or associatively related primes (e.g., *rabbit-carrot*), while 21-month-olds only show systematic priming effects when primed by a taxonomically and associatively related prime.

Similar results are reported in studies using different paradigms. For instance, Torkildsen et al. (2007) measured ERPs in 24-month-old children as they listened to pairs of words that were either members of the same basic-level category (*dog-horse*) or unrelated (*car-apple*). They found decreased negative deflections in brain activity to pairs of related words relative to unrelated words (the N400 effect). Furthermore, Rämä, Sirri and Serres (2013) measured ERPs during an auditory priming task in 18- to 24-month-olds and report similar priming of semantically related words in 24-month-olds. They also found semantic priming effects in 18-month-olds with relatively high productive vocabularies, but these effects did not exist for 18-month-olds with relatively lower vocabulary scores. These N400 priming effects suggest that the activation of features associated with the prime word, e.g., *dog*, aids processing of the related target, i.e., *horse*. Thus, it appears that the early lexicon begins to be organized according to the semantic properties of words between 18- to 24-months of age, with the earliest links forming between strongly related items, e.g., words that are both taxonomically and associatively related, followed by later connections that are comparatively less strongly related. However, as discussed next, this picture is complicated by problems associated with the paradigm typically used to test such effects.

The "closed set"

One potential critique of the studies reviewed above is that the paradigms used might bias the pattern of results. Consider the eye-tracking studies reported above, where children are presented with a prime and a target label while responses to the presented target image are measured. It is possible that the pattern of results is driven by children seeing the target image (and hearing the target label) and only then detecting the semantic overlap between the prime and target labels (sometimes referred to as the problem of the *closed set* in the visual world paradigm; e.g., Dahan & Tanenhaus, 2004). Since these paradigms typically present the related target and measure responses to this target, we cannot ascertain whether the target label is retrieved upon hearing the prime, or whether detection of the overlap between the target and the prime is facilitated by the presentation of the target image. Additionally, it is also possible that facilitated processing of the target label is not due to the target label being retrieved upon hearing the prime but due to retrieval of the features shared by prime and target, e.g., that both dog and horse are animate, four-legged, etc. This in turn, implies that we cannot be certain whether these findings are indicative of lexical links between words in the early lexicon or merely of links between words and the features (phonological or semantic) associated with these words. A similar criticism applies to ERP studies examining brain activity time-locked to the presentation of a related target.

One potential work-around to the closed-set problem is proposed in work with adults (Marslen-Wilson & Zwitserlood, 1989; Yee & Sedivy, 2006) and young children (Huang & Snedeker, 2010; Mani et al., 2012). For instance, Mani et al. (2013) presented participants with a picture prime (in silence), e.g., a plane, followed by two images, e.g., a spoon and a ball. Twenty-four-month-olds, in this study, looked longer at the target *spoon* when primed by *plane* compared to when primed by *cat*. Typically, such results are explained by suggesting that presentation of the prime *plane* leads to retrieval of words that sound similar to *plane*, in this case, the onset-overlapping word *plate*, which in turn primes recognition of the semantically related target *spoon*. Since the intermediate prime, *plate*, is never explicitly presented to participants, the most plausible way to explain these results is to suggest either that the word *plate* is retrieved due to phonological overlap with the prime *plane* or due to semantic overlap with the target image, i.e., spoon. Either way, these results present more convincing evidence of the retrieval of lexical items in the processing of related words, and consequently, of lexical links between related words in the early lexicon.

The developmental time course of lexical structure

The findings from previous semantic and phonological priming studies together highlight a common developmental time course that might shed light on the origins of phonological and semantic structure in the early lexicon. In particular, both phonological and semantic priming studies highlight an important change between 18 and 24 months of age. Briefly: a) 18-month-olds show no effects of priming in behavioral semantic priming tasks (Arias-Trejo & Plunkett, 2009); b) only 18-month-olds with larger vocabularies display semantic priming effects even using electrophysiological measures (Rämä et al., 2013); and c) dramatically different patterns of results are obtained in phonological priming tasks with 18- and 24-month-olds (Mani & Plunkett, 2010; 2011). These results highlight the volatility of the period between 18 and 24 months of age, suggesting that development of lexical links between phonologically or semantically related words emerges somewhere during this time. The change from 18 to 24 months can be explained by at least two potential changes in the fundamental processes that underlie word recognition. Either a) lexical connections between words form as the child's vocabulary size grows: most 18-month-olds know too few words to draw strong connections between phonologically or semantically related words; or b) inhibitory connections between words develop as the child's vocabulary size grows: as children learn more words, they must refine the pattern of lexical activation to inhibit activation of unrelated meanings during lexical recognition (see Mayor & Plunkett, 2014, for computational evidence supporting this argument). These inhibitory connections, in turn, would lead to the emergence of differential activation for related and unrelated lexical items. Both of these arguments implicate the increasing vocabulary size of young children in the developmental shift from 18 to 24 months—a suggestion that is supported by the findings of Rämä et al. (2013) that only 18-month-olds with larger vocabularies pattern with the older children. Thus, the findings reviewed above suggest that lexical structure emerges in young children across time, and that its emergence may be directly tied to the growth of the child's vocabulary during this time period.

Are all semantic relationships equal?

The above studies simply ask whether children recognize links among related word meanings without delving too deeply into the nature of these connections. Conceptual representations can overlap in a number of ways, including via perceptual, categorical/taxonomic and associative/thematic relationships. Next, we consider the impact of such overlap on processing the linguistic and conceptual features of word-referent mappings in infancy.

There is considerable literature examining the extent to which links among words are organized via perceptual overlap, e.g., the words *tomato* and *moon*, whose referents are both round, or the words *tomato* and *fire-truck*, whose referents overlap in color. Research examining children's extension of object names to other objects often reports finding a shape bias: 3- to 4-year-olds who are taught a new name for a novel object typically extend this name to other objects overlapping in shape but not to objects overlapping in color, texture or size (the *shape* bias; Jones et al., 1991; Landau et al., 1988). However, other studies find that 2-year-olds extend labels to objects overlapping in function or intent, in preference over objects overlapping in shape (e.g., Gelman & Bloom, 2000; Kemler et al., 2000). Regardless of whether children prefer shape over other object properties in extending a label to other objects (see Cimpian & Markman, 2005, for a series of experiments arguing for the absence of a shape bias), the studies reviewed above highlight that young children encode perceptual information about newly learned words, including information about the shape, color and function of the object, and they connect these perceptual features to other items in their lexicon.

More recently, developmental scientists have sought to examine the extent to which familiar words prime other words whose referents overlap perceptually with the referent of the familiar word (Johnson et al., 2011; Mani et al., 2013). Using a design minimally different from Arias-Trejo and Plunkett (2009), Johnson and colleagues reported evidence for color priming in young children, with children looking longer at the image of a green ball when primed by a color-matching prime word, i.e., *frog*, relative to a color mismatching prime, e.g., *bed*. Mani, Johnson, McQueen and Huettig (2013) extended this work to examine the time-course of retrieval of semantic and color information and found that looks to semantically matching targets, e.g., *frog-bird*, occurred one second prior to looks to color-matching targets. These results suggest not only that perceptual information associated with words is retrieved during lexical processing but also highlight the prioritization of certain kinds of information relative to others, in this case, the prioritization of taxonomic information over color information in 2-year-olds.

Implications for word learning

Thus far we have focused on studies that examine the extent to which familiar words influence processing of other familiar words and objects. As young children repeatedly encounter unfamiliar words that they have never heard before, a critical question remains as to the extent to which children's acquisition of novel words is influenced by their existing lexical structure. Studies examining this issue report both facilitatory and interfering accounts of already familiar words on novel word learning. For instance, Swingley and Aslin (2007) examined the ease with which toddlers learned pseudo word-object associations that either sounded similar to a highly frequent word known to most toddlers, e.g., *tog*, a variant of *dog*, or words that did not overlap substantially with other words known to children, e.g., *meb*. They found that toddlers found it more difficult to learn the novel word-object associations when the novel word sounded similar to another highly familiar word, i.e., *tog*. They interpret this result in terms of competition between lexical entries such that the presence of a highly familiar word in the child's lexicon interferes with the child's acquisition of a highly similar-sounding word—similar to the phonological priming studies on early word recognition reviewed above (Mani & Plunkett, 2011).

However, these results do not tell the full story with regard to competitive and facilitatory effects of word knowledge on later lexical acquisition: Newman, Samuelson and Gupta (2008) find that familiarity with the phonotactic form of words may help children acquire other similar-sounding words. For instance, familiarity with a number of words taking the form Xat, e.g., *cat, rat, hat, mat*, facilitates children's learning of a novel word overlapping in structure with this phonotactic sequence, e.g., *wat*, relative to a word whose form is infrequent in the child's repertoire, e.g., *fowk*. Similarly, Altvater-Mackensen and Mani (2013) find that familiarity with word forms facilitates even earlier stages of lexical acquisition, i.e., children's segmentation of words from fluent speech. Here, young infants familiarized with words like *tasse* (German for *cup*), found it easier to segment similar-sounding nonwords like *tacke* from fluent speech, showing that this critical step towards later lexical learning may benefit from the influence of previously known words. This claim is in keeping with recent proposals that dense phonological neighborhoods may help learners form connections between known and novel words (Storkel, 2006).

Similar results are obtained when examining the effect of visual and semantic overlap between novel lexical entries. Wojcik and Saffron (2013) show that toddlers encode visual similarities between referents in learning words, such that toddlers listened longer to pairs of novel words when these words had previously been associated with visually similar referents compared to visually dissimilar referents. Borovsky, Ellis, Evans and Elman (2016b) find that 2-year-olds show facilitated recognition of novel words that come from more densely structured semantic categories. These studies suggest that semantic network density may help learners identify relevant dimensions over which they can recognize correspondences in features between known and novel words (Borovsky & Elman, 2006; Smith et al., 2002). For example, Smith et al. (2002) find that children who were trained on novel label-object mappings that had shape as a relevant organizing dimension subsequently more easily learned additional untrained words that could also be categorized according to shape. The authors suggest that these gains in vocabulary learning were driven by the earlier vocabulary training, which had attuned young children to recognize shape as a relevant dimension over which novel items may be similarly categorized.

It is also important to note here that the notion of familiarity takes on a new meaning in developmental research. Very often the associations between words and their referents formed by young children may not map on to the associations referred to by more experienced language users. It is, therefore, also vital to examine the extent to which these partial or potentially incorrect associations influence the learning of other novel word-object associations. Recent work by Swingley (2007) and Fennell (2011) suggests that familiarity with either the form of a word, i.e., how the word sounds, or the objects alone can help children to map words onto their referents in later referential training. Furthermore, Yurovsky, Fricker, Yu and Smith (2014) suggest that such partial knowledge may actually aid acquisition of other novel word-object associations for one of two reasons. On the one hand, concurrent learning of one partially mapped association and one completely novel association may be eased by the limited resources required to merely complete learning of the partially acquired item. Alternatively, even partial knowledge of the association between a word and its referent may help learners rule out potential ambiguities such that it becomes easier for the child to learn a completely novel word-object association in the presence of a partially mapped association. Thus, while early lexical associations may not completely map onto more developed lexical representations, it is likely that even such partial knowledge may positively influence later lexical acquisition.

Together, these findings suggest that increasing familiarity with an increasing number of words may rapidly begin to impact the kinds of words that children acquire as well as the ease with which children acquire words. Thus, the early lexicon and its associated structure may have important implications for the shape and structure of more advanced lexicons.

Future directions and conclusions

Children begin to achieve tremendous rates of vocabulary growth, often before their second year of life. While there is not yet empirical evidence for a direct connection between the vocabulary spurt and growing organization in the lexicon, there are significant reasons to believe this relation does exist. The evidence that we have reviewed suggests that children are continually (re)organizing their lexical representations along adult-like dimensions from at least the age of 2, if not earlier. As we have discussed earlier, such lexical organization has a number of advantages and potential disadvantages. Most intriguingly, the available research suggests that recognizing these links between words can even assist young children in learning new vocabulary. The available findings highlight a number of potential avenues for future study that we consider below.

An important first question is whether and how multiple organizational dimensions of the lexicon interact. For instance, do children recognize competing semantic and phonological codes simultaneously during real-time language processing, or can this information differentially drive vocabulary acquisition at various ages? Work in adults (Marslen-Wilson & Zwitserlood, 1989; Yee & Sedivy, 2006) and children (Huang & Snedeker, 2010; Mani et al., 2012) suggests that lexical recognition results in the cascaded activation of both phonologically and semantically related words. Future work is needed to elucidate how this interactivity emerges with respect to the growing lexicon. Indeed, there is evidence from Storkel (2009) that phonological, lexical and semantic factors may have differential relations to the infant lexicon across age. Namely, phonological dimensions have a constant association with vocabulary from 16–30 months, while semantic dimensions generally increase connections with the infant's lexicons over time. Additional work is needed to directly explore how these factors interact across development.

An exploration of these questions has the potential to yield enormous benefits for those who have a stake in understanding early developmental processes in the child's lexicon. One question that could be potentially addressed is whether and how early vocabulary instruction might benefit from training words in clusters organized according to sound and meaning. Indeed, Smith et al. (2002) suggest that highlighting shape relations among words may be especially useful, and there are likely other semantic and phonological dimensions that could potentially interact and boost these kinds of learning effects over time.

Another important consequence of an understanding of lexical structure lies in the potential to identify children with early language learning delays. Findings such as those by Beckage, Smith and Hills (2011) suggest that early semantic network structure may be particularly impaired in late-talking children, who may also be at greater risk for developing later language delays or impairments. These authors note a variety of potential explanations for this outcome ranging from the child's own preference for "oddball" words, to natural variation in the child's environment. Although each of these possibilities suggests different directions for potential intervention, in general, these findings support the possibility that training novel items in a semantically clustered fashion could be beneficial for children who initially struggle in early language skills.

Another area of increasing interest is how lexical organization develops in children who are learning two or more languages simultaneously. While research into this question is now emerging in young children and suggests interactivity between a bilingual child's two languages at the phonological and the lexical level (Von Holzen & Mani, 2012), a number of questions still remain with great potential for significant advances in future directions.

The research we have reviewed here has demonstrated that not only do young children begin to structure their vocabularies from their earliest words among various phonological and semantic dimensions, but that they use this growing organization to promote further vocabulary growth. The practical applications of this knowledge are tremendous. We are especially excited by the potential to leverage children's own knowledge to promote fundamental language skills for children in a variety of early language environments and who vary in individual skill and see this as a particularly noteworthy direction to pursue in future research.

References

Altmann, G.T.M., & Kamide, Y. (1999). Incremental interpretation at verbs: Restricting the domain of subsequent reference. *Cognition, 73,* 247–264.

Altvater-Mackensen, N., & Mani, N. (2013). Word-form familiarity bootstraps infant speech segmentation. *Developmental Science, 16,* 980–990.

Arias-Trejo, N., & Plunkett, K. (2009). Lexical priming effects during infancy. *Philosophical Transaction of the Royal Society: B: Biological Sciences, 364,* 3633–3647.

Arias-Trejo, N., & Plunkett, K. (2013). What's in a link: Associative and taxonomic priming effects in the early lexicon. *Cognition, 128,* 214–227.

Beckage, N., Smith, L.B., & Hills, T. (2011). Small worlds and semantic network growth in typical and late talkers. *PLoS One, 6*(5), e19348.

Becker, A., Schild, U., & Friedrich, C.K. (2014). ERP correlates of word onset priming in infants and young children. *Developmental Cognitive Neuroscience, 9,* 44–55.

Borovsky, A., Ellis, E.M., Evans, J.L., & Elman, J.L.(2016a). Semantic density interacts with lexical and sentence processing in infancy. *Child Development, 87*(6), 1893–1908.

Borovsky, A., Ellis, E.M., Evans, J.L., & Elman, J.L. (2016b). Lexical leverage: Category knowledge boosts real-time novel word recognition in two-year-olds. *Developmental Science, 19*(6), 918–932.

Borovsky, A., & Elman, J. (2006). Language input and categories: A relation between cognition and early word learning. *Journal of Child Language, 33*(3), 759–790.

Borovsky, A., Elman, J.L., & Fernald, A. (2012). Knowing a lot for one's age: Vocabulary skill and not age is associated with the time course of incremental sentence interpretation in children and adults. *Journal of Experimental Child Psychology, 112,* 417–436.

Cimpian, A., & Markman, E.M. (2005). The absence of a shape bias in children's word learning. *Developmental Psychology, 41,* 1003–1019.

Dahan, D., & Tanenhaus, M.K. (2004). Continuous mapping from sound to meaning in spoken language comprehension: Immediate effects of verb-based thematic constraints. *Journal of Experimental Psychology: Learning, Memory and Cognition, 30,* 498–513.

Dahan, D., & Tanenhaus, M.K. (2005). Looking at the rope when looking for the snake: Conceptually mediated eye movements during spoken-word recognition. *Psychonomic Bulletin & Review, 12,* 453–459.

Fennell, C.T. (2011). Object familiarity enhances infants' use of phonetic detail in novel words. *Infancy, 16,* 1–15.

Gelman, S.A., & Bloom, P. (2000). Young children are sensitive to how an object was created when deciding how to name it. *Cognition, 76,* 911–103.

Hills, T., Maouene, M., Maouene, J., Sheya, A., & Smith, L. (2009). Longitudinal analysis of early semantic networks: Preferential attachment or preferential acquisition? *Psychological Science, 20,* 729–739.

Huang, Y.-T., & Snedeker, J. (2010). Cascading activation across levels of representation in children's lexical processing. *Journal of Child Language, 26,* 1–18.

Huettig, F., & Altmann, G.T.M. (2007). Visual-shape competition during language-mediated attention is based on lexical input and not modulated by contextual appropriateness. *Visual Cognition, 15,* 985–1018.

Johnson, E.K., McQueen, J.M., & Huettig, F. (2011). Toddlers' language mediated visual search: They need not have the words for it. *The Quarterly Journal of Experimental Psychology, 64,* 1672–1682.

Jones, S.S., Smith, L.B., & Landua, B. (1991). Object properties and knowledge in early lexical learning. *Child Development, 62,* 499–512.

Kamide, Y., Altmann, G.T.M., & Haywood, S.L. (2003). The time-course of prediction in incremental sentence processing: Evidence from anticipatory eye-movements. *Journal of Memory and Language, 49,* 133–159.

Kemler Nelson, D.G., Russell, R., Duke, N., & Jones, K. (2000). Two year olds will name artifacts by their function. *Child Development, 71,* 1271–1288.

Landau, B., Smith, L.B., & Jones, S.S. (1988). The importance of shape in early lexical learning. *Cognitive Development, 3,* 299–321.

Mani, N., Durrant, S., & Floccia, C. (2012). Activation of phonological and semantic codes in toddlers. *Journal of Memory and Language, 66,* 612–622.

Mani, N., & Huettig, F. (2012). Prediction during language processing is a piece of cake—but only for skilled producers. *Journal of Experimental Psychology: Human Perception and Performance, 38,* 843–847.

Mani, N., Johnson, E., McQueen, J.M., & Huettig, F. (2013). How yellow is your banana? Toddlers' language-mediated visual search in referent-present tasks. *Developmental Psychology, 49,* 1036–1044.

Mani, N., & Plunkett, K. (2010). In the infant's mind's ear: Evidence for implicit naming in infancy. *Psychological Science, 21,* 908–913.

Mani, N., & Plunkett. K. (2011). Phonological priming and cohort effects in toddlers. *Cognition, 121,* 196–206.

Marslen-Wilson, W.D., & Zwitserlood, P. (1989). Accessing spoken word: The importance of word onsets. *Journal of Experimental Psychology: Human Perception and Performance, 15,* 576–585.

Mayor, J., & Plunkett, K. (2014). Infant word recognition: Insights from TRACE simulations. *Journal of Memory and Language, 71,* 89–123.

Meints, K., Plunkett, K., & Harris, P.L. (1999). When does an ostrich become a bird? The role of typicality in early word comprehension. *Developmental Psychology, 35,* 1072–1078.

Meyer, D.E., & Schvaneveldt, R.W. (1971). Facilitation in recognizing pairs of words: Evidence of dependence between retrieval operations. *Journal of Experimental Psychology*, *90*, 227–234.

Newman, R., Samuelson, L., & Gupta, P. (2008). Learning novel neighbors: Distributed mappings help children and connectionist models. *Proceedings of the 30th Annual Conference of the Cognitive Science Society*, 29–34.

Rämä, P., Sirri, L., & Serres, J. (2013). Development of lexical-semantic language system: N400 priming effect for spoken words in 18- and 24-month old children. *Brain and Language*, *125*, 1–10.

Slowiaczek, L.M., Nusbaum, H.C., & Pisoni, D.B. (1987). Phonological priming in auditory word recognition. *Journal of Experimental Psychology: Learning, Memory and Cognition*, *13*, 64–75.

Smith, L.B., Jones, S.S., Landau, B., Gershkoff-Stowe, L., & Samuelson, L. (2002). Object name learning provides on-the-job training for attention. *Psychological Science*, *13*, 13–19.

Steyvers, M., & Tenenbaum, J.B. (2005). The large-scale structure of semantic networks: Statistical analyses and a model of semantic growth. *Cognitive Science*, *29*, 41–78.

Storkel, H.L. (2006). Do children still pick and choose? The relationship between phonological knowledge and lexical acquisition beyond 50-words. *Clinical Linguistics & Phonetics*, *20*, 523–529.

Storkel, H.L. (2009). Developmental differences in the effects of phonological, lexical, and semantic variables on word learning by infants. *Journal of Child Language*, *36*, 291–321.

Styles, S.J., & Plunkett, K. (2009). How do infants build a semantic system? *Language and Cognition*, *1*, 1–24.

Swingley, D. (2007). Lexical exposure and word-form encoding in 1.5-year-olds. *Developmental Psychology*, *43*, 454–464.

Swingley, D. (2009). Onsets and codas in 1.5-year-olds' word recognition. *Journal of Memory and Language*, *60*, 252–269.

Swingley, D., & Aslin, R.N. (2007). Lexical competition in young children's word learning. *Cognitive Psychology*, *54*, 99–132.

Swingley, D., Pinto, J., & Fernald, A. (1999). Continuous processing in word recognition at 24-months. *Cognition*, *71*, 73–108.

Torkildsen, J.V.K., Syversen, G., Simonsen, H.G., Moen, I., & Lindgren M. (2007). Electrophysiological correlates of auditory semantic priming in 24-month-olds. *Journal of Neurolinguistics*, *20*, 332–351.

Von Holzen, K., & Mani, N. (2012). Language non-selective lexical access in bilingual toddlers. *Journal of Experimental Child Psychology*, *113*, 569–86.

Willits, J.A., Wojcik, E.H., Seidenberg, M.S., & Saffran, J.R. (2013). Toddlers activate lexical semantic knowledge in the absence of visual referents: Evidence from auditory priming. *Infancy*, *18*, doi: 10.1111/infa.12026.

Wojcik, E.H., & Saffran, J.R. (2013). The ontogeny of lexical networks: Toddlers encode the relationships among referents when learning novel words. *Psychological Science*, *24*, 1898–1905.

Yee, E., & Sedivy, J. (2006). Eye movements to pictures reveal transient semantic activation during spoken word recognition. *Journal of Experimental Psychology: Learning, Memory, and Cognition*, *32*, 1–14.

Yurovsky, D., Fricker, D., Yu, C., & Smith, L.B. (2014). The role of partial knowledge in statistical word learning. *Psychonomic Bulletin & Review*, *21*, 1–22.

6

VERBS

Learning how speakers use words to refer to actions

Jane B. Childers, Angeline Bottera, and Tyler Howard

DEPARTMENT OF PSYCHOLOGY, TRINITY UNIVERSITY, USA

Children grow up in a complex world and must acquire their native language from a dynamic environment. From infancy, they need to segment the continuous stream of action that surrounds them into meaningful events and figure out how parents use words to describe these events. Verbs vary by language so parents speaking different languages may use different verbs to refer to different events or parts of events (e.g., Talmy, 1975). Thus, learning a new verb has been described as solving a "packaging problem" (e.g,. Gleitman & Gleitman, 1992) because what children need to do when faced with learning a new verb is to conceptually package dynamic, transient events in just those ways that fit a particular verb in their language (Gentner, 1982; Gentner & Boroditsky, 2001).

More specifically, imagine a young child faced with learning the following verbs, probably heard within the same day or week: *eat, kick, scoop, go, want, cook,* and *bathe*. (This child would be learning English, and in other languages may learn similar verbs but not synonyms, and perhaps not even as verbs but as other predicate terms with related meanings.) The young child has to parse an ongoing stream of action around him or her and deduce just what part of the scene is linked to an individual verb (e.g., for *kick*, the movement of the leg; for *eat*, the act of ingestion; for *bathe*, the use of liquid to change state from dirty to clean). Verbs vary in the size or scope of their meaning (with some being described as "heavy" verbs and some as "light" verbs, e.g., Theakston et al., 2004; Maouene et al., 2011), and languages vary in which elements of meaning they typically include in many verbs, with some including path more often (Spanish), and others including manner more often (e.g., English; Talmy, 1975). Although across languages early productive vocabularies are often dominated by nouns (Gentner, 1982; Gentner & Boroditsky, 2001), a key predictor of whether a verb is produced in early vocabularies appears not to be the complexity of the event to which it refers, but the frequency with which it is heard in the input (e.g., Tomasello, 1992; Naigles & Hoff-Ginsberg, 1998). Given variations across verbs, and the variation of the verb category itself across languages, it seems likely that the process of learning a new verb will be an active process which could include multiple mechanisms. After all, multiple mechanisms have been proposed to explain early noun learning (see Monaghan, Kalashnikova, and Mattock, this volume; Horst, this volume), including use of a shape bias (Landau et al., 1988; 1998), fast mapping (Carey & Bartlett, 1978), or different sets of constraints (Markman, 1990) and, in some ways, learning a new noun is less challenging than is learning a new verb. In any case, determining what an individual new verb means, and how to produce it in sentences, is a difficult and important problem children face.

Although children learn enough of the verbs of their language to be native speakers of at least one language by 4 or 5 years, the mechanism(s) that underlie verb learning are still in question. This is an exciting moment for verb researchers because only one wave of theories of verb learning has been proposed and tested, with a second wave just emerging. We began this chapter with a glimpse into the problem of verb learning. Next, we will explore the two most influential verb learning theories—syntactic bootstrapping and the verb island/usage-based account—both of which addressed how children initially link a single event with a new verb (e.g., Gleitman, 1990; Tomasello, 1992; 2000; 2003). One focus of current research is to ask how children go beyond this initial link to productively and appropriately extend a new verb to new situational or syntactic contexts. This is also a knotty problem for young children, one that likely benefits from cross-situational learning. Therefore, three current views proposed to explain cross-situational verb learning will be described with the goal of asking whether children may use one or more of these mechanisms at different stages of the verb acquisition process. Following this discussion, we will ask whether the two prior verb theories should be linked to these new approaches and, if so, how? Our current view is that children use multiple strategies when faced with the tough problem of learning and extending a new verb, and that it is worth considering which strategies are likely to fit together. In the end, we hope that this exploration of available theories will highlight unanswered questions that could inform future research.

Two key verb learning theories: Syntactic bootstrapping and the usage based/verb island view

Two key competing mechanisms have been proposed to initially address the question of verb learning, and both have been tested experimentally in studies in which children need to link a new verb to a single relevant event (e.g., Naigles, 1990; Fisher et al., 1994; Tomasello & Barton, 1994; Olguin & Tomasello, 1993). These two theories have existed as competitors, with one taking a domain-specific, nativist stance (syntactic bootstrapping), and one taking a domain-general and non-nativist stance (the verb island/now usage-based view). Unfortunately, not only were the starting points for each view in direct opposition to each other, but each camp used a particular procedure that the other did not use, with syntactic bootstrapping studies relying on a preferential looking procedure (e.g., Naigles, 1990; Fisher et al., 1994), and studies taking the verb island view relying on enactment and verbal production (e.g., Tomasello & Barton, 1994; Olguin & Tomasello, 1993; but see Dittmar et al., 2008). Given the strengths and weaknesses of each procedure, it was difficult for the field to compare results across studies and come up with a set of studies that could either rule out one of these theories or integrate them.

In fact, they cannot be integrated in their strongest (original) forms because their starting points are in direct opposition. In syntactic bootstrapping theory (Gleitman, 1990), children start with universal grammar, setting parameters as they hear key sentences in their native language, probably completing most of their parameter setting by 3 or 4 years. With this starting point, children understand grammatical categories—including subject and direct object, noun and verb—and understand the syntactic structure of intransitive and transitive sentences by 2½ years. They can then use the syntax across a set of sentences in which a new verb is heard to narrow down a verb's meaning (e.g., see Fisher et al., 1994).

Several studies now show that young 2-year-old children hearing transitive sentences expect the verb to refer to a causative scene (e.g., a duck pushing on a bunny to make the bunny squat), and children hearing intransitive sentences expect that new verb to refer to a non-causative event (e.g., a duck and a bunny moving their arms in a circular motion) (Naigles, 1990; Naigles & Kako, 1993; Fisher et al., 1994; Fisher, 2002; Gertner et al., 2006). More recently, syntactic bootstrapping has been described a little less formally (Fisher, 2002), with young children succeeding in these comprehension tasks perhaps because they have formed links between sentences with two arguments and scenes with two entities in a relation, and sentences expressing one argument with actions made by a single participant. Before 3 years, children may still be working out how formal syntactic categories (subject, direct object) are expressed in their language. Even so, they could be influenced by a growing understanding of syntactic structure, which could help them deduce the meaning of a novel verb. In Gertner et al. (2006), syntactic bootstrapping provides children with initial constraints about sentence structure that the item-specific usage-based account does not include, and these initial constraints help children abstract across grammatical and semantic categories as they learn verbs (also see Fisher, Gertner, Scott & Yuan, 2010).

Yet, one reason to look beyond the syntactic bootstrapping view is that these initial links do not fully specify meaning (e.g., between different causative events that are present). Although Gleitman (1990) initially showed that a blind child could differentiate "look" from "see" (and eight other verbs) based on the range of frames in which each verb was heard, few experimental studies within the syntactic bootstrapping view show that children younger than 3 years attend to a range of frames (though in Yuan & Fisher, 2009, children can learn from a dialogue between speakers). If children are collecting sets of syntactic frames for each verb, they would then need to deduce how specific sets of frames link to different types of meanings. This would be a complex process.

An alternate account to syntactic bootstrapping that was proposed around this same time was the "verb island view" of verb learning (Tomasello, 1992). In this view, children form representations for each new verb based on patterns they hear in the input. For example, children hearing the verb *draw* would listen to short sentences including this verb spoken by adults around them, and would store those sentences or constructions in relatively isolated representations specific only to that verb. They would then produce sentences using that verb in their own productions that would reflect uses heard in the input. Thus, children are not creative verb users, at least early in verb learning, and they are not decomposing the sentences in which a verb occurs, analyzing them in term of grammatical categories or structure. They also do not generalize across similar verbs, so do not produce similar verbs in the same constructions; instead their knowledge seems more piecemeal, with children initially producing verbs only in constructions heard in the input.

Evidence for this view first came from a diary study of a child's use of verbs in the second year of life. Tomasello (1992) found that the best predictor of sentences including a particular verb was previous sentences with that verb that the child had produced, with only minor increases in complexity. Verbs that were semantically similar were not used by the child in similar syntactic frames (e.g., *push* and *pull*); references to agents or objects were found only for a few verbs when these references could have been extended more widely to other verbs, and verb morphology also was produced only for specific verbs. Since then, many experiments have shown that children aged 2 to 2½ years using a newly learned verb are conservative in their verb productions (e.g., Childers & Tomasello, 2001; Olguin & Tomasello, 1993; Tomasello, 2000), often failing to extend new verbs to sentence types not heard in the input. Children may have some developing grammatical knowledge that is "weak" (Abbot-Smith et al., 2008) and 2-year-olds have some understanding of links between word order and semantic roles (Dittmar et al., 2011). Strengths of the verb island view are that it describes how children could build up a verb vocabulary specific to their language, and it predicts conservative verb productions that fit production data. A weakness is that it does not explain how the child transitions to knowledge that fits adult grammar, unless one accepts a view of adult knowledge that moves away from formal grammar (e.g., construction grammar, see Tomasello, 2003; Goldberg, 2003).

One more point to consider here is that this usage-based account describes how children could come to know how particular verbs should be used in sentences. Yet, learning a new verb also means figuring out how speakers use a particular word to refer to aspects of an ongoing event. While Tomasello was developing his verb island view, he was proposing a socio-pragmatic approach to language learning at the same time, which linked to verb meaning. He reminded us that children are learning verbs in a rich social environment in which some events are predictable, and some cues to an adult's intentions are available (Tomasello, 1992; 2000). Children faced with the complex problem of packaging transient elements of dynamic scenes in varied ways across verbs would benefit from attention to what the parent is intending to say. This "mind reading" could be even more necessary in verb learning than noun learning because different verbs take different perspectives on a single event (e.g., hearing "scoop" and "pour" while playing in a sandbox). Pragmatic or social cues also will not definitively lead to a single verb meaning, but they could help the child if s/he guesses about what parents typically focus on or do in a particular location or time of day, and what they are wanting their child to do.

Could children have a robust understanding of syntax but still progress through a stage in verb learning in which individual verbs are relatively isolated from other verbs? Is syntactic knowledge so powerful that pragmatic knowledge is not useful? In their original forms, it is true that syntactic bootstrapping and the verb island view are incompatible, mostly because they stand opposed to each other at the beginning state and, because the child begins differently, the assumed level of syntactic information available to him/her at 2 years differs. If we strip away the initial state from these mechanisms and ask, at 2 years and beyond, what mechanisms do children use in verb learning, is there any usefulness in trying to integrate these views? Perhaps children have either "turned on" or constructed enough syntactic knowledge to make some use of simple transitive and intransitive sentence structure by 2 years (e.g., Naigles, 1990; Fisher et al., 1994). In addition, they seem attuned to the social world in complex ways, attending to adult eye gaze during word learning (e.g., Baldwin et al., 2001), and understanding some adult intentions (e.g., Meltzoff, 1995), including a sense of differing desires by 18 months (Repacholi and Gopnik, 1997). Even if they are sophisticated syntactic thinkers, children act conservatively for a time in their verb uses (e.g., Roberts, 1983; Huttenlocher et al., 1983; Childers & Tomasello, 2001), showing rigidity when extending verbs to events that differ from the initial learning contexts in which the verb was heard (e.g., Behrend, 1990; Forbes & Farrar, 1995; Maguire et al., 2008). In fact, adults also are sensitive to experiences with particular verbs in specific sentence structures (Fisher, 2002).

In sum, syntactic bootstrapping and the verb island/usage-based view have been the two leading views of verb acquisition, mostly tested in studies in which children were asked to learn a new verb from a single relevant event. Yet recently, verb researchers have begun to ask what attention to and use of cross-situational information could add to children's verb learning. That is, instead of asking whether children's developing productivity is explained only by whether their syntactic knowledge is innate or mostly constructed, researchers are asking if children's initial conservatism in their verb uses is overcome by attention to multiple examples. Three new views of cross-situational learning have yet to be integrated with these two older theories. Thus, in the next section we will consider these more recent views, and then attempt to link them to one or more of the existing verb learning theories just described.

Emerging theories to explain cross-situational verb learning

One reason to posit that cross-situational information will be especially important to verb learning is that hearing a new verb and seeing a complex, dynamic event still leaves the learner with multiple possible meanings for that verb. For example, a child at a volleyball game could wonder if the parent is talking about spiking the ball, hitting it, serving it, rotating positions, walking off of the court, or blowing a whistle—all of which could be present at the same moment the child hears the parent say a new verb. From a single sentence, a transitive verb could fit any of the causative actions, the child could store a particular utterance linked to an item without knowing initially which event links to that item, and the parent's eye gaze (or other social cue) could be ambiguous. Thus, it is not surprising that verb researchers have commented that cross-situational information should be important (e.g., Behrend, 1995; Fisher et al., 1994; Pinker, 1989). In fact, both leading theories just described have assumed some cross-situational learning. In syntactic bootstrapping, it is the range of sentences in which a new verb is heard that informs the learner, and in the verb island view, it is the set of constructions heard to co-occur with the new verb (see Abbot-Smith & Tomasello, 2006 for discussion of how categorization could help learners extend verbs). Yet, it is important to pick up this question of cross-situational learning explicitly and consider it in itself, partly because if we claim that this type of learning is important, we should describe how we think situations (or sentences) *are actually compared* across time. And this seems to be what three leading views currently are seeking to do (interestingly, mostly using domain-general mechanisms).

Additionally, experimentally, verb researchers have begun to ask how children may be comparing events as they learn a verb (e.g., Scott & Fisher, 2012; Waxman et al., 2009; Childers & Paik, 2009; Haryu et al., 2011). These experiments have shown that 2½-year-old children can track the co-occurrence of a specific verb to a repeated event across a set of trials, even when both a target and distractor event are shown at the same time (Scott & Fisher, 2012). Children at this age can preserve a repeated element in an event (either action or result) when they have seen three related events (Childers, 2011). Also, both English- and Korean-speaking children, if shown three varied events (with different numbers of objects and different object roles) as opposed to three similar events, enact more varied events when asked to extend a verb at test (Childers & Paik, 2009). At the same time, processing varied examples is difficult. In two studies, Haryu et al. (2011) showed with 3- and 4-year-old Japanese speakers that if seeing a single event and then extending a verb, object similarity across the two contexts helps. However, if given multiple examples of events that can be compared, less object similarity is needed to extend the verb. Other studies also show that children who are encouraged to compare some events and contrast other events also show better verb learning than do children without these experiences (Waxman et al., 2009; Childers et al., 2014).

These experimental studies are informed by three emerging theories that specifically address how learners could use the information that is available to them across a range of examples. One is that they may use associationist processes in word learning (e.g., Yu & Smith, 2007), a second is that they may structurally align elements from one example to another and draw conclusions from these alignments (e.g., Gentner, 1983; 1989), and a third is that they form a hypothesis that they later test as they see multiple examples (e.g., Medina et al., 2011; Trueswell et al., 2013). We will briefly outline the basics of each approach in the following paragraphs, exploring them from the most bottom-up approach (associations), to the most top-down approach (hypothesis testing). As we describe each view, we will include a brief description of the evidence for the view, and then consider in what ways these views are orthogonal to each other.

In the associationist account, learners who hear two words while seeing two objects will not be sure which word/object pairing holds until they hear the same new word a second time at least (Tilles & Fontanari, 2012). Once they have seen a second pair of objects while hearing the same new word, they can track the probability of the word/object pairing across examples and learn the word (similar to statistical learning in speech segmentation, Saffran et al., 1996, and artificial grammar learning, Gomez & Gerken, 1999; see Monaghan, this volume). Experimentally testing this view, Smith and Yu (2008) have shown that 12- and 14-month-old infants could learn six object-word pairings over thirty training trials. A question that arises then is whether sheer associations of events with particular verbs can explain verb learning. In a recent verb-learning study (Scott & Fisher, 2012), 2½-year-old children saw three pairs of events in six presentations and, during each pair, they heard two different novel verbs. Their looking behavior to each event was coded frame-by-frame as the sentence with the two verbs unfolded. Starting in the second trial, or once children had heard a specific verb twice, children looked longer at a specific event that co-occurred with that verb as opposed to a distractor event. This is a complex task for these young children, and thus their performance is impressive. However, a second study showed that this level of accuracy was present only for events that were simple body movements; if events were shown with an agent and an object, only high vocabulary children at this age succeeded. In addition, these events were whole events, prepackaged for the child. In everyday contexts, children see dynamic sets of events that must be parsed, and specific verbs are used to refer to different sets of elements within these events.

Yet, what if children *started* learning a new verb using this association mechanism? This mechanism could help them begin to collect whole scenes linked to an individual verb. If children are associating an entire unconstrained memory of a dynamic event, then how do they compare it to the new event before them that also co-occurs with the same verb? How do either children or adults converge on relevant and irrelevant elements of actions across scenes? This is an easier task for nouns, or for pre-individuated events, than it is in the "real world," and the associationist view does not include an explanation of how this mental comparison of dynamic events unfolds. If children form a collection of scene-to-verb links, the other two mechanisms that have been proposed may then be ones they use to get beyond whole scenes and focus on relevant objects and relations.

One of these other mechanisms, and one we have focused on in our research, is structural alignment. In structural alignment theory, the way in which two events are compared to each other is that the observer aligns specific elements of one event to elements of another based on the relational structure of each event (e.g., Gentner, 1983; 1989; Gentner & Markman, 1994; 1997). For example, children seeing a scene in which a soccer player kicks a ball (Event 1) and then a scene in which an American football player punts a ball (drops and then kicks it before it hits the ground) (Event 2) could align these two events based on their common structure. Specifically, children could recognize that there is a kicker in Event 1 and align it with the kicker in Event 2 and recognize there is something kicked in Event 1 and align it with the kicked object in Event 2. These alignments are initially guided by the perceptual similarity of objects across the two events, and there can be different numbers of elements in each event (nonalignable differences). The alignment of elements across events highlights their common relational structure (e.g., Gentner et al., 2003). A benefit of this alignment and resulting comparison is that it allows children to draw inferences. One inference would be whether to extend the new verb to a new scene, a decision guided by the child's attention to the similarities and differences across the initial two events, and his or her alignment of the new event with these prior events. Because this theory takes event structure into account, and demonstrates attention to that event structure as well as an explanation of how that event structure is analyzed, it seems especially well suited to studies of cross-situational verb learning.

Interestingly, both Fisher and Tomasello have described how structural alignment could help children link event structures to sentence structures. Fisher (2002) noted that structural alignment could be used by children to align a conceptual structure of an event with a semantic structure of a sentence. This would give children some constraints to guide verb learning but also allow for the cross-linguistic variation in verbs and the verb category that is present. Additionally, Tomasello (2000) describes how structural alignment could help children abstract across a range of constructions by noting that two constructions can be considered analogous if a "good" structure mapping between them is found both on the level of linguistic form and on the level of communicative function. Several studies in our lab have shown that children comparing events produce behavior at test that is consistent with the structural alignment account (e.g., Childers, 2011; Childers & Paik, 2009; Childers et al., 2014; Childers et al., 2016), yet to our knowledge, no study yet has examined the more complex view that structural alignment of conceptual and syntactic structures is useful in verb learning in young children.

Taken together, there is a growing body of evidence to show that children compare multiple events, and this evidence is consistent with predictions made in structural alignment theory. Even so, does this rule out associationist processes at work in cross-situational verb learning? No—children could still begin with associations between events and specific verbs, and the process of aligning multiple examples based on their relational structure would then describe in more detail how children compare these events. Another question is whether these two views are incompatible with syntactic bootstrapping or the verb island view/usage based account. We will return to this question at the end of the chapter.

A third main mechanism proposed for cross-situational learning is the hypothesis testing approach (Medina et al., 2011). In this view, learners form a hypothesis the first time they hear a new word and see an object (or event). When they hear additional uses of that word, they test that hypothesis to determine whether it holds in the new context and, if not, they revise it, abandoning hypotheses that fail. In a recent paper, two studies with adults show that, for adults learning new nouns, the order of the examples influences their learning (Medina et al., 2011). This result is used as evidence for the hypothesis testing view since order should not be as influential if learners are computing associations. In a subsequent paper, three studies show adults learning new nouns performed in ways consistent with the hypothesis testing account, using both explicit and looking measures (Trueswell et al., 2013). In theory, this approach could be extended to verb learning, though given the complexities of the "packaging problem" (i.e., determining which elements in an event are relevant) described previously, it may be difficult for children to form an effective first hypothesis. Could hypothesis testing be invoked after children have created some associations between whole events and specific verbs? Yes, these views seem compatible with each other. Of course the associationist approach (proposed by Smith and Yu, 2008) is a domain-general, non-nativist account, and thus, the question is whether it can completely explain cross-situational verb learning without additional (possibly domain-specific) mechanisms. We believe the answer to this is that it cannot because it does not explain how children decompose and compare events. It does seem likely that children could start with associations, and thus the question is whether domain-general *and* domain-specific mechanisms could be at work, and this seems possible.

Furthermore, at this point, it is unclear to us whether children would need both structural alignment and hypothesis testing following initial associations, though if children use all three mechanisms, perhaps structural alignment could lead children to good hypotheses.

What evidence is needed to distinguish one mechanism as solely responsible for cross-situational verb learning? It seems difficult to think of evidence that will rule out the associationist account, or children's formation of associations between a set of events and a single verb, except to note that this does not on its own fully explain cross-situational verb learning. The difference between the structural alignment and hypothesis testing accounts is that, in hypothesis testing, an initial guess is created which is then tested across examples, while in structural alignment, as examples are aligned, the alignment process leads the observer to attend to certain surface and deeper commonalities—which leads them to a guess of what a particular verb may mean. Thus, in one theory, the order in which specific events are encountered could make a key difference if some events support a key hypothesis better than other events, while in the other, the ability of events to be aligned affects their comparison and inferences. Perhaps studies varying event structure and event order will be able to show whether both mechanisms are at work or whether one subsumes the other.

Putting it all together

In this chapter, we discussed the two key verb acquisition theories that have driven language development research since the 1980s. We then explored three emerging theories that verb researchers are beginning to test to deal with the question of cross-situational processing. Verb researchers have known that cross-situational processing must be important in verb learning because the process of learning a verb is so complex, idiosyncratic, and difficult, but we have only just begun exploring how children may deal with information across multiple situational and syntactic contexts. In this final section of this chapter, we want to return to the two key verb theories and ask how these theories fit together.

One way to start is to sort views based on their nativist or non-nativist stance. Thus, syntactic bootstrapping and hypothesis testing fit together (both nativist views). That leaves the associationist, structural alignment and verb island/usage-based account as the other set, which would fit together. One way researchers could proceed would be to test one set against the other.

Yet, is there a way to group these theories while arguing that innate parameters give the child too much innate knowledge, and associations give the child too little? So is there a middle ground, with a mix of mechanisms, and is it worth pursuing? In our reading and discussions with others in the field, this seems to be one direction many are considering. Additionally, do children start with construction grammar or syntactic bootstrapping, and then do cross-situational processing (because this is the order in which our theories have been birthed)? Or, is cross-situational processing the way in which grammars are constructed or parameters are set? What if children start with associations and then use structural alignment and/or hypothesis testing? (It seems likely that these could emerge early.) Does this lead them to grammar (constructed or innate)? On this account, cross-situational learning helps children learn the meaning of individual new verbs, and children could then attend to the frames or constructions in which that verb appears. Or cross-situational learning could help children learn the meaning of individual new verbs, which are also heard in sentences with a grammatical structure. Those sets of frames could help children group verbs into transitive or intransitive verb categories, guiding them to focus on causative or non-causative events within larger, dynamic scenes. Which causative event within a scene is important to an individual verb's meaning is informed by the set of scenes that have been linked to that verb (so could syntactic bootstrapping + associations be enough?). We confess that we do not have all the answers to all of these questions (as should be clear to readers by now!), but we would like to propose that verb-learning researchers consider some of these questions. At the core of our questions should be the idea that verb learning is so complex that multiple mechanisms are likely used. And, that this may be why researchers from different traditions and with different mechanisms can find some experimental evidence for all of these competing theories. As theories are developed to explain verb learning, we hope that competing theories can be considered together, perhaps as sets of mechanisms or with the acknowledgment that mechanisms may interact with each other. We believe that this type of approach to theory building and testing will be important in the future of verb research.

References

Abbot-Smith, K., Lieven, E., & Tomasello, M. (2008). Graded representations in the acquisition of English and German transitive constructions. *Cognitive Development, 23*, 48–66.

Abbot-Smith, K., & Tomasello, M. (2006). Exemplar-learning and schematization in a usage-based account of syntactic acquisition. *Linguistic Review, 23*, 275–290.

Baldwin, D.A., Baird, J.A., Saylor, M.M., & Clark, M.A. (2001). Infants parse dynamic action. *Child Development, 72*(3), 708–717.

Behrend, D.A. (1990). The development of verb concepts: Children's use of verbs to label familiar and novel events. *Child Development, 61*, 681–696.

Behrend, D.A. (1995). Processes involved in the initial mapping of verb meanings. In M. Tomasello & W.E. Merriman (Eds.), *Beyond names for things: Young children's acquisition of verbs*, 251–273. Hillsdale, NJ: Erlbaum.

Carey, S., & Bartlett, E. (1978). Acquiring a single new word. *Papers and Reports on Child Language Development, 15*, 17–29.

Childers, J.B. (2011). Attention to multiple events helps two-and-a-half-year-olds extend new verbs. *First Language, 31*(1), 3–22.

Childers, J.B., Hirshkowitz, A. & Benavides, K. (2014). Attention to explicit and implicit contrast in verb learning. *Journal of Cognition and Development, 15*(2), 213–237.

Childers, J.B., & Paik, J.H. (2009). Korean- and English-speaking children use cross-situational information to learn novel predicate terms. *Journal of Child Language, 36*(1), 201–224.

Childers, J.B., & Parrish, R., Olson, C., Fung, G., & McIntyre, K. (2016). Experience comparing similar events helps children extend new verbs. *Journal of Cognition and Development, 17*, 41–66.

Childers, J.B., & Tomasello, M. (2001). The role of pronouns in young children's acquisition of the English transitive construction. *Developmental Psychology, 37*(6), 739–748.

Dittmar, M., Abbot-Smith, K., Lieven, E., & Tomasello, M. (2008). Young German children's early syntactic competence: A preferential looking study. *Developmental Science, 11*(4), 575–582.

Dittmar, M., Abbot-Smith, K., Lieven, E., & Tomasello, M. (2011). Children aged 2;1 use transitive syntax to make a semantic role interpretation in a pointing task. *Journal of Child Language, 38*, 1109–1123.

Fisher, C. (2002). Structural limits on verb mapping: The role of abstract structure in 2.5-year-olds' interpretations of novel verbs. *Developmental Science, 5*(1), 55–64.

Fisher, C., Hall, D.G., Rakowitz, S., & Gleitman, L. (1994). When it is better to receive than to give: Syntactic and conceptual constraints on vocabulary growth. *Lingua, 92*, 333–375.

Fisher, C., Gertner, Y., Scott, R.M., & Yuan, S. (2010). Syntactic bootstrapping. *Wiley Interdisciplinary Reviews: Cognitive Science, 1*(2), 143–149.

Forbes, J.N., & Farrar, M.J. (1995). Learning to represent word meaning: What initial training events reveal about children's developing action verb concepts. *Cognitive Development, 10*, 1–20.

Gentner, D. (1982). Why nouns are learned before verbs: Linguistic relativity versus natural partitioning. In S.A. Kuczaj, II (Ed.), *Language development, vol. 2: Language, thought and culture*. Hillsdale, NJ: Erlbaum.

Gentner, D. (1983). Structure-mapping: A theoretical framework for analogy. *Cognitive Science, 7*, 155–170.

Gentner, D. (1989). The mechanisms of analogical learning. In S. Vosniadou & A. Ortony (Eds.), *Similarity and analogical reasoning*, 199–241. Cambridge: Cambridge University Press.

Gentner, D., & Boroditsky, L. (2001). Individuation, relativity, and early word learning. *Language Acquisition and Conceptual Development*, *3*, 215.

Gentner, D., Loewenstein, J., & Thompson, L. (2003). Learning and transfer: A general role for analogical encoding. *Journal of Educational Psychology*, *95*(2), 393.

Gentner, D., & Markman, A.B. (1994). Structural alignment in comparison: No difference without similarity. *Psychological Science*, *5*, 152–158.

Gentner, D., & Markman, A.B. (1997). Structure mapping in analogy and similarity. *American Psychologist*, *52*, 45–56.

Gertner, Y., Fisher, C., & Eisengart, J. (2006). Learning words and rules: Abstract knowledge of word order in early sentence comprehension. *Psychological Science*, *17*(8), 684–691.

Gleitman, L. (1990). The structural sources of verb meanings. *Language Acquisition*, *1*(1), 3–55.

Gleitman, L., & Gleitman, H. (1992). A picture is worth a thousand words, but that's the problem: The role of syntax in vocabulary acquisition. *Current Directions in Psychological Science*, *1*, 31–35.

Goldberg, A.E. (2003). Constructions: A new theoretical approach to language. *Trends in Cognitive Science*, *7*(5), 219–224.

Gomez, R.L., & Gerken, L. (1999). Artificial grammar learning by 1-year-olds leads to specific and abstract knowledge. *Cognition*, *70*(2), 109–135.

Haryu, E., Imai, M., & Okada, H. (2011). Object similarity bootstraps young children to action-based verb extension. *Child Development*, *82*(2), 674–686.

Huttenlocher, J., Smiley, P., & Charney, R. (1983). Emergence of action categories in the child: Evidence from verb meanings. *Psychological Review*, *90*(1), 72.

Landau, B., Smith, L., & Jones, S. (1998). Object shape, object function, and object name. *Journal of Memory and Language*, *38*(1), 1–27.

Landau, B., Smith, L.B., & Jones, S.S. (1988). The importance of shape in early lexical learning. *Cognitive Development*, *3*(3), 299–321.

Maguire, M.J., Hirsh-Pasek, K., Golinkoff, R., & Brandone, A.C. (2008). Focusing on the relation: Fewer examples facilitate children's initial verb learning and extension. *Developmental Science*, *11*(4), 628–634.

Maouene, J., Laakso, A., & Smith, L.B. (2011). Object associations of early-learned light and heavy English verbs. *First Language*, *31*, 109–132.

Markman, E.M. (1990). Constraints children place on word meanings. *Cognitive Science*, *14*(1), 57–77.

Medina, T.N., Snedeker, J., Trueswell, J.C., & Gleitman, L.R. (2011). How words can and cannot be learned by observation. *Proceedings of the National Academy of Sciences*, *108*(22), 9014–9019.

Meltzoff, A.N. (1995). Understanding the intentions of others: Re-enactment of intended acts by 18-month-old children. *Developmental psychology*, *31*(5), 838–850.

Naigles, L. (1990). Children use syntax to learn verb meanings. *Journal of Child Language*, *17*, 357–374.

Naigles, L.G., & Kako, E.T. (1993). First contact in verb acquisition: Defining a role for syntax. *Child Development*, *64*(6), 1665–1687.

Naigles, L.R., & Hoff-Ginsberg, E. (1998). Why are some verbs learned before other verbs? Effects of input frequency and structure on children's early verb use. *Journal of Child Language*, *25*(1), 95–120.

Olguin, R., & Tomasello, M. (1993). Twenty-five-month-old children do not have a grammatical category of verb. *Cognitive Development*, *8*, 245–272.

Pinker, S. (1989). *Learnability and cognition*. Cambridge, MA: MIT Press.

Repacholi, B.M., & Gopnik, A. (1997). Early reasoning about desires: Evidence from 14- and 18-month-olds. *Developmental Psychology*, *33*(1), 12–21.

Roberts, K. (1983). Comprehension and production of word order in Stage I. *Child Development*, *54*(2), 443–449.

Saffran, J.R., Aslin, R.N., & Newport, E.L. (1996). Statistical learning by 8-month-old infants. *Science*, *274*(5294), 1926–1928.

Scott, R.M., & Fisher, C. (2012). 2.5-year-olds use cross-situational consistency to learn verbs under referential uncertainty. *Cognition*, *122*(2), 163–180.

Smith, L., & Yu, C. (2008). Infants rapidly learn word-referent mappings via cross-situational statistics. *Cognition*, *106*(3), 1558–1568.

Talmy, L. (1975). Semantics and syntax of motion. *Syntax and Semantics*, *4*, 181–238.

Theakston, A.L., Lieven, E.V., Pine, J.M., & Rowland, C.F. (2004). Semantic generality, input frequency and the acquisition of syntax. *Journal of Child Language*, *31*(01), 61–99.

Tilles, P.F., & Fontanari, J.F. (2012). Minimal model of associative learning for cross-situational lexicon acquisition. *Journal of Mathematical Psychology*, *56*(6), 396–403.

Tomasello, M. (1992). *First verbs: A case study of early grammatical development*. Cambridge: Cambridge University Press.

Tomasello, M. (2000). Do young children have adult syntactic competence? *Cognition*, *74*, 209–253.

Tomasello, M. (2003). *Constructing a language: A usage-based theory of language acquisition*. Cambridge, MA: Harvard University Press.

Tomasello, M., & Barton, M.E. (1994). Learning words in nonostensive contexts. *Developmental Psychology*, *30*(5), 639–650.

Trueswell, J.C., Medina, T.N., Hafri, A., & Gleitman, L.R. (2013). Propose but verify: Fast mapping meets cross-situational word learning. *Cognitive Psychology*, *66*(1), 126–156.

Waxman, S.R., Lidz, J.L., Braun, I.E., & Lavin, T. (2009). Twenty-four-month-old infants' interpretations of novel verbs and nouns in dynamic scenes. *Cognitive Psychology*, *59*(1), 67–95.

Yu, C., & Smith, L.B. (2007). Rapid word learning under uncertainty via cross-situational statistics. *Psychological Science*, *18*(5), 414–420.

Yuan, S., & Fisher, C. (2009). "Really? She blicked the baby?" Two-year-olds learn combinatorial facts about verbs by listening. *Psychological Science*, *20*(5), 619–626.

7

LISTENING TO (AND LISTENING THROUGH) VARIABILITY DURING WORD LEARNING

Katherine S. White

DEPARTMENT OF PSYCHOLOGY, UNIVERSITY OF WATERLOO, CANADA

Introduction

Word learning is a central part of language development—all aspects of language intersect at the level of the word. And it is a surprisingly difficult task. In addition to determining the set of referents to which a word should be mapped, learners must also determine the set of acoustic tokens that constitute the same word. This is a nontrivial problem because no two instances of a word are acoustically identical. Both within and across speakers, words may be realized differently due to lexically irrelevant changes in rate, emotion, and voice quality. When words are mispronounced or produced by speakers with different accents, changes can also occur along lexically relevant dimensions. In the case of mispronunciations, the changes are typically unsystematic and should be ignored. In the case of accents, the changes are systematic and should be learned, not only to facilitate future processing, but also because they transmit social information about speakers. Therefore, not all variability should be treated in the same way. To complicate matters more, what counts as lexically relevant can differ across languages. Some acoustic properties that English speakers consider to be irrelevant for lexical identity, like pitch, are lexically relevant in other languages (e.g., tone languages).

How might this variability affect young learners? On the one hand, if they do not know what acoustic-phonetic dimensions to focus on, they might be overly accepting of meaningful phonological differences. In this case, their lexical categories would be too broad, and they would be attempting to map many disparate properties (meanings, grammatical properties) to the "same" lexical item. On the other hand, they might expect a match along too many dimensions. In this case, their lexical categories would be too narrow, leading them to over-lexicalize (create new lexical entries where none exist), again making it hard to learn the properties of words. And even if they do know what dimensions to pay attention to, what happens when words do not sound as expected (as in the case of unfamiliar accents)?

This chapter considers how infants and toddlers cope with various types of variability in the pronunciation of words. Because many words are highly similar, word representations must be phonologically precise to avoid confusion (no one wants to mistake a warning about a "bear" for a comment about a "pear"). At the same time, given the variability of the speech signal, the recognition process must be flexible and responsive to context. In the sections that follow, I explore these two sides of word recognition in young word learners. I begin with infants' treatment of lexically irrelevant variability and then turn to mispronunciations and accents.

Lexically irrelevant variability: Is Mom's "dog" the same as Dad's "dog"?

Because languages differ in their inventories of speech sounds and in the acoustic-phonetic dimensions they employ for lexical contrast, infants cannot begin life knowing about the sound systems of particular languages. To acquire the sound system of a language, infants must be able to determine language-specific speech categories from the input—and they must be able to do so despite the fact that speech sounds differ along non-linguistic dimensions (see Benders & Altvater-Mackensen, this volume).

By 6 months, infants detect the equivalence of speech sounds in different phonological contexts and when produced by different speakers (Eimas, 1999; Hochmann & Papeo, 2014; Kuhl, 1983), suggesting that they are prioritizing the phonetic dimensions that may be employed to distinguish words. For example, when they are reinforced for turning in response to a particular speech sound, 6-month-olds selectively turn for members of that category, despite the presence of pitch and talker variability across tokens (Kuhl, 1983). However, during the early stages of word learning, infants' word processing can still be disrupted by changes along such lexically irrelevant dimensions.

Infants segment and recognize newly familiarized words around the middle of the first year (Bortfeld et al., 2005; Jusczyk & Aslin, 1995). At this stage, infants appear to rely heavily on the degree of acoustic similarity between tokens. For example, 7.5-month-olds familiarized with isolated words produced by one talker do not later recognize those same words in sentences spoken by a different talker (Houston & Jusczyk, 2000). Similarly, they do not recognize words when the affect, pitch, or emphatic stress changes between familiarization and test, even for a single talker (Bortfeld & Morgan, 2010; Singh et al., 2004; Singh et al., 2008). Infants' failure to recognize words across lexically irrelevant changes is consistent with the storage of such detail in lexical representations (Jusczyk, 1993; Werker & Curtin, 2005).

Word recognition in adults is not immune to the acoustic realizations of words, either (e.g., Bradlow et al., 1999; Creel et al., 2008; Goldinger, 1998). But in adults, phonological information is clearly privileged; lexically irrelevant changes do not block word recognition—they simply slow processing. Why are these sorts of variability more disruptive for infants? One possibility is that infants have not yet determined which dimensions of acoustic-phonetic variability are meaningful for lexical identity. For example, if a particular word has always been heard in a high pitch, infants may assume that pitch is as relevant to the word's identity as its segmental content.

If so, this would suggest that young word learners are conservative, tracking any reliably co-occurring information across tokens that could *potentially* be relevant for signaling lexical contrast. And, indeed, acoustic properties that convey information about talker and affect, such as pitch (Banse & Scherer, 1996; Williams & Stevens, 1972), are phonologically relevant (used to signal lexical distinctions) in many languages. For example, in tonal languages, pitch contours can distinguish words, and in languages with lexical stress, relative pitch is a key cue to stress. A conservative learning strategy of tracking potentially meaningful dimensions would be beneficial for infants who do not know in advance what dimensions are important for lexical contrast in the languages they are learning. This overreliance on similarity along lexically irrelevant dimensions appears to be overcome by 10.5 months (Houston & Jusczyk, 2000; Singh et al., 2004), suggesting that development involves the down-weighting of or abstracting over these dimensions.

But if infants younger than 10.5 months cannot recognize words in their natural environments across changes in, e.g., affect or talker, word learning would be difficult indeed—a failure to group acoustically distinct tokens of the same word would make it very hard to discover semantic and grammatical properties of words. Fortunately, in naturalistic input, lexically irrelevant properties of words are more likely to vary across tokens than they do in laboratory experiments. Therefore, a strategy of tracking reliably co-occurring properties across tokens would likely lead to the prioritizing of appropriate phonetic detail during naturalistic learning. Indeed, in lab studies where the familiarization phase incorporates more variability, infants are not thrown by a subsequent change of speaker or affect (Singh, 2008; Van Heugten & Johnson, 2012). And even 6-month-olds can recognize known words in the lab when they are presented in a never-before-heard voice (Tincoff & Jusczyk, 2012) or when they are presented in different pitches across familiarization and test (Singh et al., 2008). This may indicate that young infants have observed that familiar words in their environment vary along lexically irrelevant dimensions, but have not yet made the generalization that this is true for all words.

Alternatively, it may be that young infants have made this generalization (or prioritize lexically relevant dimensions even earlier in word learning), but that in situations with high processing demands they can be disrupted by salient acoustic information. In most tests of word recognition, words are embedded in sentences. This is computationally demanding (as it requires segmentation) and also introduces additional acoustic differences between the familiarization and test stimuli (words in isolation are very different acoustically than words in fluent speech). It may be that these demands may increase infants' reliance on perceptual similarity until they have had more experience with the task of word recognition. In fact, this might explain why infants sometimes fail to recognize the equivalence of acoustically different word tokens at 7.5 months, even though they recognize the equivalence of speech sounds that vary along the same dimensions when they are presented (in single syllables) in discrimination and categorization tasks.

Lexically relevant variability: When is a "tog" a "dog"?

By 10.5 months, infants focus on meaningful dimensions of acoustic-phonetic variability during word processing. But what happens if the input deviates along these dimensions because words are mispronounced or the speaker has an unfamiliar accent?

Mispronunciations

The effect of mispronunciations on word-form recognition

Although 11-month-old infants normally prefer to listen to familiar words over unfamiliar words (Hallé & de Boysson-Bardies, 1994), this preference is eliminated when the known words are mispronounced by even one phonetic feature (e.g., "*dog*" pronounced as "*tog*"), suggesting that the mispronunciations block recognition (Hallé & de Boysson-Bardies, 1996; Swingley, 2005; Vihman et al., 2004). At this age, the location of the mispronunciation seems to matter: English and Dutch 11-month-olds are more sensitive to onset mispronunciations, whereas French infants are more sensitive to word-medial mispronunciations. This is likely due to differences in the salience of phonetic contrasts in these positions caused by differences in lexical stress in the two languages. The type of mispronunciation may matter as well, with some researchers suggesting that consonant mispronunciations are more disruptive than vowel mispronunciations (Poltrock & Nazzi, 2015), though this may differ over development and across languages.

Thus, infants' long-term lexical representations of familiar words are detailed, and infants use this detail during processing. While this degree of sensitivity is essential for discriminating similar, but distinct, lexical items, some flexibility is required to arrive at the intended word when speakers do produce mispronunciations. In the real world, words are often accompanied by contextual information that might facilitate lexical access, as in the studies described below.

The effect of mispronunciations on word comprehension

Although early studies reported that children were insensitive to some phonological distinctions in referential tasks (in which they needed to access the meanings of words; Barton, 1980; Garnica, 1973; Schvachkin, 1973), subsequent work has demonstrated that toddlers are extremely sensitive to phonological distinctions during word comprehension. Most of this work tests toddlers' sensitivity to mispronunciations using the intermodal preferential looking paradigm, which provides an online measure of the degree to which a heard pronunciation activates a lexical representation.

For example, toddlers look more slowly and less overall at an object when its label is mispronounced, by even a single phonetic feature (consonant or vowel), and even in coda position (Mani & Plunkett, 2007; Swingley, 2009; Swingley & Aslin, 2000, 2002; White & Morgan, 2008). Interestingly, however, for some one-feature mispronunciations, toddlers still look significantly more at the target object than at a distractor, showing that even though processing is disrupted, the token is still recognized as an instance of the word (Swingley & Aslin, 2000, 2002; White & Aslin, 2011). As mispronunciations deviate more from correct pronunciations, toddlers' looking towards distractor objects increases, at least when these distractors are unfamiliar (Ren & Morgan, 2011; White & Morgan, 2008). This sensitivity to the size of the mispronunciation parallels what is observed in children and adults (Connine et al., 1993; Creel, 2012; Milberg et al., 1988; White et al., 2013).[1]

Sometimes a "mispronunciation" is licensed by the phonological context. For example, in English, a coronal consonant followed by a labial can take the place feature of that labial (e.g., the phrase "brown bear" can be pronounced more like "*browm* bear"). At 24 months, English- and French-learning toddlers accept assimilated pronunciations, but only those present in the native language (place vs. voice assimilation, respectively) and only when they are licensed by the following context (Skoruppa et al., 2013a; Skoruppa et al., 2013b). When the same pronunciations precede words that do not license the change, toddlers' processing is disrupted.

Together, these mispronunciation studies reveal a number of continuities across development in the process of word recognition. Like adults, toddlers' interpretation of phonetic detail is not fixed, but is affected by context, both visual (e.g., presence/absence of a referent, type of distractor object) and phonological (in assimilation). Moreover, if there is contextual support, both children and adults may activate lexical representations when words are slightly mispronounced, but they show decreased activation as the mismatch grows. This allows listeners to recover intended words in a world where production errors do occur.

Accents

Mispronunciations are sporadic, and assimilation processes are learned as part of exposure to the native language. A more serious challenge for word learning is systematic variability introduced by speakers of different language communities (who may or may not share the same first language[2]). The nature and degree of variability introduced by accents can vary considerably (Cristia et al., 2012). Different accents can introduce subtle changes in the realization of particular speech sounds and can also introduce phonemic changes (like the mispronunciations in the studies described above). For example, the word "*pen*" is pronounced as "*pin*" in some dialects of American English, and a French-accented "p" may sound very much like a "b" to a native speaker of English, because of cross-linguistic differences in the realization of voiced and voiceless consonants. Accents can also vary at the suprasegmental level (e.g., at the level of lexical stress, as in the American- vs. British-English pronunciations of "laboratory," and more globally).

Because accents can introduce changes along lexically relevant dimensions, they have the potential to slow word learning; failure to recognize novel pronunciations of familiar words may lead to a search for other possible referents, particularly given biases that encourage unique mappings between words and referents (Clark, 1987; Golinkoff et al., 1994; Markman, 1990). Optimal processing of accent variability has two components: first, as for mispronunciations, processing must be flexible enough to recover the intended words; second, the correspondence between the new accent and the native accent should be learned so that the accent can be processed efficiently in the future. This learning should occur at two levels: first, the learned properties should be generalized across the lexicon so that novel pronunciations of words do not have to be learned on an item-by-item basis; and, second, the learned properties should be generalized to other speakers with the same accent.

The effect of unfamiliar accents on word-form recognition

Not surprisingly, given the trajectory described earlier for infants' treatment of lexically irrelevant variability, non-native accents disrupt infants' word processing. English-learning 9-month-olds are unable to recognize newly familiarized words when there is a change of accent (Spanish to English or vice versa) or a change of dialect (American vs. Canadian English) between familiarization and test. By 12–13 months, infants succeed (Schmale & Seidl, 2009; Schmale et al., 2010).

For naturally learned words, recognition in novel accents occurs even later. Although 15-month-olds generally prefer to listen to known words (words learned outside the lab) over unknown words, this preference disappears if the words are spoken in a non-native dialect; 19-month-olds exhibit a preference regardless of dialect (Best et al., 2009). It is not clear whether this more protracted development is due to a difference in accessing long-term representations as opposed to recognizing newly familiarized words, or instead has to do with the distance between the accents used across these studies (when unfamiliar accents deviate more from the native accent, recognition of equivalence may take longer).

Even adults have trouble recognizing words in novel accents on the fly and require a period of exposure to adapt (a period that is shorter or longer depending on the degree of deviation between accents). And it turns that even 15-month-olds can recognize familiar words in a novel accent following a period of exposure. Van Heugten & Johnson (2014) found that Canadian 15-month-olds recognized Australian-accented familiar words after exposure to the accent in a story, but *only if* their mothers had read them the same story for two weeks prior to the experimental session (a group exposed only to the story from the Australian speaker prior to testing failed). This suggests that toddlers noted the correspondence between how words in the story were pronounced in their native accent (during Mom's reading) and the Australian accent, and then generalized this correspondence to the test words (which were not present in the story).

The effect of unfamiliar accents on word comprehension

Toddlers and children also show some failures to understand known and newly trained words in referential tasks when they are produced in an unfamiliar accent. In a situation in which two familiar objects were presented on the screen, Australian 15-month-olds who heard Jamaican-accented words failed to look at the correct object, although toddlers with higher vocabularies were more successful (Mulak et al., 2013). Similarly, English-learning 24-month-olds were unable to interpret a novel word when they were trained on the word by an American-accented speaker and tested by a speaker with Spanish-accented English, though they succeeded in the reverse direction (Schmale et al., 2011).

However, children in these studies had no exposure to the novel accent prior to testing. When they do, performance improves. For example, White & Aslin (2011) tested 19-month-olds' comprehension of familiar words that had undergone a vowel shift. If toddlers had an exposure phase in which they were visually reinforced with the intended familiar referent while hearing the vowel-shifted pronunciations, they later understood the shifted pronunciations. More interestingly, the toddlers also understood shifted pronunciations of phonologically related words that had *not* been presented during training, suggesting that they had learned the general properties of the accent. Both this study and that of Van Heugten & Johnson (2014) suggest that lexical knowledge may help drive the reinterpretation of atypical phonetic detail, and that this detail is reinterpreted, not for individual words, but across the lexicon. This is the same process assumed to operate in adults and older children (Kraljic & Samuel, 2006; McQueen et al., 2006; McQueen et al., 2012).

Exposure may help even in the absence of lexical cues. When presented with Spanish-accented passages prior to a word-learning task, 24-month-olds successfully generalized words trained by an English speaker to a Spanish-accented test speaker. Importantly, the passages were chosen to contain content words that the children would not understand (Schmale et al., 2012). (Note, however, that familiar function words were present; it is unclear whether this is enough to trigger lexically based learning—even infants are aware of the appropriate locations and phonetic forms of function words; Shady, 1996; Shi et al., 2006.) More surprisingly, exposure to a diverse set of natively accented voices prior to the training phase also facilitates learning in this paradigm (Schmale et al., 2015).

This set of findings is consistent with an alternative mechanism for coping with accent variability—an *expansion* strategy, in which word recognition criteria are relaxed because of the presence of higher-than-normal variability in the environment (Schmale et al., 2015). An expansion strategy, in contrast to the lexically based strategy, is not a *learning* strategy. Therefore, if the same accent is encountered in the future, there should be no benefit for having heard that *particular* accent previously, as specific differences between the novel and native accents are not encoded. Rather, the presence of high variability simply leads to greater tolerance for pronunciation changes in general. It has been proposed that this type of strategy may be engaged when a novel accent is too complex to note systematic differences from the native accent or when infants do not know enough words to engage a lexical strategy. Thus far, support for the expansion account has been found exclusively in word-learning studies in which success did not require a high degree of phonological precision (as the test stimuli involved very distinct words). It is not clear that highly variable exposure (without lexical cues) facilitates the recognition of familiar words produced in a novel accent (recall that toddlers failed to recognize familiar words in Van Heugten & Johnson, 2014, following exposure to a story in the Australian voice alone).

The general picture that emerges is that, although accent variability is disruptive in some contexts, experience (both long-term and short-term) leads to an improved ability to recognize accented words. As discussed for the case of non-lexical variability, long-term experience with words varying across contexts (which is likely correlated with vocabulary size), may lead to the development of more robust, generalizable lexical representations. One proposal is that this experience with variation causes a critical shift from phonetic to phonemic representations that allow for cross-accent word recognition (Best et al., 2009). However, even at later ages (and into adulthood, when phonological representations are well established) accents continue to cause processing difficulty. For example, 4- to 7-year-olds and adults have difficulty identifying accented words in a repetition-definition task (Bent, 2014; Nathan et al., 1998) and, like younger learners, even adults often require some exposure to novel accents before they can successfully recognize words. Further, listeners of all ages are more likely to succeed in less difficult situations (for example, preschoolers have less difficulty processing unfamiliar accents in tasks that include pictured alternatives than in free response tasks (Creel et al., 2016), and even adults have more difficulty processing novel accents in noisy than in quiet environments (Munro, 1998). Therefore, there may be considerable continuity across development in the factors that affect the processing of accented words.

Long-term exposure to accent variability: What if Mom says "dog" and Dad says "dawg"?

Thus far, we have considered what happens when learners are exposed to unfamiliar accents. Very little research has been devoted to the fascinating question of how learners cope when they have long-term variability in their natural environments because of exposure to more than one accent. One way of thinking about dual accent exposure is as a case of bilingualism with high structural and lexical overlap (cognates). As in the case of bilingual exposure, one question is whether learners exposed to multiple accents maintain separate phonological and lexical representations for their accents. In one of the few existing studies on this topic, British 20-month-olds exposed to both rhotic and non-rhotic variants of English (from the community and their parents, respectively) recognized only the rhotic versions (Floccia et al., 2012). The authors concluded that the toddlers had adopted a single lexical representation, corresponding to the community pronunciation. However, in a follow-up that included only non-rhotic pronunciations during test, children from the same population recognized these versions, suggesting that they learn both variants (Durrant et al., 2017).

Another recent study similarly suggests that children store multiple variants. In that study, bi-dialectal Dutch 24-month-olds processed voicing mispronunciations differently as a function of the dialect of the speaker; voicing mispronunciations were accepted from a speaker whose dialect did not maintain voicing contrasts but disrupted processing when the speaker's dialect had voicing contrasts (Van der Feest & Johnson, 2016). These results suggest that children track talker- (and accent-) specific pronunciations (see also Creel, 2014, and Weatherhead & White, 2016, for consistent findings). However, in contrast to these demonstrations of accent-specific processing, another study found that British 20-month-olds with multi-dialectal exposure exhibited tolerance for consonant mispronunciations that were not present in either dialect (Durrant et al., 2015). If true, this could cause a more protracted word-learning trajectory since different word-forms would be categorized as the same lexical item. There is much more work to be done in the area of bi-accentual acquisition to determine the conditions under which learners do and do not maintain separate representations of their input and how flexibly they deploy these representations.

Summary

Word recognition is a balancing act. Listeners must represent and process words using precise detail (so that similar words will not be confused). At the same time, processing must be flexible because instances of words differ from one another in pitch, rate, voice, and even in whether they contain the expected sequence of sounds. Despite the seemingly intractable problem that this would appear to pose to learners who must simultaneously determine which dimensions of variability are important, infants and children show a remarkable ability to compensate for this variability. Over development, learners show an increasing ability to deal with more significant changes and with more difficult tasks. Very early in development, infants begin to ignore acoustic-phonetic changes that do not matter for lexical identity and focus on those that do. Later, they learn to be flexible in accepting words that differ along linguistically relevant dimensions, particularly when those interpretations are supported by context or prior exposure. In addition to age, there are also effects of vocabulary size in some tasks (Bent, 2014; Mulak et al., 2013), suggesting that specific lexical knowledge and more general experience with words may play a critical role in driving the ability to flexibly deal with variability. Such effects could reflect changes in representations (Best et al., 2009; Mulak et al., 2013; Werker & Curtin, 2005), better command of the types of variability that are important, stronger lexical feedback, or better use of contextual cues to drive the re-interpretation of mismatching detail. Future research should explore these possible mechanisms of developmental change. The many parallels between young learners and adults suggest that differences across development are a matter of degree, not kind. Learners appear to be well equipped to handle the daunting variability in their speech environment, a crucial foundation for their rapid word learning over the first years of life.

Notes

1 Learners show less sensitivity to changes in the pronunciation of newly learned words. Although they (correctly) ignore changes between training and test that are not lexically relevant, like vowel duration and pitch contour in English (Dietrich et al., 2007; Quam & Swingley, 2010), they are also less sensitive to phonetic contrasts present in the native language (as are adults; Stager & Werker, 1997; Werker et al., 2002; White et al., 2013). Interestingly, the presence of variability along lexically irrelevant dimensions can *enhance* toddlers' sensitivity to phonetic detail during word learning (Rost & McMurray, 2009), presumably by making the critical phonetic properties of the words apparent.
2 Although the terms "dialect" and "accent" are typically used for speakers who share and do not share the same first language, respectively, the word "accent" will be used as the more general term for this type of variability.

References

Banse, R., & Scherer, K.R. (1996). Acoustic profiles in vocal emotion expression. *Journal of Personality and Social Psychology*, 70, 614–636.

Barton, D. (1980). Phonemic perception in children. In G. Yeni-Komshian, J. Kavanaugh, & C. Ferguson (Eds.), *Child phonology: Perception, vol. 2*, 97–116. New York: Academic Press.

Bent, T. (2014). Children's perception of foreign-accented words. *Journal of Child Language*, 41, 1334–1355.

Best, C.T., Tyler, M.D., Gooding, T.N., Orlando, C.B., & Quann, C.A. (2009). Development of phonological constancy: Toddlers' perception of native- and Jamaican-accented words. *Psychological Science*, 20, 539–542.

Bortfeld, H., & Morgan, J.L. (2010). Is early word-form processing stress-full? How natural variability supports recognition. *Cognitive Psychology*, 60, 241–266.

Bortfeld, H., Morgan, J.L., Golinkoff, R.M., & Rathbun, K. (2005). Mommy and me: Familiar names help launch babies into speech stream segmentation. *Psychological Science*, 16, 298–304.

Bradlow, A.R., Nygaard, L.C., & Pisoni, D.B. (1999). Effects of talker, rate, and amplitude variation on recognition memory for spoken words. *Perception & Psychophysics*, 61, 206–219.

Clark, E.V. (1987). The principle of contrast: a constraint on language acquisition. In B. MacWhinney (Ed.), *Mechanisms of language acquisition*, 1–33. Hillsdale, NJ: Lawrence Erlbaum Associates.

Connine, C.M., Blasko, D.M., &Titone, D.A. (1993). Do the beginnings of spoken words have a special status in auditory word recognition? *Journal of Memory and Language*, 32, 193–210.

Creel, S.C. (2012). Phonological similarity and mutual exclusivity: on-line recognition of atypical pronunciations in 3-5-year-olds. *Developmental Science*, 5, 697–713.

Creel, S.C. (2014). Impossible to _gnore: Word-form inconsistency slows preschool children's word-learning. *Language Learning and Development*, 10, 68–95.

Creel, S.C., Aslin, R.N., & Tanenhaus, M.K. (2008). Heeding the voice of experience: The role of talker variation in lexical access. *Cognition*, 106, 633–664.

Creel, S.C., Rojo, D.P., & Paullada, A.N. (2016). Effects of contextual support on preschoolers' accented speech comprehension. *Journal of Experimental Child Psychology*, 146, 156–180.

Cristia, A., Seidl, A., Vaughn, C., Schmale, R., Bradlow, A., & Floccia, C. (2012). Linguistic processing of accented speech across the lifespan. *Frontiers in Psychology*, 3, 479.

Dietrich, C., Swingley, D., & Werker, J.F. (2007). Native language governs interpretation of salient speech sound differences at 18 months. *Proceedings of the National Academy of Sciences*, 104, 16027–16031.

Durrant, S., Delle Luche, C., Cattani, A., & Floccia, C. (2015). Monodialectal and multi-dialectal infants' representation of familiar words. *Journal of Child Language, 42*, 447–465.
Durrant, S., Delle Luche, C., Chow, J., Plunkett, K., & Floccia, C. (2017, April). Rhoticity – A tale of two cities. Paper presented at the meeting of the *Society for Research in Child Development*, Austin, TX.
Eimas, P.D. (1999). Segmental and syllabic representations in the perception of speech by young infants. *Journal of the Acoustical Society of America, 105*, 1901–1911.
Floccia, C., Delle Luche, C., Durrant, S., Butler, J., & Goslin, J. (2012). Parent or community: Where do 20-month-olds exposed to two accents acquire their representations of words? *Cognition, 124*, 95–100.
Garnica, O.K. (1973). The development of phonemic speech perception. In T.E. Moore (Ed.), *Cognitive development and the acquisition of language*, 215–222. New York: Academic Press.
Goldinger, S.D. (1998). Echoes of echoes. An episodic theory of lexical access. *Psychological Review, 105*, 251–279.
Golinkoff, R.M., Mervis, C.V., & Hirsh-Pasek, K. (1994). Early object labels: The case for a developmental lexical principles framework. *Journal of Child Language, 21*, 125–155.
Hallé, P., & de Boysson-Bardies, B. (1994). Emergence of an early lexicon: Infants' recognition of words. *Infant Behavior and Development, 17*, 119–129.
Hallé, P.A., & de Boysson-Bardies, B. (1996). The format of representation of recognized words in infants' early receptive lexicon. *Infant Behavior and Development, 19*, 463–481.
Hochmann, J.-R., & Papeo, L. (2014). The invariance problem in infancy: A pupillometry study. *Psychological Science, 25*(11), 2038–2046.
Houston, D.M., & Jusczyk, P.W. (2000). The role of talker-specific information in word segmentation by infants. *Journal of Experimental Psychology: Human Perception and Performance, 26*, 1570–1582.
Jusczyk, P. (1993). From general to language-specific capacities: The WRAPSA model of how speech perception develops. *Journal of Phonetics, 21*, 3–28.
Jusczyk, P.W., & Aslin, R.N. (1995). Infants' detection of the sound patterns of words in fluent speech. *Cognitive Psychology, 29*, 1–23.
Kraljic, T., & Samuel, A.G. (2006). Generalization in perceptual learning for speech. *Psychonomic Bulletin & Review, 13*, 262–268.
Kuhl, P.K. (1983). Perception of auditory equivalence classes for speech in early infancy. *Infant Behavior and Development, 6*, 263–285.
Mani, N., & Plunkett, K. (2007). Phonological specificity of vowels and consonants in early lexical representations. *Journal of Memory and Language, 57*, 252–272.
Markman, E.M. (1990). Constraints children place on word meanings. *Cognitive Science, 14*, 57–77.
McQueen, J.M., Cutler, A., & Norris, D. (2006). Phonological abstraction in the mental lexicon. *Cognitive Science, 30*, 1113–1126.
McQueen, J.M., Tyler, M.D., & Cutler, A. (2012). Lexical retuning of children's speech perception: Evidence for knowledge about words' component sounds. *Language Learning and Development, 8*, 317–339.
Milberg, W., Blumstein, S.E., & Dworetzky, B. (1988). Phonological factors in lexical access: Evidence from an auditory lexical decision task. *Bulletin of the Psychonomic Society, 26*, 305–308.
Mulak, K.E., Best, C.T., Tyler, M.D., & Kitamura, C. (2013). Development of phonological constancy: 19-month-olds, but not 15-month-olds, identify words in a non-native regional accent. *Child Development, 84*, 2064–2078.
Munro, M.J. (1998). The effects of noise on the intelligibility of foreign-accented speech. *Studies in Second Language Acquisition, 20*, 139–154.

Nathan, L., Wells, B., & Donlan, C. (1998). Children's comprehension of unfamiliar regional accents: A preliminary investigation. *Journal of Child Language, 25*, 343–365.

Poltrock, S., & Nazzi, T. (2015). Consonant/vowel asymmetry in early word form recognition. *Journal of Experimental Child Psychology, 131*, 135–148.

Quam, C., & Swingley, D. (2010). Phonological knowledge guides 2-year-olds' and adults' interpretation of salient pitch contours in word learning. *Journal of Memory and Language, 62*, 135–150.

Ren, J., & Morgan, J.L. (2011). Developmental continuity in infants' early lexical representations. *Proceedings of the 47th Chicago Linguistic Society Annual Meeting*, April 2011, Chicago, IL.

Rost, G.C., & McMurray, B. (2009). Speaker variability augments phonological processing in early word learning. *Developmental Science, 12*, 339–349.

Schmale, R., Cristia, A., & Seidl, A. (2012). Toddlers recognize words in an unfamiliar accent after brief exposure. *Developmental Science, 15*, 732–738.

Schmale, R., Cristia, A., Seidl, A., & Johnson, E.K. (2010). Developmental changes in infants' ability to cope with dialect variation in word recognition. *Infancy, 15*, 650–662.

Schmale, R., Hollich, G., & Seidl, A. (2011). Contending with foreign accent in early word learning. *Journal of Child Language, 38*, 1096–1108.

Schmale, R., & Seidl, A. (2009). Accommodating variability in voice and foreign accent: Flexibility of early word representations. *Developmental Science, 12*, 583–601.

Schmale, R., Seidl, A., & Cristia, A. (2015). Mechanisms underlying accent accommodation in early word learning: Evidence for general expansion. *Developmental Science, 18*, 664–670.

Schvachkin, N.K. (1973). The development of phonemic speech perception in early childhood. In C. Ferguson & D. Slobin (Eds.), *Studies of child language development*, 91–127. New York: Holt, Rinehart, and Winston (originally published in 1948).

Shady, M. (1996). *Infants' sensitivity to function morphemes*. Unpublished doctoral dissertation, State University of New York, Buffalo, NY.

Shi, R., Werker, J., & Cutler, A. (2006). Recognition and representation of function words in English-learning infants. *Infancy, 10*, 187–198.

Singh, L. (2008). Influences of high and low variability on infant word recognition. *Cognition, 106*, 833–870.

Singh, L., Morgan, J.L., & White, K.S. (2004). Preference and processing: The role of speech affect in early spoken word recognition. *Journal of Memory and Language, 51*, 173–189.

Singh, L., Nestor, S.S., & Bortfeld, H. (2008). Overcoming the effects of variation in infant speech segmentation: Influences of word familiarity. *Infancy, 13*, 57–74.

Singh, L., White, K.S., & Morgan, J.L. (2008). Building a phonological lexicon in the face of variable input: Influences of pitch and amplitude on early spoken word recognition. *Language Learning and Development, 4*, 157–178.

Skoruppa, K., Mani, N., & Peperkamp, S. (2013a). Toddlers' processing of phonological alternations: Early compensation for assimilation in English and French. *Child Development, 84*, 313–330.

Skoruppa, K., Mani, N., Plunkett, K., Cabrol, D., & Peperkamp, S. (2013b). Early word recognition in sentence context: French and English 24-month-olds' sensitivity to sentence-medial mispronunciations and assimilations. *Infancy, 18*, 1007–1029.

Stager, C.L., & Werker, J.F. (1997). Infants listen for more phonetic detail in speech perception than in word learning tasks. *Nature, 388*, 381–382.

Swingley, D. (2005). 11-month-olds' knowledge of how familiar words sound. *Developmental Science, 8*, 432–443.

Swingley, D. (2009). Onsets and codas in 1.5-year-olds' word recognition. *Journal of Memory and Language, 60,* 252–269.

Swingley, D., & Aslin, R.N. (2000). Spoken word recognition and lexical representation in very young children. *Cognition, 76,* 147–166.

Swingley, D., & Aslin, R.N. (2002). Lexical neighborhoods and the word-form representations of 14-month-olds. *Psychological Science, 13,* 480–484.

Tincoff, R., & Jusczyk P.W. (2012). Six-month-olds comprehend words that refer to parts of the body. *Infancy, 17,* 432–444.

Van der Feest, S., & Johnson, E. (2016). Input driven differences in toddlers' perception of a disappearing phonological contrast. *Language Acquisition, 23,* 89–111.

Van Heugten, M., & Johnson, E.K. (2012). Infants exposed to fluent natural speech succeed at cross-gender word recognition. *Journal of Speech, Language, and Hearing Research, 55,* 554–560.

Van Heugten, M., & Johnson, E.K. (2014). Learning to contend with accents in infancy: Benefits of brief speaker exposure. *Journal of Experimental Psychology: General, 143,* 340–350.

Vihman, M.M., Nakai, S., DePaolis, R.A., & Hallé, P. (2004). The role of accentual pattern in early lexical representation. *Journal of Memory and Language, 50,* 336–353.

Weatherhead, D., & White, K.S. (2016) He says potato, she says potahto: Young infants track talker-specific accents. *Language Learning and Development, 12,* 92–103.

Werker, J.F., & Curtin, S. (2005). PRIMIR: A developmental model of speech processing. *Language Learning and Development, 1,* 197–234.

Werker, J.F., Fennell, C.T., Corcoran, K.M., & Stager, C.L. (2002). Infants' ability to learn phonetically similar words: Effects of age and vocabulary size. *Infancy, 3,* 1–30.

White, K.S., & Morgan, J.L. (2008). Sub-segmental detail in early lexical representations. *Journal of Memory and Language, 59,* 114–132.

White, K.S., & Aslin, R.N. (2011). Adaptation to novel accents by toddlers. *Developmental Science, 14,* 372–384.

White, K.S., Yee, E., Blumstein, S.E., & Morgan, J.L. (2013). Adults show less sensitivity to phonetic detail in unfamiliar words, too. *Journal of Memory and Language, 68,* 362–378.

Williams, C.E., & Stevens, K.N. (1972). Emotions and speech: Some acoustical correlates. *Journal of the Acoustical Society of America, 52,* 233–248.

8
INDIVIDUAL DIFFERENCES IN EARLY WORD LEARNING

Meredith L. Rowe
HARVARD GRADUATE SCHOOL OF EDUCATION, USA

Kathryn A. Leech
HARVARD GRADUATE SCHOOL OF EDUCATION, USA

Children vary widely in the rate and breadth of vocabulary acquisition across early childhood. Even as early as 9 months, before children utter their first words, there is variation in how many words children comprehend (Halle et al., 2009). Further, children speak their first words at a variety of ages, and wide differences in typically developing children's productive vocabularies are seen around 18 months (Weisleder & Fernald, 2013). By definition, variability in the earliest stages of word learning is small but grows with age. It is not uncommon for a 24-month-old toddler to have 200 more words in his/her productive vocabulary than another same-aged peer (Fenson et al., 1994). Where does this variability come from? In this chapter we review relevant literature on the nature of individual differences in children's early word learning, including issues relevant to measuring that learning, and we put forth several child-factors (e.g., gender, temperament) and other proximal environmental factors (family socioeconomic status, quantity and quality of speech input) that account for some of this variation.

Capturing variability in early word learning

Prior to the 1990s, systematic studies of language variation were uncommon, or were based on very small samples of children, in part because few measurement tools were available to capture vocabulary skills in larger scale and among pre-verbal children. However, more recent advances in methodology and technology have allowed researchers to sensitively measure very early language comprehension and production. The introduction of audio and video recording devices in the mid-20th century allowed researchers to capture children's productive speech in naturalistic settings and, as a result, draw comparisons between children more easily. Typically, recordings are transcribed to yield a permanent written record of the child's speech for future analysis. For example, one of the first in-depth studies of early language development was conducted by Brown (1973), who documented the emergence of morphology by recording two-hour interactions between three parent-child pairs over four years. The audio recordings were then transcribed and coded by hand to yield measures of language (e.g., mean length of utterance) that were compared across the three children. More methodological advances in the 1980s furthered the practice of recording and transcribing children's interactions in the child's natural setting. One widely cited study by Hart and Risley (1995) used methodology similar to Brown (1973) but instead used a larger sample of older children from diverse backgrounds. They recruited 42 families and recorded, transcribed, and coded hour-long interactions from when children were 10-months- to 3-years-old.

Both Brown (1973) and Hart and Risley (1995) coded and analyzed transcripts by hand, a practice that is now more systematic and automated thanks to several programs such as SALT (Miller, 2010) and the CHAT conventions in the CHILDES system (MacWhinney, 2000). For example, CHAT conventions standardize how one transcribes adult and child communication (e.g., speech, gesture, colloquial words, babbling). While this process is time consuming (MacWhinney, 2000, estimates 15 minutes of transcription for every minute of recording), the result is a rich and informative transcript. The CHILDES project also contains a large database of transcripts donated by researchers (www.talkbank.org). This database contains videos and transcripts from speakers of different languages, children of all ages, and interactions in different contexts (e.g., school, playtime, mealtimes, book reading), making it an excellent source for examining questions about individual differences in language acquisition at larger scale.

In addition to naturalistic observations of child language production, researchers can estimate children's receptive and productive vocabularies using survey methodology. While many developmental scales include items to assess language development, perhaps the most valid and in-depth measure of children's language acquisition is the MacArthur-Bates Communicative Development Inventory (MCDI) (Fenson et al., 1993), a widely used parent checklist for estimating vocabulary size among children aged 8–30 months. The MCDI was developed by Fenson and colleagues and consists of two measures: one for 8- to 16-month-old infants and another for 16- to 30-month-old toddlers. The infant checklist, for example, consists of a list of words (e.g., *car, leg, doll*), and the parent or caregiver indicates whether or not the child "understands" or "understands and says" the word. The toddler checklist focuses on language production and asks parents to indicate whether their child says particular words and grammatical constructions. The original MCDI has been normed on a sample of over 1,800 children, and has now been created and normed in 63 other languages.

Variation in early vocabulary acquisition

Word learning is an area of language that shows large variability in both size and rate of acquisition. In controlled laboratory studies, there is evidence that children can comprehend their own name as early as 4.5 months (Mandel et al., 1995), and data from the infant MCDI suggests that children begin to rapidly pick up on spoken language between 8 and 10 months (Fenson et al., 1994). On average, children's receptive vocabularies hit 50 words around their first birthdays and grow to over 150 words by 16 months (Fenson et al., 1994). Parent report measures (Fenson et al., 1994), and more recent computational modeling techniques (Mayor & Plunkett, 2011) suggest that children's productive vocabulary development lags behind receptive development by approximately 4 to 6 months. While the average 1-year-old child understands more than 50 words, his/her productive vocabulary is typically made up of fewer than 10 words (Fenson et al., 1994). By 16 months, children produce an average of 40 words (Fenson et al., 1994). Many studies note that by the time children's productive vocabularies exceed 50 words, there is a period of rapid growth where the rate of acquisition picks up drastically, typically between 18 and 24 months of age (Goldfield & Reznick, 1990). English-speaking 2-year-olds learn on average two new words per day (Bloom, 2000). By the time children reach their second birthdays, the average child utters between 200 and 500 words (Fernald et al., 2013; Fenson et al., 1994; Weisleder & Fernald, 2013).

Around 18 months, the average child's first 50 words are typically comprised mostly of nouns with very few verbs (Fenson et al., 1994). By 30 months, nouns still dominate productive vocabulary, although verb production typically increases to about 8 percent of the total productive vocabulary. There is some variability, however, across languages. In English, a subject-verb-object (SVO) language, the salience of the noun position is thought to facilitate word learning and lead to the strong noun bias (Gopnik & Choi, 1990). Children acquiring subject-object-verb languages (SOV), such as Korean, or languages in which the word order can vary more than English (e.g., Chinese) often do not display such a strong noun bias (Gopnik & Choi, 1990; Tardif, 1996). However, other studies find that in languages like Italian and Chinese, which permit word order variations, children still show a strong noun bias compared to their English-speaking peers (Caselli et al., 2000).

Further, nouns, unlike verbs, are easier for parents and adults to label during episodes of joint attention with the child. Gentner (1982) argues that verbs are less concrete (i.e., convey relational meanings between nouns) and therefore need more exposures under a variety of contexts and situations. Nelson (1973) examined the composition of English-speaking children's first 50 words and discussed variation in terms of the referential or expressive nature of the words. Referential vocabularies consist of mostly nominal acquisition (e.g., names for objects), while expressive vocabularies focus less on nouns and more on routines and word games. Within her sample, children with an expressive style acquired vocabulary at a slower rate than their same-aged peers who possessed a referential style (Nelson, 1973). The consistency of these categories has been questioned (e.g., Lieven et al., 1992), yet this work suggests that not all children acquire words in the same manner.

Children's rapid growth in vocabulary is striking, but what is even more remarkable is the variation around this typical developmental trajectory. While the composition of very early vocabulary looks similar across children, data show an asymmetry in the extent to which comprehension and production abilities vary between children learning the same language. For instance, after children's vocabularies reach 100 words, variability in vocabulary comprehension remains stable, while variability surrounding productive vocabulary continues to increase with age (Mayor & Plunkett, 2014).

In general, most data examining the size and composition of early vocabulary is taken from parent report checklists such as the MCDI. At 12 months, typically developing infants range in comprehending from 11 words to more than 154 words. Similarly, in language production at 16 months, children range from producing fewer than 10 words up to almost 200 words. Fenson and colleagues (1994) found that within their sample of typically developing children, almost 10 percent did not produce any language at 18 months. A recent study by Fernald and colleagues (2013) using observational methodology found that the word production at 18 months ranged from 5 to 503 words among a sample of children from diverse socioeconomic status backgrounds. With older children, the study by Hart and Risley (1995), mentioned above, found that 3-year-old children were observed to have cumulative vocabularies of between 500 and 1,100 words. The goal of this chapter is to consider where these wide individual differences in word learning come from. We start by considering what we call child-factors and then turn to the role of the environment.

Heritability

Like other traits, children inherit some of their linguistic abilities from their parents. Heritability estimates are typically determined by comparing performance between monozygotic and dizygotic twins on a given trait (e.g., Plomin et al., 1997). While all twin pairs are exposed to similar environments, monozygotic and dizygotic twins differ in the amount of shared human genetic material. Monozygotic twins share 100 percent of human genetic material while dizygotic twins share approximately 50 percent. Thus, if trait concordance is greater among monozygotic twins, for example, then it can be said that the trait has stronger genetic influence. Studies using twin methodologies typically find that the genetic influence on vocabulary is between .25 and .5, or that between 25–50 percent, of the variation in word learning can be attributed to genetic, or inherited, factors (Colledge et al., 2002; Dale et al., 1998; Dale et al., 2000; Stromswold, 2001). Thus, there does seem to be a genetic influence on vocabulary development, yet we urge caution in interpreting these findings, as research investigating heritability in low socioeconomic status (SES) populations finds lower heritability effects and larger environmental effects than the research that relies on primarily middle-class samples (e.g., Turkheimer et al., 2003). Whatever the heritability value, there remains variability in word learning related to other factors. As such, we devote the remaining sections to reviewing aspects of the child as well as his/her environment that lead to variation in vocabulary size and rate of acquisition.

Child gender

Gender differences in language acquisition have been documented for almost 100 years (McCarthy, 1930). While gender differences in word learning favoring girls are found in both comprehension and production, most studies find these differences are relatively small in magnitude and disappear after age 2 (Bornstein & Haynes, 1998; Nelson, 1973; Fenson et al., 1994; Huttenlocher et al., 1991; Hyde, 1981; Hyde & Linn, 1988). Fenson and colleagues (1994) found a slight female advantage in word learning prior to age 2 using data from the MCDI. More specifically, only 1–2 percent of the variance in vocabulary production on the MCDI can be attributed to gender. Parents report slight advantages for girls in language comprehension starting at 10 months and language production beginning at 14 months. Hyde (1981) was among the first to systematically review differences in language acquisition between boys and girls and concluded that the effect size (d) for general verbal ability was only +.11, or a slight advantage for girls based on a meta analysis of 168 studies. Huttenlocher et al. (1991) extended this line of research to show that the *rate* of word learning also differs, albeit slightly, between boys and girls. These analyses also demonstrated that girls' rate of acquisition slows relative to boys between 20 and 24 months, thus allowing boys to catch up to girls around age 2 (Huttenlocher et al., 1991).

Nonetheless, it is unclear exactly why these early gender differences exist. One possibility is that parents (in particular, mothers) talk to boys and girls differently. However, this hypothesis is not supported by many studies, which have found that mothers' child-directed speech is similar for boys and girls (Huttenlocher et al., 1991). Instead, it is possible that girls' maturation may be accelerated, allowing them to become better word learners slightly earlier than boys.

Birth order

Like gender, there is some evidence that birth order plays a small role in very early vocabulary comprehension and production. In general, first-born children show accelerated vocabulary development relative to later born children (Bornstein et al., 2004; Fenson et al., 1994; Hoff-Ginsberg, 1998; Jones & Adamson, 1987; Pine, 1995). First-borns are more likely to reach the 50-word milestone before later-borns (Jones & Adamson, 1987; Pine, 1995), and first-born children tend to have larger receptive and productive vocabularies between 10 and 30 months compared to later-born children (Fenson et al., 1994; Pine, 1995). This advantage also extends to the grammatical domain where first-born children tend to begin producing multiword combinations earlier than later-born children (Fenson et al., 1994). Bornstein and colleagues (2004) found, however, that this advantage is only seen in maternal report of language ability rather than through child speech recordings or experimenter-administered assessments. This first-born advantage may be because for at least part of their life, first-born children are only-children, allowing them to receive more direct speech from parents and participate in more conversational exchanges with parents since they are not competing with siblings for the parents' attention. There is some support for this explanation, as mothers tend to use more responsive and complex language with their first-borns than they do with later-borns of the same age (Hoff-Ginsberg, 1998; Jones & Adamson, 1987; McCartney et al., 1991). In turn, studies find that first-born children tend to direct more utterances to mothers than later-born children at 21 months (Hoff-Ginsberg, 1998). However, this first-born advantage seems be more influential in explaining differences in vocabulary prior to 20 months, whereas other environmental factors (e.g., parent speech variations) seem to be more important after 20 months (e.g., Huttenlocher et al., 1991).

First-born advantages in vocabulary acquisition may seem surprising if one assumes that later-borns have the advantage of hearing input from parents and overheard speech from parents directed to older siblings. While overheard speech does not appear to offer the same benefits as child-directed speech (Shneidman & Goldin-Meadow, 2012; Weisleder & Fernald, 2013; but see Dunn & Shatz, 1989, for an exception), there is some evidence that this overheard input has targeted effects on structures such as conversational skills (Hoff-Ginsberg, 1998) and pronoun acquisition (Oshima-Takane et al., 1996).

Temperament and attentional factors

Some children may be better word learners than others in part because they possess particular traits that allow them to pay attention to the relevant cues that help with the word learning task. Many argue that temperament traits play a role in the rate and size of children's language acquisition (e.g., Bloom, 1993). In general, children high on positive sociability (also known as approach/withdrawal, positive emotionality, extraversion) tend to show advanced language comprehension at 10 months and advanced language production at 20 and 21 months (Dixon & Shore, 1997; Dixon & Smith, 2000). Additionally, children high on this attention dimension also learn words at a faster rate between age 24 and 36 months (Slomkowski et al., 1992). These personality traits may lead children to form more social relationships and result in more rich and frequent social interactions with others.

Another important consideration is that a longer attention span may be an important mechanism driving typical language development (Bloom, 1993). Children who demonstrate longer attention spans (measured through laboratory assessments and parent report) are more likely to use a referential language style as described by Nelson (1973) and have higher MCDI scores at 24 months (Dixon & Shore, 1997; Salley & Dixon, 2007). Control over the attentional system is also thought to allow children to enter into and stay in more frequent episodes of joint attention, a context in which rich word learning opportunities are present (Tomasello & Farrar, 1986), as discussed in more detail below.

In addition to the child factors discussed above, there are environmental factors that contribute to children's word learning. In particular, the speech that children are exposed to during the early childhood period is consistently strongly related to the rate and breadth of vocabulary acquisition. In this section we summarize the research to date on the predictors and consequences of the quantity and quality of parents' child-directed speech for children's word learning.

Quantity and quality of child-directed speech

Our discussion focuses on parents' speech to children, yet research looking at preschool teachers' speech, while more limited in scope, is very complementary to that of parent speech. In the 1990s there were several seminal studies showing that the amount of speech parents directed to their children predicted children's vocabulary development (Bornstein et al., 1998; Hart & Risley, 1995; Hoff-Ginsberg, 1991; Huttenlocher et al., 1991). In short, children who heard more words had larger vocabularies and faster vocabulary growth during early childhood than children who heard fewer words from their parents. The variability in Hart and Risley's study (1995) was dramatic and highlighted the fact that, on average, there were large social-class differences in the amount that parents talked with their children, favoring the higher-SES parents, and these average differences led to faster vocabulary growth for the children from higher- versus lower-SES families. However, Huttenlocher and colleagues (1991) made it clear that there was significant variability in child-directed speech even within a relatively small and homogeneous sample of middle-class families, and this variability also related to children's word learning. Subsequently, research looking within low-income samples has found the same—that there is wide variability in input related to child vocabulary outcomes *within* low-SES samples (Pan et al., 2005; Shimpi et al., 2012). More recent work by Fernald and colleagues (Weisleder & Fernald, 2013), also within a low-SES sample, indicates that children who hear more words addressed to them are more efficient at processing language input than children exposed to fewer words, and the relation between input and vocabulary is mediated by processing ability. Thus, the quantity of words children hear likely helps improve their ability to process spoken language and to map words to referents leading to faster word learning during early childhood.

In addition to quantity of input playing a role, many studies have demonstrated that the *quality* of child-directed speech is important as well, and in many cases is more important than quantity (e.g., Rowe, 2012). Quality can be measured in a variety of ways. Here we summarize the literature on specific features of child-directed speech that relate to word learning. We organize the literature developmentally by highlighting the features of input that appear particularly useful for word learning during different periods across early development, as word learning is a process that unfolds over a relatively long period of time when the child is also gaining in other related cognitive skills.

Infancy (birth–18 months)

During the earliest stages of word learning, input that consists of shorter utterances and repetition of words can be useful (McRoberts et al., 2009). While hearing repeated uses of a vocabulary word assists children in learning the meaning of that word, young children are also able to learn vocabulary words from single exposures, especially if the exposure includes contextual supports for word learning. Joint attention, introduced earlier, refers to episodes in which both members of a dyad are sharing their attention to the same object or event for an extended period of time. Such episodes facilitate word learning in that they provide the child with a nonlinguistic referential framework onto which they can map linguistic information. Parent-child dyads vary in the frequency with which they establish and maintain joint attention, and engaging in more joint attention episodes is related to greater word learning in young children (Carpenter et al., 1998; Mundy & Newell, 2007; Tomasello & Farrar, 1986; Tomasello & Todd, 1983). Research indicates that the informative nonverbal contextual cues parents provide when communicating with children during episodes of joint attention help children to map the linguistic input to the referents, enhancing word learning (e.g., Cartmill et al., 2013). When parents label objects during play that are visually dominant in the infants' view, the infant is more likely to learn the label for that object than when the object is not visually dominant (Yu & Smith, 2012). Further, parent gesture use, particularly the amount and variety of objects parents point to, positively relates to children's own gestures and vocabulary development (e.g., Rowe & Goldin-Meadow, 2009). Additional evidence for the facilitative effect of joint attention comes from work showing that while the amount of child-directed speech is positively related to vocabulary learning, overheard speech does not play a role (Shneidman & Goldin-Meadow, 2012; Weisleder & Fernald, 2013). In sum, during the earliest stages of language learning, talking to children about objects or events in a joint focus, repeating words, and offering nonverbal support for understanding, can all help to facilitate word learning.

Toddlerhood (18 months–3 years)

Across early childhood, input that is responsive to the child's vocalizations is positively associated with children's vocabulary development likely because it fosters children's pragmatic understanding of language as a social tool to share information, but also because parents' responses are often informative (providing a label for the object a child is pointing to) and temporally linked to children's actions and utterances (e.g., Tamis-LeMonda et al. 2014).

Parents' conversation-eliciting speech, in particular their questions, is positively related to child vocabulary (e.g., Cristofaro & Tamis-LeMonda, 2012). Parents' questions typically require a verbal response from the child, which helps to promote language use and foster language learning. Certain types of questions are more beneficial than others. For example, *wh*-questions—questions that begin with *who*, *what*, *where*, *when*, *why*, or *how*—are found to elicit more responses and longer responses from children and positively relate to child vocabulary skill (Rowe et al., 2017), as well as children's own questioning abilities (Rowland et al., 2003). In contrast to the positive effects of questions, studies have found negative effects of parents' directives and prohibitives on children's language development

(McCathren et al., 1995; Murray & Hornbaker, 1997; Rowe, 2008). Neither directives nor prohibitives invite follow-up dialogue or support autonomy in the way conversation-eliciting and responsive utterances do, and both are negatively correlated with children's vocabulary development.

While during infancy it is often helpful to repeat vocabulary words, during the toddler period parents who use more diverse vocabularies have children with larger vocabularies who show faster word learning (e.g., Huttenlocher et al, 1991; Pan et al., 2005). Further, it is not just diversity that matters, but also vocabulary sophistication. By the time children are about 2 years old and have built up a knowledge base of common vocabulary words, hearing more unusual or rare vocabulary in their input is helpful. Vocabulary sophistication is often measured as the number or proportion of words in the input that are rare words or dictionary words not included in the most common 3,000–4,000 words understood by fourth graders (Weizman & Snow, 2001). During the toddler period parents who use more diverse vocabulary and a larger proportion of rare words (the average is about 6 percent) have children with larger vocabularies one year later than parents who use less diverse and sophisticated vocabularies (Rowe, 2012).

While syntactic diversity in the input best predicts syntactic diversity in child speech, and vocabulary diversity in the input best predicts vocabulary diversity in child speech (Huttenlocher et al., 2010), there is some evidence that syntactic properties of the input can play a role as well in word learning. For example, one measure of syntactic complexity is mean length of utterance (MLU) or the average number of morphemes per utterance. MLU in parent speech to toddlers predicts the child's vocabulary development and MLU across early childhood (Hoff & Naigles, 2002). Additionally, research suggests that the more flexibly a novel verb is used in child-directed speech the more flexible its use becomes by that child. That is, when a child hears a verb used in multiple sentence frames, that child is likely to use that verb in more sentence frames than a child who hears a verb used in mostly one sentence frame (e.g., utterance-final) (Naigles & Hoff-Ginsberg, 1995; 1998). According to the syntactic bootstrapping theory this is because different sentence frames provide different contextual clues about how to interpret the meaning and proper use of the target verb (see also Childers, Bottera, and Howard, this volume).

Finally, during this developmental period children often make lexical (e.g., using *moon* to refer to the streetlight) and morphological (e.g., *goed* instead of *went*) overgeneralization errors (see Ambridge et al., 2013, for a review). While the research on adult responses to child errors is mixed, there is some evidence suggesting that parents' corrective feedback in the form of recasts may positively influence children's language development (e.g., Chouinard & Clark, 2003).

Preschool (3–5 years)

Decontextualized language, including narrative talk that is abstract and removed from the here and now as well as explanations that make causal connections about how things work in the world, are challenging forms of input to toddlers and preschoolers that are associated with positive vocabulary outcomes. This type of input is challenging because it requires a higher level of analysis on the part of the child than comprehending talk that is focused on the here or now, such as object labels. By exposing children to these types of challenging talk, parents provide them with practice in the forms of abstract discourse they must come to master in school. Beginning around age 30 months and through the preschool years, uses of decontextualized language input relate to children's vocabulary and narrative skills (Demir et al., 2015; Rowe, 2012; Dickinson & Tabors, 2001).

Specifically, parents of 2.5- through 5-year-olds who provide more explanations and use more narrative talk about the past or future have children with larger vocabularies than parents who provide fewer explanations and narrative talk (Demir et al., 2015; Rowe, 2012). These relationships are found even when you control for the total quantity of parent talk parents are producing. Parents also vary in their reminiscing style, and these individual differences appear to be associated with children's narratives. Specifically, parents who tend to ask a lot of questions and produce rich, detailed descriptions of past events have children who recall more information and produce longer and more elaborate narratives of their own as compared to children of parents who talk less about the past and provide little descriptive information (Fivush, 1991; Peterson & McCabe, 1992; Reese, 1995). Further, during book reading in particular, parents who more often extend the talk beyond the book by asking prediction questions or making connections between the story and the child's life have children with greater vocabulary and narrative skills (DeTemple, 2001).

In sum, the communicative environments that children are immersed in during early childhood help shape their vocabulary development. The quantity of child-directed speech clearly has an effect on word learning, yet certain qualities or features of input often have an even stronger effect than input quantity and can inform us about the mechanisms involved in word learning. Finally, and perhaps most importantly, understanding the predictors of individual differences in word learning is of particular importance because vocabulary size during early childhood is a strong positive predictor of learning to read and school success more broadly.

References

Ambridge, B., Pine, J.M., Rowland, C.F., Chang, F., & Bidgood, A. (2013). The retreat from overgeneralization in child language acquisition: Word learning, morphology and verb argument structure. *Wiley Interdisciplinary Reviews: Cognitive Science*, 4, 47–62.

Bloom, L. (1993). *The transition from infancy to language: Acquiring the power of expression*. Cambridge, UK: Cambridge University Press.

Bloom, L. (2000). *How children learn the meanings of words*. Cambridge, MA: MIT Press.

Bornstein, M.H., & Haynes, O.M. (1998). Vocabulary competence in early childhood: Measurement, latent construct, and predictive validity. *Child Development*, 69, 654–671.

Bornstein, M.H., Leach, D.B., & Haynes, M.O. (2004). Vocabulary competence in first- and secondborn siblings of the same chronological age. *Journal of Child Language*, 31, 855–873.

Brown, R. (1973). *A first language: The early stages*. Cambridge, MA: Harvard University Press.

Carpenter, M., Nagell, K., & Tomasello, M. (1998). Cognition, joint and communicative attention, competence from 9 to 15 months of age. *The Society for Research in Child Development, Serial Monographs 63*, (4, no. 255).

Cartmill, E.A., Armstrong, B.F., Gleitman, L.R., Goldin-Meadow, S., Medina, T.N., & Trueswell, J.C. (2013). Quality of early parent input predicts child vocabulary three years later. *Proceedings of the National Academy of Sciences, 110*, 11278–11283.

Caselli, M.C., Casadio, P., & Bates, E. (2000). Lexical development in English and Italian. In M. Tomasello & E. Bates (Eds.), *Language development: The essential reading*, 76–110. Oxford: Blackwell.

Chouinard, M.M., & Clark, E.V. (2003). Adult reformulations of child errors as negative evidence. *Journal of Child Language, 30*(3), 637–669.

Colledge, E., Bishop, D.V.M., Koeppen-Schomerus, G., Price, T.S., Happ, F.G.E., Eley, T. C., & Plomin, R. (2002). The structure of language abilities at 4 years: A twin study. *Developmental Psychology, 38*, 749–757.

Cristofaro, T.N., & Tamis-LeMonda, C.S. (2012). Mother-child conversations at 36 months and at pre-kindergarten: Relations to children's school readiness. *Journal of Early Childhood Literacy, 12*, 68–97.

Dale, P., Simonoff, E., Bishop, D., Eley, T., Oliver, B., Price, T., ... & Plomin, R. (1998). Genetic influence on language delay in two-year-old children. *Nature Neuroscience, 1*(4), 324–328.

Dale, P.S., Dionne, G., Eley, T.C., & Plomin, R. (2000). Lexical and grammatical development: A behavioural genetic perspective. *Journal of Child Language, 27*, 619–642.

Demir, E., Rowe, M.L., Heller, G., Levine, S., & Goldin-Meadow, S. (2015). Vocabulary, syntax, and narrative development in typically developing children and children with early unilateral brain injury: Early parental talk about the *there-and-then* matters. *Developmental Psychology, 51*, 161–175.

DeTemple, J.M. (2001). Parents and children reading books together. In D.K. Dickinson & P.O. Tabors (Eds.), *Beginning literacy with language: Young children learning at home and school*, 31–52. Baltimore, MD: Brookes.

Dickinson D., & Tabors, P.O. (2001) *Beginning literacy with language: Young children learning at home and school*. Baltimore, MD: Brookes.

Dixon, W.E., Jr., & Shore, C. (1997). Temperamental predictors of linguistic style during multiword acquisition. *Infant Behavior and Development, 20*, 99–103.

Dixon, W.E., & Smith, P.H. (2000). Links between early temperament and language acquisition. *Merrill Palmer Quarterly, 46*, 417–440.

Dunn, J., & Shatz, M. (1989). Becoming a conversationalist despite (or because of) having an older sibling. *Child Development, 60*, 399–410.

Fenson, L., Dale, P., Reznick, J., Thal, D., Bates, E., Hartung, J., Pethick, S., & Reilly, J. (1993). *MacArthur communicative development inventories: User's guide and technical manual*. Baltimore, MD: Paul H. Brookes.

Fenson, L., Dale, P.S., Reznick, J.S., Bates, E., Thal, D.J., & Pethick, S.J. (1994). Variability in early communicative development. *Monographs of the Society for Research in Child Development, 59*, (Serial No. 242).

Fernald, A., Marchman, V.A., & Weisleder, A. (2013). SES differences in language processing skill and vocabulary are evident at 18 months. *Developmental Science, 16*, 234–248.

Fivush, R. (1991). Gender and emotion in mother–child conversations about the past. *Journal of Narrative and Life History, 1*, 325–341.

Gentner, D. (1982). Why are nouns learned before verbs: Linguistic relatively versus natural partitioning. In S. Kuczaj II (Ed.), *Language development, Vol. 2: Language, thought, and culture*. Hillsdale, NJ: Erlbaum.

Goldfield, B.A., & Reznick, J.S. (1990). Early lexical acquisition: Rate, content, and the vocabulary spurt. *Journal of Child Language, 17*, 171–183.

Gopnik, A., & Choi, S. (1990). Do linguistic differences lead to cognitive differences? A cross-linguistic study of semantic and cognitive development. *First Language, 10*, 199–215.

Halle, T., Forry, N., Hair, E., Perper, K., Wandner, L., Wessel, J., & Vick, J. (2009). Disparities in early learning and development: Lessons from the Early Childhood Longitudinal Study–Birth Cohort (ECLS-B). *Washington, DC: Child Trends*.

Hart, B., & Risley, T. (1995). *Meaningful differences in the everyday experience of young American children*. Baltimore, MD: Brookes.

Hoff, E., & Naigles, L. (2002). How children use input to acquire a lexicon. *Child Development, 73*, 418–433.

Hoff-Ginsberg, E. (1991). Mother-child conversations in different social classes and communicative settings. *Child Development, 62*, 782–796.

Hoff-Ginsberg, E. (1998). The relation of birth order and socioeconomic status to children's language experience and language development. *Applied Psycholinguistics, 19*, 603–629.

Huttenlocher, J., Haight, W., Bryk, A., Seltzer, M., & Lyons, T. (1991). Early vocabulary growth: Relation to language input and gender. *Developmental Psychology, 27*, 236–248.

Huttenlocher, J., Waterfall, H., Vasileyva, M., Vevea, J., & Hedges, L. V. (2010) Sources of variability in children's language growth. *Cognitive Psychology, 61*, 343–365.

Hyde, J.S. (1981). How large are cognitive gender differences? A meta-analysis using ω and d. *American Psychologist, 36*, 892–901.

Hyde, J.S., & Linn, M.C. (1988). Gender differences in verbal ability: A meta-analysis. *Psychological Bulletin, 104*, 53–69.

Jones, C.P., & Adamson, L.B. (1987). Language use in mother-child and mother-child-sibling interactions. *Child Development, 58*, 356–366.

Lieven, E.V., Pine, J.M., & Barnes, H.D. (1992). Individual differences in early vocabulary development: Redefining the referential-expressive distinction. *Journal of Child Language, 19*, 287–310.

MacWhinney, B. (2000). *The CHILDES project: Tools for analyzing talk (3rd ed.)*. Mahwah, NJ: Erlbaum.

Mandel, D.R., Jusczyk, P.W., & Pisoni, D.B. (1995). Infants' recognition of the sound patterns of their own names. *Psychological Science, 6*, 314–317.

Mayor, J., & Plunkett, K. (2011). A statistical estimate of infant and toddler vocabulary size from CDI analysis. *Developmental Science, 14*, 769–785.

Mayor, J., & Plunkett, K. (2014). Shared understanding and idiosyncratic expression in early vocabularies. *Developmental Science, 17*, 412-423.

McCarthy, D. (1930). *The language development of the preschool child*. Minneapolis, MN: University of Minnesota Press.

McCartney, K., Robeson, W., Jordan, E., & Mouradian, V. (1991). Mothers' language with first- and second-born children: A within-family study. In K. Pillemer & K. McCartney (Eds.), *Parent-child relations throughout life*, 125–142. Hillsdale, NJ: Erlbaum.

McCathren, R.B., Yoder, P.J., & Warren, S.F. (1995). The role of directives in early language intervention. *Journal of Early Intervention, 19*, 91-101.

McRoberts, G.W., McDonough, C., & Lakusta, L. (2009). The role of verbal repetition in the development of infant speech preferences from 4 to 14 months of age. *Infancy, 14*, 162–194.

Miller, J.F. (2010). *Systematic Analysis of Language Transcripts (Version 9)*. Computer software. Madison, WI: University of Wisconsin-Madison.

Mundy, P., & Newell, L. (2007). Attention, joint attention, and social cognition. *Current Directions in Psychological Science, 16*, 269–274.

Murray, A.D., & Hornbaker, A.V. (1997). Maternal directive and facilitative interaction styles: Associations with language and cognitive development of low-risk and high-risk toddlers. *Developmental Psychopathology, 9*, 507–516.

Naigles, L., & Hoff-Ginsberg, E. (1998). Why are some verbs learned before other verbs? Effects of input frequency and structure on children's early verb use. *Journal of Child Language, 25,* 95–120.

Naigles, L.R., & Hoff-Ginsberg, E. (1995). Input to verb learning: Evidence for the plausibility of syntactic bootstrapping. *Developmental Psychology, 31*, 827–837.

Nelson, K. (1973). Structure and strategy in learning to talk. *Monographs of the Society of Research in Child Development, 38*, (1 & 2 Serial No. 149).

Oshima-Takane, Y., Goodz, E., & Derevensky, J.L. (1996). Birth order effects on early language development: Do secondborn children learn from overheard speech? *Child Development, 67*, 621–634.

Pan, B.A., Rowe, M.L., Singer, J.D., & Snow, C.E. (2005). Maternal correlates of growth in toddler vocabulary production in low-income families. *Child Development, 76*, 763–782.

Peterson, C., & McCabe, A. (1992). Parental styles of narrative elicitation: Effect on children's narrative structure and content. *First Language, 12*, 299–321.

Pine, J.M. (1995). Variation in vocabulary development as a function of birth order. *Child Development, 66*, 272–281.

Plomin, R., DeFries, J.C., McClearn, G.E., & Rutter, M. (1997). *Behavioural genetics (3rd ed.)*. New York: W.H. Freeman.

Reese, E. (1995). Predicting children's literacy from mother-child conversations. *Cognitive Development, 10*, 381–405.

Rowe, M.L. (2008). Child-directed speech: Relation to socioeconomic status, knowledge of child development, and child vocabulary skill. *Journal of Child Language, 35*, 185–205.

Rowe, M.L. (2012). A longitudinal investigation of the role of quantity and quality of child-directed speech in vocabulary development. *Child Development, 83*, 1762–1774.

Rowe, M.L., & Goldin-Meadow, S. (2009). Differences in early gesture explain SES disparities in child vocabulary size at school entry. *Science, 323*, 951–953.

Rowe, M.L., Leech, K.A., & Cabrera, N. (2017). Going beyond input quantity: *Wh*-questions matter for toddlers' language and cognitive development. *Cognitive Science, 41*, 162–179.

Rowland, C.F., Pine, J.M., Lieven, E.V., & Theakston, A.L. (2003). Determinants of acquisition order in wh-questions: Re-evaluating the role of caregiver speech. *Journal of Child Language, 30*, 609–635.

Salley, B.J., & Dixon Jr, W.E. (2007). Temperamental and joint attentional predictors of language development. *Merrill-Palmer Quarterly, 53*, 131.

Shimpi, P.M., Fedewa, A., & Hans, S. (2012). Social and linguistic input in low-income African American mother-child dyads from 1 month through 2 years: Relations to vocabulary development. *Applied Psycholinguistics, 33*, 781–798.

Shneidman, L.A., & Goldin-Meadow, S. (2012). Language input and acquisition in a Mayan village: How important is directed speech?. *Developmental Science, 15*, 659–673.

Slomkowski, C.L., Nelson, K., Dunn, J., & Plomin, R. (1992). Temperament and language: Relations from toddlerhood to middle childhood. *Developmental Psychology, 28*, 1090–1095.

Stromswold, K. (2001). The heritability of language: A review and meta-analysis of twin, adoption, and linkage studies. *Language, 77*, 647–723.

Tamis-LeMonda, C.S., Kuchirko, Y., & Song, L. (2014). Why is infant language learning facilitated by parental responsiveness?. *Current Directions in Psychological Science, 23*(2), 121–126.

Tardif, T. (1996). Nouns are not always learned before verbs: Evidence from Mandarin speakers' early vocabularies. *Developmental Psychology, 32*, 492–504.

Tomasello, M., & Farrar, M.J. (1986). Joint attention and early language. *Child Development, 57*, 1454–1463.

Tomasello, M., & Todd, J. (1983). Joint attention and lexical acquisition style. *First Language, 4*, 197–212.

Turkheimer, E., Haley, A., Waldron, M., D'Onofrio, B., & Gottesman, I.I. (2003). Socioeconomic status modifies heritability of IQ in young children. *Psychological Science, 14*, 623–628.

Weisleder, A., & Fernald, A. (2013). Talking to children matters: Early language experience strengthens processing and builds vocabulary. *Psychological Science, 24*, 2143–2152.

Weizman, Z.O., & Snow, C.E. (2001). Lexical input as related to children's vocabulary acquisition: Effects of sophisticated exposure and support for meaning. *Developmental Psychology, 37*, 265–279.

Yu, C., & Smith, L.B. (2012). Embodied attention and word learning by toddlers. *Cognition, 125*, 244–262.

9
EARLY BILINGUAL WORD LEARNING

Christopher Fennell
UNIVERSITY OF OTTAWA, CANADA

Casey Lew-Williams
PRINCETON UNIVERSITY, USA

> Many studies have been published on child language; few on the learning of two languages by small children.
>
> *Leopold (1949/1970), p. vii*

Some global estimates of the number of bilingual children are as high as 50% (Grosjean, 2010). Yet historically, there has been little research involving word learners acquiring two or more languages. It was not until the mid-1990s that our field rose to the challenge posed by Leopold above. A PsycInfo search revealed that 90% of publications on childhood bilingualism were published in the last 20 years, with 60% in the last 10 years. These studies have primarily addressed the most common question posed to researchers studying bilingual word learning: do bilingual children have a word-learning delay or deficit in the face of more variable input than their monolingual peers?

In this chapter, we review the extant literature of bilingual lexical acquisition in the first years of life. In doing so, we demonstrate that no such general deficit is present in children learning two languages. However, that is not to say that there are no effects engendered by a dual-language environment. When comparing monolingual and bilingual infants and toddlers, researchers need to account for numerous complexities, both in designing experiments and interpreting results. Do we compare total vocabularies across monolingual and bilingual participants, or do we compare bilinguals and monolinguals on vocabulary in just one language (e.g., a bilingual's English vocabulary to the vocabulary of English monolinguals)? Do we consider each vocabulary autonomously? Can we truly compare different types of bilinguals in the first place (e.g., French-English versus Spanish-Basque infants)? Researchers have been aware of these intricacies since the first major scientific treatise on infant bilingualism (Ronjat, 1913), which highlighted issues such as infants' separation of their two languages and the effects of parental bilingual input on vocabulary.

Despite the complexities inherent in measuring the bilingual vocabulary, it is important to establish whether bilinguals and monolinguals reach similar vocabulary levels in toddlerhood in order to inform hypotheses about whether word learning processes would necessarily differ across these populations. If bilinguals and monolinguals have similar vocabularies across the board, there would be little reason to suspect that basic word learning and processing differ depending on the number of languages being acquired. Thus, this review of the early bilingual lexicon unfolds in somewhat of a reverse manner. We begin with an exploration of bilingual vocabulary in the first years of life and then address word learning. Also, as this chapter focuses on early word learning, the studies included herein only involve simultaneous bilingual infants and toddlers, i.e., children learning two languages from birth.

The nature of the initial bilingual vocabulary

The earliest "assessments" of bilingual children's vocabularies were diary studies published by linguists concerning their own bilingual children (Leopold, 1949/1970; Ronjat, 1913). These studies are informative starting points due to their rich detail, although they are necessarily limited in their generalizability—an issue acknowledged by both Ronjat and Leopold. However, to demonstrate the potential validity of these studies, we will tie early diary findings to later research with standardized measures of infant and toddler vocabularies, such as the MacArthur-Bates Communicative Development Inventory (MCDI) (Fenson et al., 1993). The MCDI is a parental report of children's vocabulary comprehension and production that has been used to assess bilinguals' vocabularies in many studies, and it has been adapted to multiple languages and cultures. Although the norms provided by the MCDI are not applicable to bilinguals, as they are based on monolingual samples, one can compare raw scores to a monolingual group of the same age. Further, and more importantly, the MCDI has been found to be a valid and reliable measure of bilingual vocabulary (Marchman & Martinez-Sussman, 2002).

Diary research shows evidence that bilingual infants and toddlers reach developmental milestones at the same time as monolinguals. Ronjat (1913) found that his bilingual son Louis produced words in both French and German starting around 9 months, comfortably inside the average onset age of word production in monolinguals. Leopold's (1949/1970) bilingual daughter, Hildegard, appeared to start comprehending words around 9 months and producing words at 10 months in both English and German. Hildegard produced 377 unique words across both languages by 24 months. If these numbers were treated as MCDI scores—an unorthodox but perhaps informative use of the data—it is interesting to note that Hildegard would be at exactly the 50th percentile based on her total vocabulary, highlighting the lack of a language delay. Indeed, Leopold stressed that "Hildegard's early speaking development was average" (p. 13).

Other diary and small-sample studies further demonstrate that infants learning two languages have similar onsets of receptive and productive vocabularies as infants learning one language (De Houwer, 1995; Petitto et al., 2001; Quay, 1995; Vihman, 1985; with Yavaş, 1995, as an exception). Further, the language milestone of the lexical spurt, where infants begin learning new words in earnest, appears in bilinguals at the same age as monolinguals: 18–24 months (Pearson & Fernández, 1994). Broadly, these findings suggest that bilinguals do not appear to be delayed or atypical in terms of lexical development (Marchman & Martinez-Sussman, 2002; Patterson, 1998). However, while bilingual infants may acquire their first word and begin an accelerated rate of word learning at approximately the same time as monolinguals, it is still possible that vocabulary size could deviate from monolinguals later in development. Indeed, Pearson and Fernández (1994) found that no child had a lexical spurt in both languages at the same time; one language always preceded the other, and growth was intimately tied to overall exposure to each language. Such differences could have direct ramifications for lexical processing, opening the possibility of weaker processing in the language with the less rich vocabulary.

In early diary studies, researchers saw quantitative differences across the language-specific vocabularies of bilingual infants and toddlers and immediately tied these differences to unequal input across the target languages. Ronjat (1913) reported that Louis had a larger initial vocabulary in German due to greater overall input in that language; however, changes in location and input (e.g., spending time with French family members) affected his language dominance. Leopold (1949/1970) reported that the relative percentage of German and English words in Hildegard's vocabulary shifted depending on her amount of German and English input (e.g., a trip to Germany increasing the proportion of German words). Other diary studies demonstrated that bilinguals' vocabularies were matched to the distribution of input. Vihman (1985) reported that Raivo, who was learning Estonian and English, spent 24% of his waking hours exposed to English, and one-quarter of his vocabulary consisted of English words. Quay's (1995) analyses of the vocabulary of an infant acquiring English and Spanish also showed tight correspondence to exposure (50% English exposure resulting in 50% English words).

Again, researchers using standardized measures with larger samples confirmed 1) different vocabulary scores across the two languages of many young bilingual children, and 2) the tight relationship between language exposure and the nature of the bilingual vocabulary (e.g., Pearson & Fernández, 1994; Pearson et al., 1993; Silvén et al., 2014; Thordardottir et al., 2006; Umbel et al., 1992). Pearson, Fernández, Lewedeg, and Oller (1997) discovered a strong positive correlation between bilingual infants' Spanish and English exposure and the presence of words from those languages in their nascent vocabularies (see also Hoff et al., 2012; Marchman & Martinez-Sussman, 2002; Place & Hoff, 2011). Spanish exposure explained nearly 70% of the variance in children's Spanish vocabulary size, which was also the case in English. This concordance between input and vocabulary matches monolingual findings: monolingual infants with higher maternal speech input have larger vocabularies (e.g., Hart & Risely, 1995), and there are relationships between types of speech input and the corresponding parts of the young child's vocabulary (e.g., mental state language, Taumoepeau & Ruffman, 2008).

Young bilinguals thus have vocabularies that are tied to input in each language, but what of the overlap between the two vocabularies? Hildegard possessed translation equivalents, i.e., words across a bilingual's languages that refer to the same concept, such as *dog* and *Hund* (Leopold, 1949/1970). Vihman (1985) reported that translation equivalents comprised 34% of Raivo's vocabulary by age 2. Similar levels were reported in a study of a Spanish-English toddler (40%; Quay, 1995) and an ASL-English toddler (37%; Brackenbury et al., 2006). Large-sample research again confirmed these levels of translation equivalents amongst bilingual infants and toddlers, with translation equivalents across studies accounting for an average of 25% of total vocabulary (Mancilla-Martinez et al., 2011), ranging from 15% (Marchman et al. 2010; Core et al., 2013) to 50% (Frank & Poulin-Dubois, 2002; Houston-Price et al., 2010; Junker & Stockman, 2002). Thus, translation equivalents are present in the vocabularies of bilingual children from the onset of their vocabulary development and comprise a sizeable proportion of words.

Bilinguals' potentially unequal vocabularies across their languages (i.e., dominance) and the fact that translation equivalents usually comprise less than half of their vocabulary have ramifications for vocabulary assessment. Comparing bilinguals' performance in only one language to monolingual learners of that language fails to account for concepts known only in their other language, especially if the vocabulary in question is their non-dominant language. Indeed, the majority of bilingual work demonstrates that young bilingual children have significantly lower vocabularies in their non-dominant language when compared to monolinguals of that language (Junker & Stockman, 2002; Patterson, 1998; Pearson & Fernández, 1994; Thordardottir et al., 2006; Umbel et al., 1992). While some large-sample studies reveal parity between the dominant language of young bilinguals and that of monolinguals of that language (e.g., Junker & Stockman, 2002; Patterson, 1998; Pearson & Fernández, 1994; Pearson et al., 1993), others continue to find smaller vocabularies even in bilinguals' stronger language (Mancilla-Martinez & Vagh, 2013; Thordardottir et al, 2006). These differences highlight the problem of using only one language as the central measure of bilingual word knowledge. Unfortunately, this is, even today, a misguided but common practice in clinical language assessment.

Thus, Pearson and her colleagues, who pioneered large-sample vocabulary assessments of bilingual infants, advocated two alternate and more representative measures of bilingual lexical knowledge: total vocabulary (i.e., adding all words across the two languages), and total conceptual vocabulary, or TCV (e.g., Pearson & Fernández, 1994; Swain, 1972). This latter measure counts translation equivalents across the two languages as only one "word," so that only words reflecting unique concepts comprise infants' vocabulary. The argument for using TCV is that the large amount of vocabulary overlap (i.e., translation equivalents) may be acting as an inflationary factor for a total vocabulary measure.

In Pearson's work, bilingual infants' total vocabularies were the same size as monolinguals' vocabularies from 8 to 30 months of age, in both production and comprehension (Pearson & Fernández, 1994; Pearson et al., 1997; Pearson et al., 1993, see also Core et al, 2013; Hoff et al., 2012; Patterson, 1998). Other research has shown that the mean total vocabulary size of bilingual infants actually exceeds that of monolinguals (Bosch & Ramon-Casas, 2014; Junker & Stockman, 2002; Silvén et al., 2014). Many bilingual studies, including Pearson's work above, indicate that the TCV measure is also the same size as monolinguals' total vocabulary (Bosch & Ramon-Casas, 2014; Junker & Stockman, 2002; Silvén et al, 2014). However, Core et al. (2013) found that bilingual English-Spanish toddlers' TCV fell below monolingual values (see also Mancilla-Martinez & Vagh, 2013; Thordardottir, et al, 2006). Core and her colleagues criticized TCV by arguing that reducing translation equivalents from two vocabulary entries to one misrepresents the complexity of the bilingual lexicon. After all, the child still needs to learn two phonological forms. Further, translation equivalents are rarely truly equivalent: there is imperfect semantic overlap across the languages for the same "words." Nevertheless, while total vocabulary size may sometimes overestimate bilingual children's vocabulary size and TCV may sometimes underestimate it, it is important to note that the majority of research shows parity between these measures of bilingual vocabulary and monolingual norms.

The above findings inform hypotheses about the word learning processes underlying lexical acquisition and vocabulary development. Bilingual children appear to possess the same *general* word learning capabilities as monolinguals, despite the complexities inherent in their language environments. The evidence for this is the similarly sized vocabularies between bilinguals and monolinguals, and the similarly timed language milestones between these groups. Bilinguals are not delayed; but they also do not initially possess a super-vocabulary, double that of monolinguals. However, because bilinguals' two languages unfurl at different rates depending on exposure to each language, this may indicate that lexical processing efficiency may differ across dominant and non-dominant languages. With these hypotheses in mind, we now turn to an exploration of lexical processes in young bilinguals.

Lexical processes in bilingual infants and toddlers

To successfully learn a word and build a vocabulary, an infant must acquire and refine both the form of the word and the concept to which it refers. The extant literature on early bilingual word learning and recognition primarily focuses on the former over the latter. Most studies examining lexical processes in young bilingual children investigated their ability to learn and/or recognize words in the face of changes to the acoustic form, especially phonological contrasts (i.e., sounds that denote lexical changes, like /b/ and /p/ in English: *bat* versus *pat*). This approach stems from literature indicating that bilingual infants may have developmentally transient difficulties in perceiving some acoustically close phonological contrasts, especially if learning related languages (e.g., Spanish-Catalan; Bosch & Sebastián-Gallés, 2003). The explanation for these difficulties is that the variation present in bilinguals' language environments may promote a greater acceptance of acoustic variation in phonemes. Small changes are normal and therefore not surprising due to the higher probability of hearing accented speech in comparison to monolinguals and the presence of cognates in the input of many bilingual infants. Thus, it logically follows that research on early bilingual lexical processing has focused on phonological changes in word forms.

Word segmentation

The only two studies exploring bilingual infants' word segmentation and recognition both examined issues relating to phonological detail (Singh & Foong, 2012; Vihman et al., 2007). Before or during attaching a meaning to a word, infants must extract the acoustic word-form candidate from continuous speech (see Chapter 2). In one study, English-learning 7.5-month-olds listened longer to passages containing word forms heard during a learning phase (e.g., *bike*) over those with phonetically similar forms (e.g., *gike*; Jusczyk & Aslin, 1995). This suggests that English-learning infants recognize familiar words in fluent speech by 7.5 months and encode word forms in sufficient detail to detect phonemic mispronunciations.

Bilingual exposure does affect word segmentation. However, the specific effects appear to depend on the languages being acquired. Singh and Foong (2012) found that Mandarin-English bilingual infants were sensitive to a phonological change present in only one of their languages (Mandarin tone changes) at 7.5 and 11 months. At 9 months, however, they appeared to generalize words across differences in lexical tone. These data mirror the U-shaped developmental pattern seen in some bilingual phoneme discrimination work that also tests infants on phonological changes unique to one of their languages (see Byers-Heinlein & Fennell, 2014, for a review). This supports the hypothesis that bilingual infants may go through a period of accepting phonemic substitutions that should signal a change in a word's meaning due to the variability present in their input.

However, Vihman et al. (2007) found that exposure to a more "stable" phonological system actually enhanced bilinguals' attention to phonological changes in comparison to their monolingual peers. In Welsh, words undergo consonant mutation for a variety of morphological and syntactic reasons. For example, the word *pont* (bridge) could be produced as /pont/, /bont/, or /font/ depending on the grammatical context. English-learning infants of 11 months preferred listening to frequent words over phonetically similar *in*frequent words. But Welsh-learning infants did not show the same preference until 12 months, perhaps due to their more variable phonological environments. However, bilingual Welsh-English infants recognized frequent words in Welsh one month earlier than their Welsh-learning peers (their performance in English matched their English peers). Thus, the bilinguals' exposure to English, a more phonologically "stable" language, supported their ability to recognize words in the comparatively more "unstable" Welsh (Vihman et al., 2007). These studies highlight the need to take language characteristics into account when interpreting bilingual performance.

Word learning

A fundamental aspect of lexical acquisition that we would expect to be similar across bilinguals and monolinguals is the ability to contemporaneously link a word form to a concept, which undergirds all word learning. Byers-Heinlein, Fennell, and Werker (2013) tested this skill in 12- and 14-month-old monolingual and bilingual infants using the Switch task. In this procedure, infants are habituated to two distinct auditory word-object combinations and then receive two test trials: a "same" trial where they experience one of the word-object combinations from habituation (e.g., Word A–Object A), and a "switch" trial where a word and object from habituation are incorrectly paired (e.g., Word A–Object B). If infants map the words to the objects, they should react with surprise to the incorrect pairing and look longer on the "switch" versus the "same" trials. While infants begin acquiring word-object correspondences in natural settings earlier in life (e.g., Bergelson & Swingley, 2012), monolingual infants usually do not succeed in this controlled laboratory task until 14 months (Werker et al., 1998). Byers-Heinlein et al. (2013) replicated that monolingual finding and extended it to bilinguals: both groups succeeded in learning the words at 14 months, but not at 12 months. As predicted, basic word learning does not appear to differ in bilingual infants.

Would these comparable results hold for bilingual infants in a more challenging word learning task? One such task is a variation of the Switch procedure where infants are required to learn two similar-sounding words (i.e., a minimal pair) rather than two distinct words. If a bilingual infant is habituated to Object A being called '/kɛm/' and Object B called '/gɛm/', they may not react with surprise to Object A receiving the label '/gɛm/' at test. After all, in their environment, words can undergo such changes (i.e., cognates). Indeed, Fennell, Byers-Heinlein, and Werker (2007) found that bilingual infants did not react to a minimally different mislabeling of the objects at test until 20 months of age, whereas monolinguals reacted to the switch in labels at 17 months. On the surface, it would appear that variation in the bilinguals' language environments led them to learn words in either a less detailed manner, or to disregard small changes in word forms.

Yet, a similar word-learning study demonstrated opposing results, casting doubt on bilinguals' purported holistic processing of word details. Mattock et al. (2010) tested French-English bilingual, English monolingual, and French monolingual infants of 17 months in the minimal pair Switch task. Although the minimal pair was the same across conditions (/bos/-/gos/), the words were either produced in a French or English manner. Monolingual infants only reacted to a violation in the learned word-object pairings when hearing native productions (e.g., French monolinguals hearing words produced in a French manner). They failed with non-native productions (e.g., French monolinguals hearing words in an English manner) or when hearing an interleaved mix of the two productions. In contrast, Mattock et al. (2010) found that bilingual infants in the mixed-production condition succeeded in noticing word-object violations. The researchers hypothesized that, compared to monolinguals, bilingual infants are better able to process a diverse array of tokens based on the phonetic variability in their environment.

However, a recent study indicates that bilingual infants do not fundamentally differ from monolinguals in these challenging word-learning tasks; both groups react to changes prevalent in their language environment. Note that bilingual infants who failed to notice a change in the target words in Fennell et al. (2007) only heard words produced by a monolingual speaker, and the successful bilingual infants in Mattock et al. (2010) heard bilingual-accented tokens. Even highly proficient simultaneous bilinguals possess slightly different accents in their native languages relative to monolinguals of those languages (Antoniou et al., 2010). Bilingual and monolingual infants may simply prefer their "native" accents, meaning that bilinguals possess neither an enhanced acceptance of variation nor impoverished word representations. Indeed, Fennell and Byers-Heinlein (2014) found that 17-month-old bilinguals succeeded in distinguishing a minimal pair when hearing a bilingual adult produce the tokens, but failed when hearing a monolingual adult, with monolingual infants showing the opposite pattern. Monolingual and bilingual infants therefore follow the same pattern of development: both groups succeed with minimal pairs at 17 months when listening to a speaker who sounds like people in their environment.

All of the word learning studies discussed above examined bilinguals' reactions to a phonological change that occurred in both of their languages. Would young bilingual learners react appropriately to a phonological change that occurs in only one of their languages, similar to their sensitivity to such changes in early segmentation (Singh & Foong, 2012)? Mandarin-English bilingual 2-year-olds successfully detect changes in lexical tone in newly learned words (tone is phonological in Mandarin, but not in English). Importantly, bilinguals acquiring English and a non-tonal language treat tone as non-phonemic at 2 years, thereby treating a word that changes in tone as a new word (Singh et al., 2014). So, the variable nature of the bilingual environment does not engender broader acceptance of non-native phonological categories. Rather, bilinguals, like monolinguals, are attuned to the possible phonemes in both their languages. This again shows that bilingual infants are as detailed in their lexical acquisition as monolinguals.

The literature reviewed above has shown that monolingual and bilingual word learning processes are highly concordant. However, this is not necessarily the case for a word learning constraint known as mutual exclusivity: the idea that monolingual children assume that objects should have one basic-level label (Markman & Wachtel, 1988; see Chapter 3 for in-depth discussions of word learning constraints). Strong adherence to this mutual exclusivity constraint would derail bilingual acquisition. If a French-English bilingual infant possesses *chien* as the word for the category dog, she must also be able to efficiently attach the word *dog* to that same category. The presence of large numbers of translation equivalents in bilinguals' early vocabularies suggests a relaxed mutual exclusivity constraint.

In one study on mutual exclusivity, Au and Glusman (1990) tested Spanish-English bilingual 3- to 5-year-olds. An English-speaking experimenter labeled an animal from a novel category (a lemur) with a novel name (*mido*). When presented with another lemur along with two individual animals from another novel category (seals), children selected another lemur when the English experimenter asked for another *mido*. A Spanish-speaking experimenter then asked the children to show her a *theri*, and interestingly, children were random in their choices: *theri* could equally be the Spanish word for lemur *or* seal (see also Davidson & Tell, 2005; but see Frank & Poulin-Dubois, 2002, for comparable results across monolinguals and bilinguals).

Two more recent studies have confirmed that infant multilinguals do not readily apply mutual exclusivity to word learning. Using English as the testing language, Houston-Price et al. (2010) showed that 17- to 22-month-old bilinguals learning English and another language did not look reliably longer to a novel object over a familiar object after hearing a novel label (*dax*), whereas monolinguals did. Byers-Heinlein and Werker (2009) showed comparable results. Monolingual 18-month-olds looked significantly longer to a novel object over a familiar one after hearing a novel label, whereas bilingual infants approached but failed to reach significance. Trilingual infants failed to show any evidence of mutual exclusivity. Further, bilingual infants with more translation equivalents in their vocabularies appear to have weaker adherence to mutual exclusivity, demonstrating an influence of the structure of the bilingual lexicon (Byers-Heinlein & Werker, 2013). Collectively, it appears that greater experience with multiple labels for a single word or category reduces the role of mutual exclusivity from the beginnings of word learning.

Word recognition

Word recognition skills may not fundamentally differ across young bilinguals and monolinguals, but may be subject to the intricacies of dual-language input. Bilingual infants' vocabularies in each of their languages are tied to exposure to each language, and non-dominant languages are more deviant from monolingual norms than dominant languages. Thus, one strong prediction would be that bilingual infants' and toddlers' word processing and recognition skills would be comparable to monolinguals in their dominant language but weaker in their non-dominant language (i.e., similar to monolinguals with low total vocabulary).

Marchman et al. (2010) investigated how Spanish-English bilingual 2-year-olds' vocabularies relate to their real-time language processing skills. Specifically, they sought to understand whether bilinguals' speed of processing familiar words is similar across their two languages, or whether processing speed in each language is tied specifically to vocabulary in each language. Participants were Spanish-English bilingual 30-month-olds with a range of exposure to each language. As in previous studies with bilinguals, vocabulary size in one language was not closely related to vocabulary size in the other language (Pearson et al., 1993), but interestingly, this was also the case for real-time processing speed. Young bilingual children's processing speed in Spanish was tied to vocabulary knowledge in Spanish, and processing speed in English was tied to vocabulary knowledge in English; neither was linked to processing speed or vocabulary in the other language.

Parra, Hoff, and Core (2011) found comparable within-language relations in 2-year-old Spanish-English bilinguals. Data were collected on children's household language exposure, vocabulary knowledge, grammatical knowledge, and ability to repeat novel words produced by an experimenter. While some evidence of language-general skill was found for phonological memory, the central finding was that exposure to each language accounted for significant variance in phonological memory skill in that language, and—in turn—phonological memory skill in each language predicted vocabulary and grammar in that language. Thus, in young bilingual children, there may be two independent tracks of cascading effects between language exposure and later language growth. Together with the study by Marchman et al. (2010), we can conclude that exposure, vocabulary, and processing travel together, such that (for example) lower vocabulary predicts slower processing, as in studies with monolingual children (e.g., Hurtado et al., 2007). Critically, this also parallels the robust finding that children who hear less language in the household show lower vocabulary (Hart & Risley, 1995) and slower language processing (Weisleder & Fernald, 2013).

One final line of research on bilinguals' word recognition skills returns to the focus on bilingual phonology: testing mispronunciations of known words. In these tasks, infants see two side-by-side pictures (e.g., a doll and a car) and a target object is either named correctly (e.g., *doll*) or incorrectly (e.g., *goll*). Monolinguals as young as 11 months showed reduced looking to the target when hearing mispronunciations relative to correct pronunciations, suggesting phonologically rich lexical encoding (Swingley, 2005). However, Spanish-Catalan bilingual 17- to 24-month-olds did not detect a mispronunciation in familiar words when the vowel change corresponded to the Catalan-specific /e/-/ɛ/ contrast, unlike same-age Catalan monolinguals. Bilinguals looked to the target object equally regardless of correct or incorrect pronunciation (Ramon-Casas et al., 2009). This was not due to a general inability to hear the distinction, as early discrimination problems resolve by 12 months. Their failure, however, does seem to be restricted to the Catalan-specific contrast, since mispronunciations consisting of contrasts common to both Spanish and Catalan hindered word recognition. Further, Ramon-Casas and Bosch (2010) noted that this study only used cognate words, which may have driven bilinguals' acceptance of mispronunciations. Indeed, they found that Spanish-Catalan bilinguals of the same age detected /e/-/ɛ/ mispronunciations when target words were not cognates (see Chapter 5 for further discussions of phonological encoding, including effects of input variability).

Conclusion

Research on bilingual lexical acquisition reveals striking similarities between bilingual and monolingual infants and toddlers. In the face of more variable input, infants acquiring multiple languages still reach similar milestones, have similar sized total vocabularies, and learn word-concept pairings in similar ways as their monolingual peers. Further, although input affects lexical processes in both populations, this link is more clearly revealed in bilingual infants due to the presence of two languages. The few discrepancies between the populations are primarily attributable to the presence of multiple labels for individual concepts, which increases children's willingness to map two words onto one object and engenders a greater acceptance of certain mispronunciations. Critically, these conclusions may shift as the field makes progress in understanding the intricacies of bilingual word learning.

References

Antoniou, M., Best, C.T., Tyler, M.D., & Kroos, C. (2010). Language context elicits native-like stop voicing in early bilinguals' productions in both L1 and L2. *Journal of Phonetics, 38*(4), 640–653.

Au, T.K.F., & Glusman, M. (1990). The principle of mutual exclusivity in word learning: To honor or not to honor?. *Child Development, 61*(5), 1474–1490.

Bergelson, E., & Swingley, D. (2012). At 6–9 months, human infants know the meanings of many common nouns. *Proceedings of the National Academy of Sciences, 109*(9), 3253–3258.

Bosch, L., & Ramon-Casas, M. (2014). First translation equivalents in bilingual toddlers' expressive vocabulary: Does form similarity matter? *International Journal of Behavioral Development, 38*(4), 317–322.

Bosch, L., & Sebastián-Gallés, N. (2003). Simultaneous bilingualism and the perception of a language-specific vowel contrast in the first year of life. *Language and Speech, 46*(2–3), 217–243.

Brackenbury, T., Ryan, T., & Messenheimer, T. (2006). Incidental word learning in a hearing child of deaf adults. *Journal of Deaf Studies and Deaf Education, 11*(1), 76–93.

Byers-Heinlein, K., & Fennell, C.T. (2014). Perceptual narrowing in the context of increased variation: insights from bilingual infants. *Developmental Psychobiology, 56*(2), 274–291.

Byers-Heinlein, K., Fennell, C.T., & Werker, J.F. (2013). The development of associative word learning in monolingual and bilingual infants. *Bilingualism: Language and Cognition, 16*(1), 198–205.

Byers-Heinlein, K., & Werker, J.F. (2009). Monolingual, bilingual, trilingual: Infants' language experience influences the development of a word-learning heuristic. *Developmental Science, 12*(5), 815–823.

Byers-Heinlein, K., & Werker, J.F. (2013). Lexicon structure and the disambiguation of novel words: Evidence from bilingual infants. *Cognition, 128*, 407–416.

Core, C., Hoff, E., Rumiche, R., & Señor, M. (2013). Total and conceptual vocabulary in Spanish–English bilinguals from 22 to 30 months: Implications for assessment. *Journal of Speech, Language, and Hearing Research, 56*, 1637–1649.

Davidson, D., & Tell, D. (2005). Monolingual and bilingual children's use of mutual exclusivity in the naming of whole objects. *Journal of Experimental Child Psychology, 92*(1), 25–45.

De Houwer, A. (1995). Bilingual language acquisition. In P. Fletcher & B. MacWhinney (Eds.), *The handbook of child language*, 219–250. Oxford: Blackwell.

Fennell, C., & Byers-Heinlein, K. (2014). You sound like Mommy: Bilingual and monolingual infants learn words best from speakers typical of their language environments. *International Journal of Behavioral Development, 38*(4), 309–316.

Fennell, C.T., Byers-Heinlein, K., & Werker, J.F. (2007). Using speech sounds to guide word learning: The case of bilingual infants. *Child Development, 78*(5), 1510–1525.

Fenson, L, Dale, P., Reznick, J.S., Thal, D., Bates, E, Hartung, J., Pethick, S., & Reilly, J. (1993). *The MacArthur communicative development inventories: User's guide and technical manual*. San Diego, CA: Singular Publishing Group.

Frank, I., & Poulin-Dubois, D. (2002). Young monolingual and bilingual children's responses to violation of the mutual exclusivity principle. *Journal of Bilingualism, 6*(2), 125–146.

Grosjean, F. (2010). *Bilingual: Life and reality*. Cambridge, MA: Harvard University Press.

Hart, B., & Risley, T.R. (1995). *Meaningful differences in the everyday experience of young American children*. Baltimore, MD: Brookes.

Hoff, E. Core, C., Place, S., Rumiche, R., Señor, M., & Parra, M. (2012). Dual language exposure and early bilingual development. *Journal of Child Language, 39*(1), 1–27.

Houston-Price, C., Caloghiris, Z., & Raviglione, E. (2010). Language experience shapes the development of the mutual exclusivity bias. *Infancy, 15*(2), 125–150.

Hurtado, N., Marchman, V. A., & Fernald, A. (2007). Spoken word recognition by Latino children learning Spanish as their first language. *Journal of Child Language, 33*, 227–249.

Junker, D. A., & Stockman, I. J. (2002). Expressive vocabulary of German-English bilingual toddlers. *American Journal of Speech-Language Pathology, 11*, 381–394.

Jusczyk, P.W., & Aslin, R.N. (1995). Infants' detection of the sound patterns of words in fluent speech. *Cognitive Psychology, 29*(1), 1–23. doi: 10.1006/cogp.1995.1010

Leopold, W. (1949/1970). *Speech development of a bilingual child, vol. 4*. Evanston, IL: Northwestern University Press.

Mancilla-Martinez, J., Pan, B.A., & Vagh, S.B. (2011). Assessing the productive vocabulary of Spanish-English bilingual toddlers from low-income families. *Applied Psycholinguistics, 32*, 333–357.

Mancilla-Martinez, J., & Vagh, S.B. (2013). Growth in toddlers' Spanish, English, and conceptual vocabulary knowledge. *Early Childhood Research Quarterly, 28*(3), 555–567.

Marchman, V.A., Fernald, A., & Hurtado, N. (2010). How vocabulary size in two languages relates to efficiency in spoken word recognition by young Spanish-English bilinguals. *Journal of Child Language, 37*, 817–840.

Marchman, V.A., & Martinez-Sussmann, C. (2002). Concurrent validity of caregiver/parent report measures of language for children who are learning both English and Spanish. *Journal of Speech, Language, and Hearing Research, 45*(5), 983–997.

Markman, E.M., & Wachtel, G.F. (1988). Children's use of mutual exclusivity to constrain the meanings of words. *Cognitive Psychology, 20*, 121–157.

Mattock, K., Polka, L., Rvachew, S., & Krehm, M. (2010). The first steps in word learning are easier when the shoes fit: Comparing monolingual and bilingual infants. *Developmental Science, 13*(1), 229–243.

Parra, M., Hoff, E., & Core, C. (2011). Relations among language exposure, phonological memory, and language development in Spanish-English bilingually developing 2-year-olds. *Journal of Experimental Child Psychology, 108*, 113–125.

Patterson, J.L. (1998). Expressive vocabulary development and word combinations of Spanish-English bilingual toddlers. *American Journal of Speech-Language Pathology, 7*, 46–56.

Pearson, B.Z., & Fernández, S.C. (1994). Patterns of interaction in the lexical growth in two languages of bilingual infants and toddlers. *Language Learning, 44*(4), 617–653.

Pearson, B.Z., Fernández, S.C., Lewedeg, V., & Oller, D.K. (1997). The relation of input factors to lexical learning by bilingual infants. *Applied Psycholinguistics, 18*(1), 41–58.

Pearson, B.Z., Fernández, S.C., & Oller, D.K. (1993). Lexical development in bilingual infants and toddlers: Comparison to monolingual norms. *Language Learning, 43*(1), 93–120.

Petitto, L.A., Katerelos, M., Levy, B.G., Gauna, K. Tétreault, K., & Ferraro, V. (2001). Bilingual signed and spoken language acquisition from birth: Implications for the mechanisms underlying early bilingual language acquisition. *Journal of Child Language, 28*(2), 453–496.

Place, S., & Hoff, E. (2011). Properties of dual language exposure that influence 2-year-olds' bilingual proficiency. *Child Development, 82*(6), 1834–1849.

Quay, S. (1995). The bilingual lexicon: Implications for studies of language choice. *Journal of Child Language, 22*(2), 369–387.

Ramon-Casas, M., & Bosch, L. (2010). Are non-cognate words phonologically better specified than cognates in the early lexicon of bilingual children. In *Proceedings of the 4th Conference on Laboratory Approaches to Spanish Phonology*, 31–36.

Ramon-Casas, M., Swingley, D., Sebastián-Gallés, N., & Bosch, L. (2009). Vowel categorization during word recognition in bilingual toddlers. *Cognitive Psychology, 59*(1), 96–121.

Ronjat, J. (1913). *Le développement du langage observé chez un enfant bilingue*. Paris: Champion.

Silvén, M., Voeten, M., Kouvo, A., & Lundén, M. (2014). Speech perception and vocabulary growth: A longitudinal study of Finnish-Russian bilinguals and Finnish monolinguals from infancy to three years. *International Journal of Behavioral Development*, *38*(4), 323–332.

Singh, L., & Foong, J. (2012). Influences of lexical tone and pitch on word recognition in bilingual infants. *Cognition*, *124*(2), 128–142.

Singh, L., Hui, T.J., Chan, C., & Golinkoff, R.M. (2014). Influences of vowel and tone variation on emergent word knowledge: A cross-linguistic investigation. *Developmental Science*, *17*(1), 94–109.

Swain, M. K. (1972). *Bilingualism as a first language*. PhD thesis. University of California, Irvine, CA.

Swingley, D. (2005). 11-month-olds' knowledge of how familiar words sound. *Developmental Science*, *8*(5), 432–443.

Taumoepeau, M., & Ruffman, T. (2008). Stepping stones to others' minds: Maternal talk relates to child mental state language and emotion understanding at 15, 24, and 33 months. *Child Development*, *79*, 284–302.

Thordardottir, E., Rothenberg, A., Rivard, M.-E., & Naves, R. (2006). Bilingual assessment: Can overall proficiency be estimated from separate measurement of two languages? *Journal of Multilingual Communication Disorders*, *4*(1), 1–21.

Umbel, V.M., Pearson, B.Z., Fernández, M.C., & Oller, D.K. (1992). Measuring bilingual children's receptive vocabularies. *Child Development*, *63*(4), 1012–1020.

Vihman, M.M. (1985). A developmental perspective on codeswitching: Conversations between a pair of bilingual siblings. *The International Journal of Bilingualism*, *2*(1), 45–84.

Vihman, M.M., Thierry, G., Lum, J., Keren-Portnoy, T., & Martin, P. (2007). Onset of word form recognition in English, Welsh, and English–Welsh bilingual infants. *Applied Psycholinguistics*, *28*(3), 475–493.

Weisleder, A., & Fernald, A. (2013). Talking to children matters: Early language experience strengthens processing and builds vocabulary. *Psychological Science*, *24*(11), 2143–2152.

Werker, J.F., Cohen, L.B., Lloyd, V.L., Casasola, M., & Stager, C.L. (1998). Acquisition of word–object associations by 14-month-old infants. *Developmental Psychology*, *34*(6), 1289.

Yavaş, M. (1995). Phonological selectivity in the first fifty words of a bilingual child. *Language and Speech*, *38*(2), 189–202.

10

ERP INDICES OF WORD LEARNING

What do they reflect and what do they tell us about the neural representations of early words?

Manuela Friedrich

HUMBOLDT-UNIVERSITY BERLIN, INSTITUTE OF PSYCHOLOGY, GERMANY. MAX PLANCK INSTITUTE FOR HUMAN COGNITIVE AND BRAIN SCIENCES, DEPARTMENT OF NEUROPSYCHOLOGY, LEIPZIG, GERMANY

Introduction

At a certain point in development, infants' mental representations of word meanings shift from low-level visual-auditory associations to higher-level connections that referentially bind word forms with semantic representations. This view of a representational transition from so-called "proto-words" to "genuine words" (Nazzi & Bertoncini, 2003) is widely accepted, but how such a change happens has been largely unknown. Does a particular state of brain maturation have to be achieved before elementary semantic representations can be established? Do genuine words develop from first-established proto-words? Do proto-words and genuine words develop independently at successive developmental stages, or does the emergence of genuine words begin parallel to the further establishments of proto-words? Until recently, it has not been investigated on which factors the transition from proto-words to genuine words depends. Moreover, even though the shift from perceptual-associative to referential semantic representations was claimed to underlie changes in infants' behavioral development, such as the emergence of the fast mapping ability or the onset of the vocabulary spurt (e.g., Nazzi & Bertoncini, 2003), it has been unknown when exactly the supposed transition in infants' word representations occurs.

The presence of genuine words is hard to prove. Behavioral methods cannot directly differentiate between knowledge based on perceptual memory and knowledge based on semantic memory. In behavioral measures, a distinction between perceptual and semantic memory can only be made by varying the kind of knowledge, e.g., by testing concrete vs. abstract words (e.g., Bergelson & Swingley, 2013). However, this kind of dissociation of proto-words and genuine words involves an interference with the developmental trajectory of the acquisition of concrete and abstract knowledge.

This means infants might be able to represent concrete knowledge in semantic memory, already before they are able to acquire abstract words.

Thus, the question on the first emergence of genuine words and a large range of other issues of early word learning cannot be resolved by means of behavioral methods alone. Measuring the infants' brain activity through event-related potentials (ERP) is one method to complement behavioral data and to provide information that may contribute to specify the nature of infants' early words.

The ERP represents voltage fluctuations at the scalp surface, which result from activity within brain structures involved in the processing of a certain stimulus type. It is calculated by averaging segments of the electroencephalogram (EEG) time-locked to the onset of a specified stimulus condition. Since ERPs access brain activity with high temporal resolution, they allow for distinguishing discrete stages of stimulus processing, such as perceptual and semantic stages of word processing.

The ERP consists of so-called "components." An ERP component is characterized by its positive or negative deflection (polarity), the temporal occurrence of its onset or its maximum with respect to stimulus onset (onset latency or peak latency), and its magnitude (amplitude). ERP components have typical spatial distributions over the scalp surface, they systematically vary with experimental manipulations, and they are assumed to reflect specific neural processes. Various components of the adult ERP are known to reflect unique perceptual, attentional, cognitive, and language-specific aspects of stimulus processing. ERP components can therefore mark the presence or absence of a certain processing stage, they can attest a particular ability, they may indicate processing speed, the amount of resources allocated, or the effort necessary to realize a particular task.

Despite their potential great benefit in providing brain signatures of certain abilities or defined developmental states, ERP studies in infants have been rare for a long time. This was only partly due to the fact that specific experimental equipment and special knowhow is required to perform an infant ERP study. The main reason was that we cannot generally equate infant ERPs with adult ERPs. Although some infant ERP components appear to be functionally equivalent to those of adults, other components are quite different from that of adults. These differences reflect the infants' early stages of brain maturation and their low developed perceptual, cognitive, and language abilities, as well as the commonly different experimental settings used in ERP studies with infants and adults. Even though we know the typical pattern of components in a visually or acoustically evoked infant ERP, until now, we are far from being able to assign a definite functional role to each component. Nevertheless, while we are still in the process of decoding of what an individual infant ERP component may reflect, some ERP components can already be utilized to contribute to specific issues of infant development.

The present chapter reflects this ambiguous situation. Before deducing mechanisms of word learning from the presence, absence, or responsiveness of certain ERP components, we have to know what neural processes these components indicate. Therefore, in the first part of the chapter, I review those infant ERP components that have been observed to be involved in the processing of words, and I summarize what brain mechanisms they appear to reflect. The second part of the chapter illustrates what kind of conclusions can be drawn when applying the ERP method to infant research. This part focuses on the experimentally induced acquisition of novel word meanings in infants from 3 to 16 months of age. Here, infant ERP components are utilized to determine the nature of infants' newly established words in both temporary and long-term memory. It is shown that the representational format of new word meanings does not only depend on the infant's age as an indicator of brain maturation and developmental stage, but also on the complexity of the learning environment and the infant's brain state subsequent to the initial acquisition of new word meanings. The results of a recent study particularly highlight the role of infant sleep in transferring individual experiences stored in temporary memory into semantic representations of long-term memory.

ERP components involved in word processing

Infant ERPs to words in isolation

N200–500

In early pioneering studies, Mills and colleagues (1993, 1997) investigated the ERP response to known words in groups of 13- to 17- and 20-month-old infants and compared the response with those to unknown words and backward presented words (nonwords). In these first infant ERP studies with unimodal acoustic word presentation, Mills and colleagues observed two early negative components, which were characterized by peak latencies of 200 ms and 350/375 ms, respectively, and were therefore called N200 and N350 (in 20-month-olds) or N375 (in 13- to 17-month-olds). In both age groups these early negative components were significantly larger for comprehended than for unknown words and nonwords. Since here, as well as in subsequent studies, the two early negative peaks responded similarly to the experimental manipulations, in further studies they were often integrated into a unitary component, the N200–400 (e.g., Mills et al., 2004) or, as we call it here, the N200–500 (e.g., Mills et al., 2005).

From these early findings one might conclude that the N200–500 reflects comprehension, that is, the presence of a certain word meaning in long-term memory and its activation when perceiving the appropriate word. However, a study with 10-month-olds demonstrated that during familiarization with repeatedly presented, initially unfamiliar words a broadly distributed N200–500 with frontal maximum emerged within an experimental session, even though only word forms were presented, such that infants had no opportunity to acquire the meanings of words (Kooijman et al., 2005). This finding suggests that the negativity in the 200–500 ms range reflects the perceptual processing of word forms, that is, the process of acoustic-phonological structure building during the perception of a word, which is facilitated by the repeated presentation of the word. This notion is still compatible with the findings of Mills and colleagues, because the perceptual experience with comprehended words is commonly much higher than that with unknown words.

On this view, exposure to comprehended words, i.e., word repetitions in the past, had specified and strengthened the phonological representations of the perceived words, which led to more efficient or more effortless perceptual processing of comprehended words. Thus, the N200–500 effect appears to indicate the eased acoustic-phonological word processing, which is based on the increase of either the short-term or the long-term familiarity with word forms. This N200–500 familiarity effect can therefore be utilized as an indicator of both temporary and long-term memory of word forms.

Late comprehension negativity

In the early studies of Mills and colleagues, an additional late negative component ranging from 600 to 1200 ms in 13- to 17-month-olds (called N600–1200 by the authors) and from 600 to 900 ms in 20-month-olds (called N600–900) responded to word comprehension. Again, this component was larger to comprehended than to unknown words, but only in the younger infant group with poor language abilities (as measured by their rated vocabulary), and neither in the 13- to 17-month-old infants with better language development nor in the older 20-month-olds (Mills et al., 1993, 1997). These findings suggest that the late negative component represents a rather immature response that reflects any brain mechanism that is particularly involved in the initial stages of word comprehension. Even though this late comprehension negativity has been interpreted as a sign of enhanced attention (Conboy and Mills, 2006), based on existing data, we can only speculate about the brain mechanisms reflected by this component.

Infant and adult ERPs to words in meaningful contexts

In studies with single words presented in isolation we cannot distinguish the effect of word comprehension from that of word familiarity. When aiming to investigate word comprehension without interference of familiarity, priming effects are favored. Priming effects for words indicate how word processing is affected by the immediately preceding presentation of a prime stimulus that contains information related to the target word. Providing that the underlying mechanisms of the relevant ERP components are specified, or that appropriate distinguishing experimental manipulations are created, ERP priming effects can reveal at which stage (e.g., phonological or semantic) the processing of the target word is altered by the prime information. Of particular interest in the context of word learning is, when semantic priming of word meanings emerges, that is, at what point in development a semantic word processing stage is eased by the immediately preceding presentation of semantically related information (see also Mani and Borovsky, this volume). The emergence of semantic word priming during the course of development could give hints about when the proposed transition from proto-words into genuine words occurs.

Adult N400 priming effect

In adults, semantic priming is indicated by the N400 in the ERP, a component with negative polarity, peak latency of about 400 ms, and amplitude maximum over the mid-central and mid-parietal brain regions (Kutas & Hillyard, 1980). A multitude of studies have consistently shown that the presentation of semantically related information prior to a target stimulus reduces the N400 amplitude to that target (for reviews, see Kutas & Federmeier, 2000, 2011). This N400 semantic priming effect indicates that the pre-activation of semantic information, which has been triggered by a word, a sentence, a picture, or any other semantically related context, eases the semantic processing of the subsequent target stimulus.

Infant priming effects: N400 and N200–500

Our first infant ERP studies on word comprehension were intended to find out whether an N400 priming effect can be observed in infants, and if so, at what age it emerges. We designed a picture–word priming study for German infants (Friedrich & Friederici, 2004, 2005a, 2005b) in which pictures of known objects presented on a screen were followed by combinations of acoustically presented indefinite articles *ein* (a, masculine/neuter) or *eine* (a, feminine) with real words or with word-like stimuli, e.g., *ein Ball* (a ball) or *ein Fless* (a fless). Words either named the object correctly (congruous condition) or named a different object (incongruous condition). Word-like stimuli were either pseudowords that followed the phonotactic regularities of German and could be viewed as unknown words (e.g., *Fless*), or nonwords that violated the phonotactic regularities of German and could not be considered as potential words (e.g., *Rlink*). In this design, each word occurred in both congruous and incongruous conditions, such that familiarity was held constant between the word conditions. In contrast, pseudowords and nonwords differed in the familiarity with their word forms insofar as pseudowords were constructed from familiar phoneme combinations, while the first syllable of nonwords contained phoneme clusters that, at word onset, German infants had never heard before.

We applied this cross-modal priming design to 12-, 14-, and 19-month-old infants as well as to adults (Friedrich & Friederici, 2004, 2005a, 2005b). In 19-month-olds, we observed two priming effects for the congruous word condition. First, from around 400 ms the broadly distributed negativity with centro-parietal maximum was reduced for congruous as compared to incongruous words (Fig. 10.1b: PZ), an effect that is similar to the N400 priming effect observed in adults (Fig. 10.1a: PZ; Friedrich & Friederici, 2005a). Therefore, this effect was interpreted as an infant N400 priming effect. And second, despite the fact that words presented in congruous and incongruous conditions were exactly the same, and thus did not differ in familiarity or word comprehension, the negativity over the outer lateral frontal regions in the 200–500 ms range was increased for congruous as compared to incongruous words (Fig. 10.1b: F7). Since the picture context was the only aspect that differed between word conditions, this early effect indicates that a word

128 Friedrich

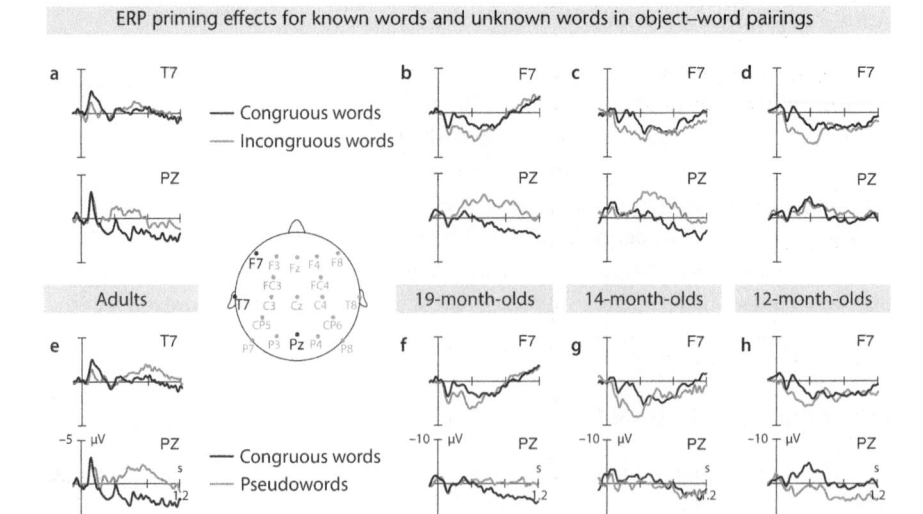

FIGURE 10.1 (modified from Friedrich & Friederici, 2005a, b)

a–d) ERP responses to congruous and incongruous words in the picture-word priming design with known objects and known words (real words). Note that due to conventions in ERP research, negativity is plotted upward. **a)** Adults (N=20): N200–500 word form priming effect at T7 and N400 semantic priming effect at PZ. **b)** 19-month-old infants (N=47): N200–500 word form priming effect at F7 and N400 semantic priming effect at PZ. **c)** 14-month-old infants (N=30): N200–500 word form priming effect at F7 and N400 semantic priming effect at PZ. **d)** 12-month-old infants (N=46): N200–500 word form priming effect at F7, no evidence for N400 semantic priming. **e–h)** ERP responses to congruous words and unknown words (pseudowords) in the picture-word priming design with known objects. **e)** Adults (N=20): N200–500 word form priming effect at T7 and N400 semantic priming effect at PZ. **f)** 19-month-old infants (N=47): N200–500 word form priming effect at F7 and N400 semantic priming effect at PZ. **g)** 14-month-old infants (N=27): N200–500 word form priming effect at F7, missing N400 semantic priming effect. **h)** 12-month-old infants (N=46): N200–500 word form priming effect at both F7 and PZ, no evidence for N400 semantic priming, late comprehension negativity at PZ.

processing stage prior to semantic processing was altered by the picture prime. We interpreted this N200–500 priming effect as being caused by the pre-activation of the acoustic-phonological structure of the expected congruous words, i.e., as a word form priming effect (Friedrich & Friederici, 2004, 2005a).

In 14-month-old infants the same priming effects as in 19-month-olds were observed (Friedrich & Friederici, 2005b; Fig. 10.1c), but in 12-month-olds, N200–500 word form priming occurred without responsiveness of the N400 (Friedrich & Friederici, 2005a; Fig. 10.1d). These results revealed that N400 priming to known words emerges between 12 and 14 months of age. The presence of semantic priming from objects to words in 14- and 19-month-olds clearly speaks for the presence of referential connections between words and their meanings from 14 months onwards. Since word form priming can be caused by both higher-level lexical-semantic connections and low-level perceptually based associations, the presence of N200–500 word form priming without co-occurring N400 semantic priming in

12-month-olds might suggests that up to 12-months-of-age infants have only non-referential associative connections between visual representations of objects and phonological representations of words available. Nevertheless, at that stage of research, we did not definitely know whether generally missing referential connections between words and their meanings are the reason for why semantic priming is lacking in infants up to 12 months of age. The missing maturation of brain structures involved in the particular semantic processing stage reflected in the N400, or the infants' insufficient memory development due to low experience or weak memory consolidation may also prevent an N400 effect (for discussions of this issue, see Friedrich, 2010, and Friedrich & Friederici, 2010).

Subsequent studies and post-hoc analyses of the data from these first studies provided evidence that the occurrence of the N400 priming effect as well as its strength, latency, and hemispheric distribution is related to the infants' state of behavioral language development. Infants with better early language abilities (high word production) displayed an N400 semantic priming effect already at 12 months, while infants with low to normal early language abilities did not show an N400 effect at that age, not even for those words that parents rated to be comprehended by their child (Friedrich & Friederici, 2010). At 19 months, children with lower comprehension abilities showed only a small N400 priming effect in the left hemisphere that occurred with a very late onset latency, while children with high comprehension abilities displayed a large N400 priming effect with much earlier onset latency, in which the right hemisphere was strongly involved (Friedrich & Friederici, 2004). When children were retrospectively grouped according to their verbal performance in a language test at 30 months, children with later age-adequate expressive language skills displayed a prominent N400 at 19 months, but children with later poor expressive language skills, who were at risk for a developmental language disorder, did not (Friedrich & Friederici, 2006). Similarly, in children at familial risk for developmental dyslexia, the N400 priming effect was absent at 20 months, while an N400 priming effect was present in the peers of the control group (Torkildsen et al., 2007). Importantly, in the two latter studies, the N200–500 priming effect was still present or even much enhanced, prolonged, and more broadly distributed in those groups that did not show an N400 priming effect, i.e., in the children at familial risk for dyslexia and in children with poor language skills later on. These results support the view that, compared to the N400, the N200–500 reflects a less demanding word processing stage that requires only a lower state of brain maturation or a lower state of language development.

Adult N200–500 priming effect

When applying the same picture-word priming design to adults, not only the expected N400 semantic priming effect, but also the N200–500 priming effect was detectable in the adult ERP (although with shorter latency and slightly more temporal distribution) (Friedrich & Friederici, 2005a; Fig. 10.1a: T7). This was the first time that N200–500 object–word priming was described for adults. We hypothesize that this unexpected adult ERP effect was caused by the experimental design specifically developed for infants, in which words were always presented at the basic level (e.g., the target word for the picture of a beach ball was *Ball* [ball] and not *Spielzeug* [toy] or *Wasserball* [beach ball]). The basic level is the most frequent and most familiar level of naming, making the appropriate word form highly expectable. In addition, the presentation of the word stimuli with a fixed time lag after the indefinite article provides information about the temporal occurrence of the word onset. Together, these methodological details induce a fully determined and temporally precise expectation about the occurrence of a certain word form with its specific phoneme combinations. This expectation is reflected in the N200–500 priming effect.

Infant N200–500 familiarity effect

The analyses of the ERPs to the unknown word-like stimuli revealed several additional aspects. For the focus of the present chapter two results are relevant. First, even though pseudowords and nonwords were both unknown, i.e., had an unfamiliar word form and were not comprehended, in 19-month-olds, the N200–500 was enhanced to pseudowords when compared with nonwords, an effect that appeared to be caused by the infants' familiarity with the phonotactically regular phoneme clusters of their language (Friedrich & Friederici, 2005a). This finding strengthens the interpretation that the N200–500 reflects a perceptually based stage of word processing, i.e., the acoustic-phonological processing of word forms.

Late negativity

Second, in 12-month-olds, pseudowords and congruous words did not only differ in the broadly distributed N200–500 (Fig. 10.1e: F7 and PZ), but also in a late negativity ranging from 500 to 1200 ms (Friedrich & Friederici, 2005a; Fig. 10.1h: PZ). This enhanced negative response to (at least partly) known words compared with pseudowords (i.e. fully unknown words) and resembled the late negativity (N600–1200) observed for comprehended words in the unimodal study with 13- to 17-month-olds (Mills et al., 1997). This effect was not seen in the older 19-month-old infants (Fig. 10.1g) and not even in 14-month-olds (Fig. 10.1f), although the N200–500 effect was present in all infant age groups (Fig. 10.1f–h: F7). However, when comparing incongruous words with pseudowords, i.e., conditions that were both unprimed by the picture context, incongruous words elicited a more negative response than pseudowords (compare Fig. 10.1 b and f and Fig. 10.1 c and g), suggesting that in 14- and 19-month-olds, the late negativity was present to congruous words as well, but was masked by an overlap with the temporally extended N400 semantic priming effect.

Summary of infant ERP components reflecting word processing

At this point we know three ERP components that indicate different aspects of word comprehension in infancy: first, the late negativity to known words, the reflection of a brain mechanism particularly involved in initial stages of word comprehension; second, the N200–500 that represents acoustic-phonological aspects of word processing and can account for any neural pathway between the representations of objects and words; and third, the N400 that indicates a semantic word processing stage and can prove the existence of referential connections between word forms and semantic representations, i.e. the presence of genuine words.

Learning-related changes in the infant ERP to words

Once we know these components, we can use them to observe how the infant brain acquires novel word meanings in experimental training sessions. The emergence of a particular priming effect can be taken to determine the nature of word representations built after a specified training phase in infants at a certain age. The comparison of priming effects during training with priming effects during a delayed memory test session moreover provides information about the retention, the decay, or the qualitative modification of these new word representations, that is, about whether they are transferred from temporary into long-term memory and how they are stored for long term.

The learning and retention of object–word mappings

In a first cross-modal infant word learning study, we showed that the ERP of 14-month-old infants effectively reflects the acquisition of new word meanings (Friedrich & Friederici, 2008). In the training session, infants were repeatedly exposed to pairs of initially unknown objects and initially unknown words. Eight object–word pairs were each repeated eight times, allowing the learning of object–word pairings. To remove pure repetition effects, in a control condition, eight other objects and eight other words were presented in pairs eight times too, but here each object was paired with each word once, such that only word forms and not word meanings could be learned. The comparison of these conditions revealed that consistently paired words elicited an N200–500 word form priming effect already within the first four presentations, indicating that infants had rapidly associated objects and words. In the second four presentations, an N400 priming effect emerged, suggesting that semantic representations had been established and linked with the appropriate word representations (Fig. 10.2a). In the memory test session one day later, the consistently paired words of the training session were presented each four times in correct (trained picture context) or incorrect conditions (untrained picture context). The presence of an N400 priming effect for the correctly paired words (Fig.10.2d) showed that infants had retained the newly acquired object–word mappings in lexical-semantic long-term memory.

Next, we adapted the design to younger infants by using the same word stimuli as in the initial design, but simpler, more brightly colored objects, and applied this modified design to 6-month-olds (Friedrich & Friederici, 2011). As in the older

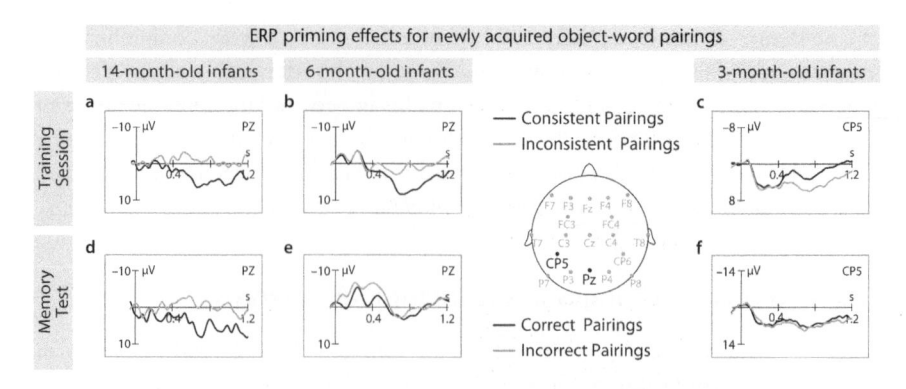

FIGURE 10.2 (modified from Friedrich & Friederici, 2008, 2011, 2015)

a–c) ERP responses to consistent and inconsistent pairings presented during the second half of the training session. **d–f)** ERP responses to correct and incorrect pairings in the memory test. **a, d)** N400 semantic priming effect in 14-month-old infants during both the second half of the training session (N=31) and the memory test one day later (N=16), indicating the learning and retention of genuine words. **b, e)** N400 semantic priming effect in the training session of 6-month-olds (N=44), but no evidence of N400 priming in the memory test one day later (N=39), revealing the temporary formation of genuine words and their missing retention. **c, f)** Late negativity in 3-month-olds during the training session (N=61), but no effect during the first half of the memory test one day later (N=31), indicating the rapid acquisition of proto-words and their missing retention.

infants, an N400 priming effect emerged during the second four presentations of the object–word pairings (Fig. 10.2b), suggesting that these young infants are already able to build semantic representations and link them to word forms presented together with these objects. Within the first four presentations, priming was not present, but three different word repetition effects were observed, including the increase in the N200–500. Interestingly, all these repetition-based effects occurred as priming effects for correctly paired words in the memory test, even though the N400 did not respond to the kind of pairing the next day (Fig. 10.2e). From the presence of N200–500 word form priming without co-occurring N400 semantic priming in the memory test of 6-month-old infants (which is a similar response pattern as observed for known words in 12-month-olds) we concluded that infants had retained any knowledge about the pairings of objects and words, but either the semantic representations established during learning or the referential link to them were not sufficiently consolidated in long-term memory.

The finding that 6-month-old infants are able to learn pairings of objects and words fits with behavioral observations that first signs of word comprehension are present from 6 months on (Shukla et al., 2011; Bergelson & Swingley, 2013). The more surprising result that, for temporary memory, an N400 semantic priming effect was observed in this young age group strongly suggests that basic semantic processing routines are functioning at 6 months of age, and, moreover, that these processing routines operate over at least simple genuine words.

The combined results of these ERP word learning studies in infants imply that, temporarily, referential connections between word forms and word meanings can be established very quickly and even at an early age, but they are not retained in long-term memory until 14 months of age (Friedrich & Friederici, 2005a, 2005b, 2008). However, the presence of N200–500 word form priming in the memory test of 6-months-olds suggests that non-semantic associative connections between objects and words exist in the infants' long-term memory from 6 months on.

In principle, however, infants might be able to learn object–word pairings even much earlier, because several abilities that are necessary for the acquisition of such pairings develop within an infant's very first months. In particular, already from birth, infants are able to associate auditory and visual information (Slater et al., 1999). Also, very early, they can detect statistic regularities (Kirkham et al., 2007; Bulf et al., 2011; Addyman & Mareschal, 2013), and at about 3 months, they categorize complex visual patterns, such as pictures of dogs and cats (Mareschal & Quinn, 2001; French et al., 2004). Thus, in order to explore the precursors of word learning, we applied the object–word learning design to a group of 3-month-olds (Friedrich & Friederici, 2015). In these very young infants, an N400 effect was not present, not even during learning, indicating that 3-month-olds do not involve a semantic processing stage when encoding pairs of objects and words. However, a late left-lateralized negativity from 500 to 1000 ms (similar to that found for known words in the unimodal study of Mills and colleagues) emerged to consistently paired words (Fig. 10.2c), revealing that infants had acquired object–word pairings after only a few presentations. In the learning test at the next day, this response disappeared (Fig. 10.2f), suggesting that the 3-month-old infants had forgotten the pairings. With increasing repetition, however, the late left negativity emerged again, this time in combination with an N200–500 effect, which clearly indicates that the 3-months-old infants had relearned the pairings even in the more difficult test phase, in which a certain object and a certain word were paired consistently in only half of their overall pairings.

Although, we still do not know, what particular brain mechanism the late negativity reflects, it indicates the rapid non-referential learning of object–word pairings by the immature brain that is known to already be able to associate the visual patterns of objects and related sounds. Thus, the late negativity in infants can be taken as a brain signature for the presence of proto-words in infant temporary memory.

The consolidation of simultaneously acquired object–word and category–word pairings

In current studies we focus on the consolidation of word meanings, that is, on the transfer of temporarily encoded information about words and their meaningful contexts into longer-lasting lexical-semantic memory (Friedrich et al., 2015). In our first consolidation study, 9- to 16-month-old infants were trained with both object–word pairings (specific word meanings) and category–word pairings (more

134 Friedrich

general word meanings). In this complex design with 24 initially novel words, 16 individual objects, and 64 objects forming 8 similarity-based categories, infants were able to acquire the specific object–word pairings (Fig. 10.3a), but not the general category–word pairings (Fig. 10.3b). For the object–word pairings, the late negativity was increased for consistently paired words, but the expected N200–500 and N400 priming effects remained missing, even in the older infants of the sample. Thus, infants had acquired low-level associations between objects and related word sounds instead of genuine words. This result suggests that the acquisition of object–word pairings remains at initial stages of word comprehension when the design is too complex for the investigated age group.

The absence of a comprehension effect in the category–word condition implies that infants did not encode general information about the category–word pairings.

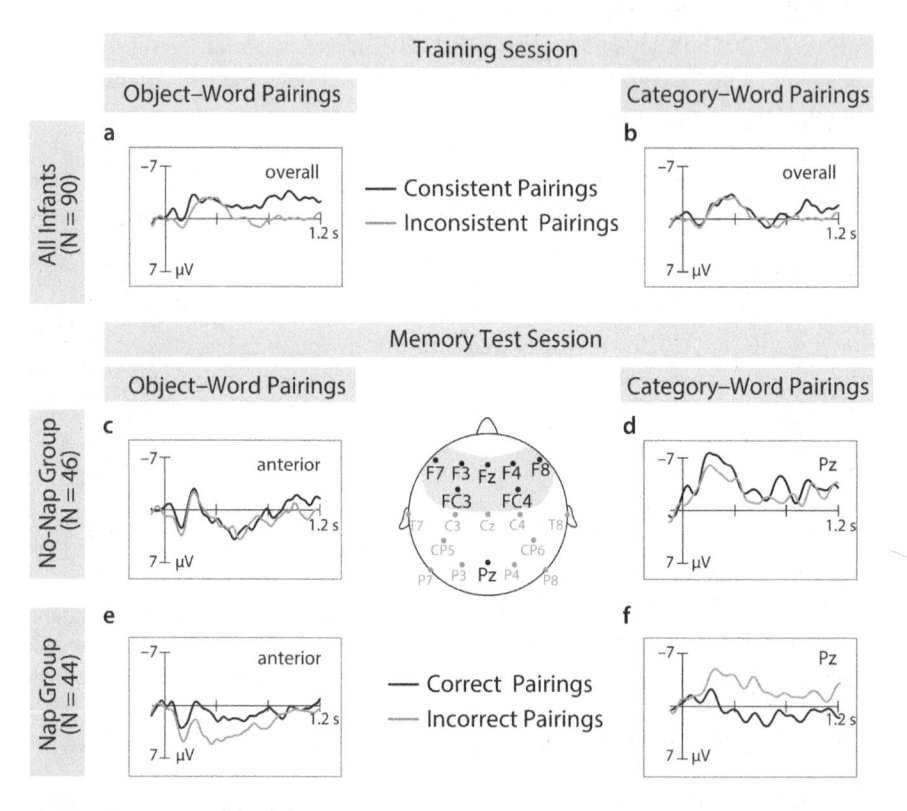

FIGURE 10.3 (modified from Friedrich & Friederici, 2015)

a–b) ERP responses to consistent and inconsistent pairings averaged over all electrode sites presented during the second half of the training session. **a)** Late negativity indicating temporary associative memory of the object–word pairings. **b)** No evidence for the learning of category–word pairings. **c–f)** ERP responses to correct and incorrect pairings in the memory test. **c)** No evidence for the retention of object–word pairings in the no-nap group. **d)** No evidence for the formation of category–word pairings in the no-nap group. **e)** N200–500 word form priming effect over anterior sites, indicating non-referential long-term memory for the object–word pairings in the nap group. **f)** N400 semantic priming effect at PZ indicating the existence of generalized genuine word meanings in the long-term memory of the nap group.

The missing effect, however, does not imply that infants did not acquire any knowledge in this condition. As the result of the memory test suggests, infants had encoded information about the pairings between individual category members and related individual words, but the encoding of these individual pairings could not cause a comprehension effect because category exemplars were not repeated.

In the memory test session about 1.5 hours later, infants, who had napped in the retention period, displayed an N200–500 priming effect for words that were correctly paired with the same objects as in the training phase (Fig. 10.3e), showing that infants of the nap group had transferred the newly encoded object–word associations from temporary into long-term memory. Importantly, for words that were correctly paired with novel, i.e., previously unseen category exemplars, an N400 priming effect was present in the infants of the nap group (Fig. 10.3f), revealing that during their nap, infants had built semantic categories and had linked them with the appropriate words. Thus, while sleeping, infants had created genuine words. In contrast, infants who did not nap forgot the object–word pairings acquired in the training session (Fig. 10.3c) and did also not create genuine words within the retention period (Fig. 10.3d). The results of this study show that the specific brain state subsequent to the initial acquisition of object-word pairings strongly affects the later memory for the pairings. While the wake state leads to rapid forgetting, sleep as the brain's offline state enables both the retention of the pairings, its reorganization, and its transfer into genuine lexical-semantic long-term memory. The study moreover implies that initially built proto-word representations that are indexed by the late negativity in the infant ERP constitute a sufficient neural base for the subsequent creation of genuine words, notably, without any further exposure to external stimuli.

Conclusions

The results of the infant ERP word learning studies have several implications for the development of word meanings and our view on the nature of infants' early words. First, from at least 3 months on, infants are able to represent their experience with co-occurring objects and words in form of perceptually based proto-words in temporary memory. Second, a semantic word processing stage is effectively established at 6 months, suggesting that word meanings built at that age can go beyond perceptually based associations. On the other hand, in complex learning tasks, even much older infants do not immediately establish referential links to semantic representations but acquire words and related meanings in the same way as 3-month-olds, that is, as pure perceptually based associations. In this case, moreover, the transition from proto-words to genuine words occurs delayed, during the brain's offline period of sleep.

According to the infant ERP word learning studies reviewed here, genuine words are present early in development, and they can arise from first established proto-words. However, proto-words are still built for a long time, even if genuine words have already been established in lexical-semantic memory. This implies that mental representations of proto-words and genuine words coexist during a period of at least several months. Thus, although the ERP priming studies with known words have shown that, generally, the quality of word representations in long-term memory depends on infants' developmental state, the results of the ERP word learning studies revealed that the transition from proto-words to genuine words does not occur at a fixed state of brain maturation. The quality of word representations in temporary and long-term memory is much more flexible than previously thought, and it is strongly affected by certain factors of the learning situation, such as the kind of learning material, the number of repetitions, the complexity of parallel exposure, and the infants' brain state subsequent to the initial acquisition of meaningful information.

References

Addyman, C., & Mareschal, D. (2013). Local redundancy governs infants' spontaneous orienting to visual-temporal sequences. *Child Development*, *84*(4), 1137–1144. doi: 10.1111/cdev.12060

Bergelson, E., & Swingley, D. (2013). The acquisition of abstract words by young infants. *Cognition*, *127*, 391–397.

Bulf, H., Johnson, S.P., & Valenza, E. (2011). Visual statistical learning in the newborn infant. *Cognition*, *121*(1), 127–132.

Conboy, B.T., & Mills, D.L. (2006). Two languages, one developing brain: Event-related potentials to words in bilingual toddlers. *Developmental Science*, *9*(1), F1–F12.

French, R.M., Mareschal, D., Mermillod, M., & Quinn, P.C. (2004). The role of bottom-up processing in perceptual categorization by 3- to 4-month-old infants: Simulations and data. *Journal of Experimental Psychology: General*, *133*(3), 382–397.

Friedrich, M. (2010). Early word learning – Reflections on behavior, connectionist models, and brain mechanisms indexed by ERP components. In J. Guendouzi, F. Loncke, & M. Williams (Eds.), *Handbook of psycholinguistic and cognitive processes: Perspectives in communication disorders*, 145–168. New York: Psychology Press.

Friedrich, M., & Friederici, A.D. (2004). N400-like semantic incongruity effect in 19-month-olds: Processing known words in picture contexts. *Journal of Cognitive Neuroscience*, *16*(8), 1465–1477.

Friedrich, M., & Friederici, A.D. (2005a). Phonotactic knowledge and lexical-semantic processing in one-year-olds: Brain responses to words and nonsense words in picture contexts. *Journal of Cognitive Neuroscience*, *17*(11), 1785–1802.

Friedrich, M., & Friederici, A.D. (2005b). Lexical priming and semantic integration reflected in the ERP of 14-month-olds. *NeuroReport*, *16*(6), 653–656.

Friedrich, M., & Friederici, A.D. (2006). Early N400 development and later language acquisition. *Psychophysiology*, *43*(1), 1–12.

Friedrich, M., & Friederici, A.D. (2008). Neurophysiological correlates of online word learning in 14-month-old infants. *NeuroReport*, *19*(18), 1757–1762.

Friedrich, M., & Friederici, A.D. (2010). Maturing brain mechanisms and developing behavioral language skills. *Brain & Language*, *114*(2), 66–71.

Friedrich, M., & Friederici, A.D. (2011). Word learning in 6-month-olds: Fast encoding – weak retention. *Journal of Cognitive Neuroscience*, *23*(11), 3228–3240.

Friedrich, M., & Friederici, A.D. (2015). The origins of word learning: Brain responses of three-month-olds indicate their rapid association of objects and words. *Developmental Science*, *20*(2). doi: 10.1111/desc.12357

Friedrich, M., Wilhelm, I., Born, J., & Friederici, A.D. (2015). Generalization of word meanings during infant sleep. *Nature Communications, 6,* 6004.

Kirkham, N.Z., Slemmer, J.A., Richardson, D.C., & Johnson, S.P. (2007). Location, location, location: Development of spatiotemporal sequence learning in infancy. *Child Development, 78*(5), 1559–1571.

Kooijman, V., Hagoort, P., & Cutler, A. (2005). Electrophysiological evidence for prelinguistic infants' word recognition in continuous speech. *Cognitive Brain Research, 24*(1), 109–116.

Kutas, M., & Federmeier, K.D. (2000). Electrophysiology reveals semantic memory use in language comprehension. *Trends in Cognitive Sciences, 4,* 463–470.

Kutas, M., & Federmeier, K.D. (2011). Thirty years and counting: Finding meaning in the N400 component of the event related brain potential (ERP). *Annual Review in Psychology, 62,* 621–647.

Kutas, M., & Hillyard, S.A. (1980). Reading senseless sentences: Brain potentials reflect semantic incongruity. *Science, 207,* 203–205.

Mareschal, D., & Quinn, P. (2001). Categorization in infancy. *Trends in Cognitive Sciences, 5*(10), 443–450.

Mills, D., Plunkett, K., Prat, C., & Schafer, G. (2005). Watching the infant brain learn words: Effects of language and experience. *Cognitive Development, 20,* 19–31.

Mills, D., Prat, C., Stager, C., Zangl, R., Neville, H., & Werker, J. (2004). Language experience and the organization of brain activity to phonetically similar words: ERP evidence from 14- and 20-month olds. *Journal of Cognitive Neuroscience, 16,* 1452–1464.

Mills, D.L., Coffey-Corina, S.A., & Neville, H.J. (1993). Language acquisition and cerebral specialization in 20-month-old infants. *Journal of Cognitive Neuroscience, 5,* 317–334.

Mills, D.L., Coffey-Corina, S.A., & Neville, H.J. (1997). Language comprehension and cerebral specialization from 13 to 20 months. *Developmental Neuropsychology, 13,* 397–445.

Nazzi, T., & Bertoncini, J. (2003). Before and after the vocabulary spurt: Two modes of word acquisition? *Developmental Science, 6*(2), 136–142.

Shukla, M., White, K.S., & Aslin, R.N. (2011). Prosody guides the rapid mapping of auditory word forms onto visual objects in 6-mo-old infants. *Proceedings of the National Academy of Science, 108*(15), 6038–6043.

Slater, A., Quinn, P.C., Brown, E., & Hayes, R. (1999). Intermodal perception at birth: Intersensory redundancy guides newborn infants' learning of arbitrary auditory–visual pairings. *Developmental Science, 2*(3), 333–338.

Torkildsen, J.V.K., Syversen, G., Simonsen, H.G., Moen, I., & Lindgren, M. (2007). Brain responses to lexical–semantic priming in children at-risk for dyslexia. *Brain and Language, 102,* 243–261.

11

COMPUTATIONAL MODELS OF WORD LEARNING

Gert Westermann and Katherine Twomey

DEPARTMENT OF PSYCHOLOGY, LANCASTER UNIVERSITY, UK

Introduction

Computational models of word learning have made important contributions to understanding the mechanisms underlying this process. Different models have addressed virtually all the aspects of word learning discussed in the other chapters of this book, from learning speech sounds and segmenting words from speech, to mapping words to objects and acquiring a lexicon. In this chapter we first motivate the computational modeling approach and discuss what it can contribute to our understanding of cognitive development in general and to word learning in particular. We then explain the basic principles of one widely used type of computational model—artificial neural networks. Finally, we review and evaluate several word learning models and their contributions to our understanding of this process.

Why computational modeling?

Computational models are computer programs that mimic some aspect of psychological processing. If their performance matches human behavior on a set of defined criteria, the mechanisms implemented in the model can serve as an explanation for the simulated human behavior. One way to look at a model is as a restricted artificial organism with a very limited set of specific behaviors. Such a model can be exposed to data similar to that experienced by humans in an experimental task (such as a speech segmentation task) or in their natural environment (such as hearing parental language), and the performance of the model (e.g., looking times in response to a set of stimuli) can then be compared with human data. It is then possible to manipulate the model, for example, by changing its internal processing mechanisms or the data to which it is exposed, to examine changes in performance. This approach can lead to predictions about human behavior in new situations which can be tested in experiments with human participants. In developmental psychology, computational models are often used to account for the change in cognitive abilities across age, allowing researchers to examine the effects of accumulating experience and changes in learning processes on the observed developmental trajectories.

One class of computational models that have been particularly powerful in furthering our understanding of cognitive development, and on which we focus in this chapter, are artificial neural network models, also called connectionist models (Mareschal & Thomas, 2007; Munakata & McClelland, 2003; Quinlan, 2003; Westermann & Plunkett, 2007). On a relatively abstract level these models are inspired by the functioning of neural networks in the brain. The basic idea here is that cognition arises from the complex interactions of many simple processing units (neurons in the brain). Consequently, connectionist models aim to show precisely how network structure, processing mechanisms and experience with the environment can give rise to such high-level processes. The most important property of connectionist models is that they can learn from experience with the environment (as detailed in the next section), making them ideally suited to model children's cognitive development as an interaction between internal learning processes and experience with an environment.

A large number of connectionist models have been applied to various aspects of word learning (e.g., Althaus & Mareschal, 2013; Aslin et al., 2006; Li et al., 2007; Mayor & Plunkett, 2010; McMurray et al., 2012; Räsänen, 2011; Samuelson et al., 2009; for an overview, see Westermann et al., 2009). These models suggest how such diverse empirical findings as vocabulary spurts, overextensions of meaning, the effects of labels on object categorization and many others can arise from general learning mechanisms. This chapter will review such computational approaches to word learning with a focus on artificial neural networks that link cognitive development to processes in the brain.

We first describe the principles of artificial neural networks and specifically the three most common types used in models of word learning. Instead of focusing on the minutiae of the models' functioning we hope to achieve two things. First, we discuss the overall design decisions that modelers face when developing a model. This point is often neglected but we think it might be interesting to non-modelers in helping to assess the usefulness of a model. Second, we discuss the general principles and contributions made by models to our understanding of numerous aspects of word learning discussed in other chapters in this book.

Principles of artificial neural networks

Artificial neural networks (ANNs) consist of often large numbers of simple processing units with weighted connections between these units. Although a variety of specific modeling paradigms exist, they share some common principles. In all models the units can be activated, and activation then flows through the connections to other units. How much activation flows through a connection depends on the strength (weight) of this connection, which can be positive or negative (or indeed, zero). Each unit typically sums up the activation it receives through these connections (or directly from the environment), and if this activation is greater than a certain threshold, or if it falls within a certain range, the unit becomes active itself and in turn sends activation through its outgoing connections. ANNs are loosely inspired by the basic principles of the functioning of biological neurons in the brain. These neurons receive activation through synaptic connections with other neurons, and if this incoming activation exceeds the neuron's firing threshold it creates a spike that then travels through its axon to the synaptic connections with further neurons.

Despite these superficial similarities between artificial and biological neural networks, ANNs should not be seen as attempts to implement the specific biological networks underlying cognitive development and processing—the function of biological neurons is, of course, far more complex than the described principles, and the number of neurons involved in a specific function in the brain are by several orders of magnitude larger than the number of units in even the largest ANNs. Nevertheless, ANNs show how even complex cognitive functions can emerge from the interactions of large numbers of simple nonlinear associative processors.

The most important property of ANNs for modeling cognitive development is their ability to learn from experience. Learning occurs through changes to the weights of the connections between neurons, resulting in changes in the activation patterns across the network. Different types of models vary in the specific way in which weights are updated, and they will be discussed below.

How a model experiences the world

Information is presented to neural network models in the form of strings of numbers that translate into the activation values of input units. For example, phonemes are often encoded by the presence or absence of phonetic features such as voiced, labial and plosive for consonants, and frontal and low for vowels. An input will include all possible features, set to 1 when the feature is present, and to 0 otherwise. Similarities between inputs can therefore easily be represented. For example, the only difference between the representations for /p/ and /b/ is that the "voiced" feature is set to 0 for /p/ and to 1 for /b/, while both phonemes have 1s for "bilabial" and "plosive" and 0 for all other features (depending on the specific feature description). Representations such as these, where similarities are reflected, are called *distributed* representations and they are chosen when similarity is assumed to play a role in processing (e.g., in modeling mispronunciations, priming, or categorization). In contrast, *localist* representations allocate a separate input for each item, for example, a word in a model of word-object mapping. This encoding scheme assumes that similarities between different inputs are irrelevant for the simulated process (such as mapping two distinct words to two distinct objects).

Another important aspect of computational models is the statistical structure of the environment. As discussed, neural network models learn from experience, and the more often a specific input or a class of inputs is experienced, the more the model learns from it. Therefore, many models of word learning aim to reflect

Computational models of word learning **141**

the statistical structure of a child's experience. For example, a model of vocabulary development could present words to the model according to the frequency with which these words are uttered to children (gleaned from corpora of child-directed speech).

Together, these factors show that the modeler has to make specific assumptions at each step of the modeling process. A computational model thus not only comprises the processing architecture but also the representation scheme of environmental information and the statistical structure of the environment of the system—an aspect that is sometimes forgotten when discussing and evaluating models.

We will now discuss the most common types of ANN that form the basis for many of the models of word learning.

Supervised learning

In supervised learning, a model receives an input and has to learn to generate a specific output as a response. Supervised models are usually arranged in a layered structure with an input layer that receives information from the environment, an output layer that generates a response, and a variable number of intermediate (hidden) layers (often just one; Figure 11.1). Often all units in one layer send outputs

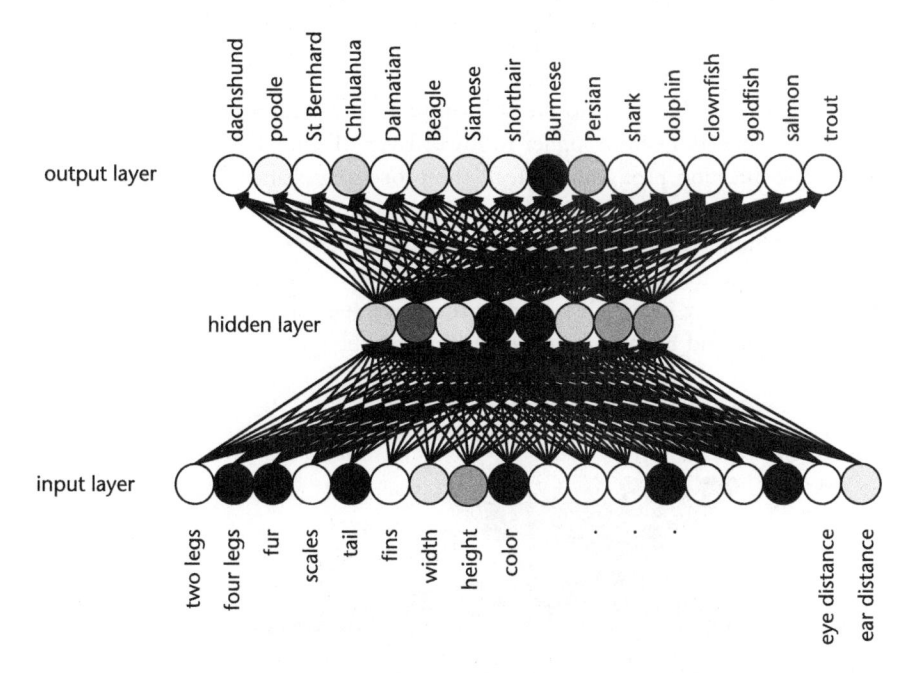

FIGURE 11.1 A three-layer neural network. This illustrative model learns the mapping from a set of features to an animal. Activation values are indicated by grayscale. Some activations on the input layer are binary (e.g., four legs: yes/no), others are continuous (e.g., width). On the output layer, several units can be activated to different degrees, reflecting the uncertainty of the model.

to all units in the next layer through weighted connections: strong connections send more information than weak ones. There can also be negative connection values so that one unit can inhibit the activation of a downstream unit. Recent "deep learning" models contain many more hidden layers but work on the same basic principles as these simpler models (Zorzi et al., 2013).

When an input is presented to a supervised model, the respective units on the input layer are activated and send activation to the hidden layer. Each unit in the hidden layer sums up the incoming activation and computes its own activation value as a function of this incoming activation. The hidden units then send their activation through outgoing connections to the output layer. There again, units become active as a function of their incoming activation. The pattern of output unit activations is then interpreted by the modeler as a response.

In a supervised model, the pattern of output activations is compared with a desired (target) pattern. Then, for each unit, the incoming weights are adjusted so that the actual output will become closer to the target output. In effect, when a unit's output is lower than the target value, its incoming connections from active units are strengthened. Conversely, when the output is higher than the target, connection weights are weakened. The most popular weight change algorithm that enables this process for multiple network layers is the backpropagation algorithm (Rumelhart et al., 1986). In effect, this algorithm sends error signals backwards through the network to generate target values for the internal (hidden) units that do not have an explicit target from the environment.

An interesting extension to "feed-forward" supervised models are those with recurrent connections from higher to lower layers (Figure 11.2). This apparently simple modification profoundly affects the processing characteristics of a model: now it can represent time and thereby process sequences. In the most common model, the Simple Recurrent Network (SRN; Elman, 1990), the hidden activation pattern for one input is presented to the input layer alongside the next input. Therefore, the way in which a model processes a specific input is affected by the previous input and becomes context dependent: the same input in two different

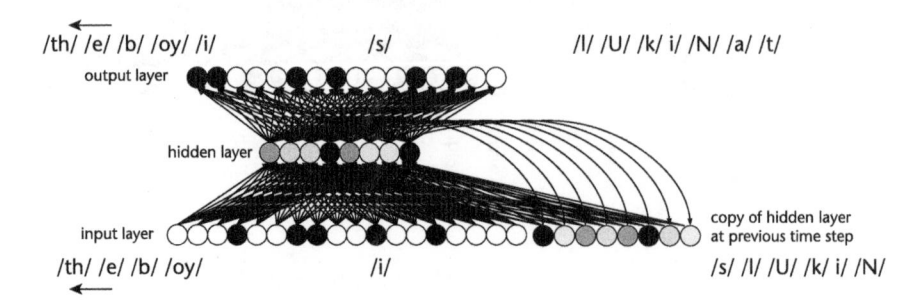

FIGURE 11.2 A simple recurrent network. This model is here presented with an unsegmented sequence of phonemes and has the task to predict the next phoneme in the stream.

contexts (i.e., with two different previous inputs and therefore two different hidden unit activation patterns) will lead to different activation patterns across the network. Recurrent models are presented with sequences of inputs and often the task of such a model is to predict the next item in the sequence (i.e., produce the next upcoming input on the output layer, before this input is actually presented to the model)—a task that is impossible to get correct all the time, but since predictability of the next item in a sequence often varies (such as in sentences: compare "She __" and "She switched on the __"), the model's prediction accuracy at each step is informative.

Unsupervised learning

In unsupervised learning, there is no target for learning. Instead the model learns independently, from the environmental information. One way in which this can happen is through *Hebbian learning*. Here, a connection between two units is strengthened when both units are active at the same time. Hebbian learning is thus well suited for learning associations between stimuli. Variations of this process exist. For example, connections can be weakened when the two units are active at different times, or they can decay when no unit activation occurs.

A second type of unsupervised learning that is often used in models of word learning is the self-organizing feature map (SOM; Kohonen, 1998). Here, units are arranged on a two-dimensional map (Figure 11.3). Inputs are presented to an input layer and activation flows through connections to all units on the map. The unit on the map that is maximally responsive to a specific input then changes its incoming connection weights so that at the next presentation of the same input, it will respond even more strongly. Importantly, all units in a predefined radius or

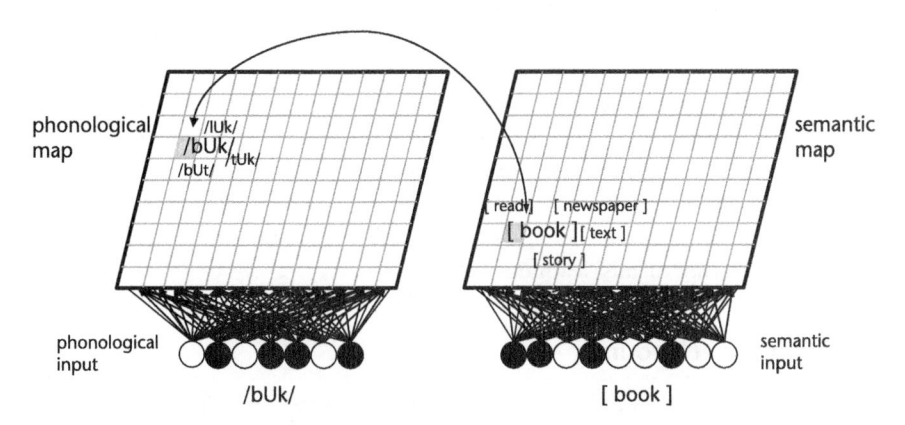

FIGURE 11.3 A model that consists of two self-organizing feature maps that are linked with Hebbian connections. In this illustrative example, the model learns, through co-occurrence, the link between a word and its meaning. On the phonological map, similar-sounding words cluster together, whereas on the semantic map, concepts with overlapping meanings are clustered.

"neighborhood" around this winning unit also change their weights in a similar way. Thus, regions on the map become responsive to similar inputs. The update radius is gradually reduced during learning so that learning becomes progressively more fine grained.

The final structure of an SOM reflects the statistical structure of the environment and similarity relationships between inputs. For example, a map that is trained on phonemes would usually develop one region for consonants and one for vowels (because of overlapping and distinct feature-based representations of both classes). Within each region, similarities between phonemes would be reflected, with similar phonemes located close together. This type of learning therefore only makes sense with distributed representations where similar inputs have overlapping activation patterns.

Self-supervised learning

Self-supervised learning falls between supervised and unsupervised learning. Here, the model is trained as in supervised learning, but it extracts the target without need for an external teacher. For example, in "auto-encoder" models, the target is the same as the input: the model has to learn to reproduce its input on the output layer. This is a useful task because in order to do so, the model has to extract and represent regularities in the input. As a consequence the model also learns to generalize what it has encountered to new information in meaningful ways. For example, when familiarized with a category of items, the model can generalize this learned category when tested with a novel object (Mareschal & French, 2000). The activation patterns of the hidden layer in the network can then be examined to understand how the model internally represents such information. Typically, as in SOMs, similar inputs lead to similar activation patterns of the hidden units.

Several other types of ANN exist, but those described here capture the majority of models of the various stages of word learning.

We now turn to a description of the contributions that specific models have made to our understanding of various aspects of word learning. While we focus on ANNs, we also discuss related models which employ different frameworks to illustrate ways in which different modeling techniques can be used to simulate the same phenomenon, and consequently make different predictions about the mechanisms driving infants' learning.

Learning speech sounds

As described by Benders and Altvater-Mackensen (this volume), the first task of the language learner is to develop a phonemic repertoire of the native language. Computational models have simulated this process to investigate the links between perception and production and the role of parental reinforcement in this process. Westermann & Miranda (2004) directly addressed the interactions between the auditory and motor system in shaping a speech sound repertoire. The model consisted of two neural maps. A motor map contained neurons that activated a number of articulatory "muscles" in a speech synthesizer simulating human speech production. An auditory map was activated by heard vowel sounds. Both maps were linked with Hebbian connections that were strengthened when motor and auditory units were co-active. The model babbled by randomly generating motor settings and producing the resulting sound, and as a consequence the links between motor settings and their resulting sounds were reinforced. Importantly, activation flowing through the between-map links affected the representations on each map so that articulatory-auditory pairs that were produced with high reliability became prototypical. In this way, nonlinearities in the articulation-sound mappings biased the model to preferentially produce and perceive certain sounds. The model also learned to adapt to an external language environment: speech sounds that were experienced in the environment selectively strengthened connections from the relevant auditory units to their associated articulatory settings. As a consequence, over time speech sounds produced by the model came to reflect the speech sounds in the environment. The process implemented in this model provided a mechanistic explanation of the articulatory filter hypothesis (Vihman, 1993), according to which the sounds an infant itself produces are more salient to that infant than sounds not in its speech sound repertoire.

A shortcoming of the Westermann & Miranda model was that it did not account for the speaker normalization effect, in which different speakers' phonemes are perceived equivalently despite between-speaker variability (e.g., Bladon et al., 1984); rather, the model assumed that self-generated sounds were perceived in exactly the same way as sounds produced by external speakers. Other models which have aimed to account for this effect by integrating a parent's reinforcement demonstrate that characteristics of parental input play an important role in shaping infants' early vocalizations (Warlaumont et al., 2013; Yoshikawa et al., 2003).

Segmenting words from a continuous stream

As described by Junge (this volume), words do not occur in isolation in the child's environment; rather, they have to be segmented from a continuous auditory stream. One way in which this complex ability can be achieved is by exploiting the statistical regularities of language at different levels: differences in the probability of one phoneme following another can be reliable cues for word boundaries. On the level of whole words, transitional probabilities between different words can enable the detection of the grammatical class of a word.

The idea that phonotactic probabilities are cues to word boundaries was explored by Elman (1990) using the first SRN model. The model was trained on a simple artificial corpus of phoneme strings with no indication of word boundaries. The model saw the current phoneme as input and had the task of predicting the next phoneme in the sequence. Elman found that the model's prediction error (that is, the uncertainty about the next phoneme) was usually high at the beginning of words and then decreased within a word. Thus, as the model learned the phonotactics of language, peaks in network error coincided with word boundaries because they formed the least predictable instance within the language stream.

The seminal Elman (1990) model was subsequently improved upon, most notably by Christiansen and colleagues (1998). Their model was also an SRN but used as input a real corpus of child directed speech, which not only provided phonemic information but also relative lexical stress and utterance boundaries. While these three cues individually were not reliable indicators, when they were learned together, the model could accurately predict word boundaries. Importantly, this model showed how the combination of accessible but unreliable statistical cues can together provide reliable cues for aspects of language for which there is no direct evidence in the input, and that an associative learner can extract this information from the language input. The focus on using actual language data on the statistical cues inherent in language—and on the powerful ability of statistical learners to extract and use this information—have been important drivers in the move away from the Chomskyan argument of the "poverty of the stimulus" and the inevitability of domain-specific innate language abilities (Chomsky, 1957).

Mapping words to objects

An intuitive approach to learning word-object mappings is to imagine a pool of words and a pool of objects. Word learning then consists in establishing links between an element in the word pool and an element in the object pool (see Figure 11.3). Pioneered by Miikkulainen (1993; 1997), this approach has been directly instantiated in a number of models based on self-organizing feature maps where units on one map become linked to units on the other through Hebbian learning, and has since been adopted by others (e.g., Mayor & Plunkett, 2010). The most advanced developmental word learning model based on linked feature maps so far is DEVLEX (Li et al., 2004) and its extension DEVLEX II (Li et al., 2007). The DEVLEX models explored the effects of the detailed statistical properties of the input heard by children on their lexical development. DEVLEX II consisted of three linked SOMs. A phonological map received word forms that were based on phonetic feature vector representations. A semantic map contained semantic concepts derived from large corpora of language. Finally, an output sequence map learned to generate sequences of phonemes to produce words. The model was trained on word-object pairings so that representations formed on the respective maps. In parallel, links between the maps were trained with Hebbian learning to strengthen for co-occurring words, semantic concepts and phoneme sequences.

Word comprehension in the model was simulated by presenting a word to the phonological map. The maximally active unit on this map then propagated activation through the Hebbian links to the semantic map, activating a unit that represented a semantic concept. Production was modeled by propagating activation from the semantic to the phonological output map. Training data was based on real input to children, using 591 words from the MacArthur-Bates CDI (Fenson et al., 1993), including verbs, adjectives, nouns from different categories, and closed class words.

Word meanings were represented by the distributional co-occurrence statistics of the target word in parental input to children (from CHILDES transcripts). These representations were learned and enriched gradually as learning progressed. During learning, words were presented to the model depending on their frequency in parental input.

DEVLEX II demonstrated the feasibility of simulating word comprehension and production in an associative model, modeling a range of phenomena observed in children's lexical development. First, it displayed a vocabulary spurt in the form of a phase of rapidly increasing word-meaning mappings after initial slow learning. This emerged from the simultaneous learning of organization within each map and connections between them. Once a basic organization on the maps had been achieved, inter-map connections could be learned rapidly and accurately. Furthermore, the model showed a lag in word production relative to comprehension and individual differences between iterations of the model in the onset of the vocabulary spurt. These differences were linked to the specific learning experiences of the model, with exposure to short and frequent words leading to an earlier onset of the spurt.

During word production the model generated errors that are commonly found in word learning children, such as leaving out final consonants (e.g., *ca* for *cat*) or consonants from consonant clusters (*mile* for *smile*) and substitution of consonants (*birb* for *bird*). These errors arose from incomplete sequence learning on the output map and incomplete links from meaning to words. Importantly, then, as well as capturing children's word learning trajectories, DEVLEX II also offered a mechanism for the errors they make during this process.

DEVLEX II nicely illustrated how a model can be seen as an artificial learner embedded in the same environment as a developing child: by simulating a realistic learning environment (within the confines of a disembodied learner), it provided insights into how the precise structure of the child's experience can shape the learning process. Subsequently DEVLEX II has also been applied to bilingual word learning (Zhao & Li, 2010) to investigate how differential onset of the two languages affects structure and interaction of phonological and semantic representations on the respective maps.

A different approach to learning word-object mappings was taken in Westermann & Mareschal (2014; for an earlier related model see Plunkett et al., 1992). In feature map-based models the representations that develop on each map are unaffected by the links between the maps. Nevertheless, it is possible that the different aspects of an object representation—visual appearance, auditory and functional features, the object name etc., become integrated so that different features can affect each other. For example, research with adults suggests that objects that share a name are perceived as more similar than the same objects if they do not share a name (Lupyan et al., 2007). In development it has been found that labels affect how infants represent visual objects: they group together objects that share a common label and separate similar objects that have different names (Althaus & Westermann, 2016; Gliozzi et al., 2009; Plunkett et al., 2008). Therefore, Westermann and Mareschal (2014) modeled how developing mental representations can be affected by common labels using an auto-encoder neural network. The way in which representations of different objects relate to each other can be assessed by examining the activation profiles of the hidden units: activation patterns for objects perceived as similar will cluster together (see also Rogers & McClelland, 2004).

Westermann and Mareschal (2012; 2014) provided their model with feature-based representations of 26 different object categories from four superordinate categories. When trained without language, the model developed object representations that were based on the visual similarity between objects. But when the model was enhanced by units encoding the category name for an object, the representational space in the model became warped to that object while different labels became more dissimilar.

This and other models also address the issue of the status of labels in early word learning. Two contrasting theoretical standpoints have been put forward. According to one, labels are qualitatively separate from the perceptual representation of objects and refer to these objects (Waxman & Gelman, 2009). This viewpoint is expressed in models that have separate maps for labels (e.g., Mayor & Plunkett, 2010; Li et al., 2007). According to another theory, labels, at least in very early word learning, are mere features of objects at the same representational level as other perceptual features. This viewpoint was instantiated in a model by Gliozzi et al. (2009) in which visual features and object labels fed into a single map that developed holistic object representations. The Westermann and Mareschal (2014) model implemented a third view: here, labels were separate from visual object descriptions, but through learning became closely integrated with them, leading to an object representation that took account of visual similarity modulated by the label. The status of labels in object representations remains a topic of ongoing research (e.g., Deng & Sloutsky, 2015) and predictions made by different models will likely be able to advance our understanding about this aspect of word learning.

Word-object mapping: Hypothesis testing or association?

The discussed models of learning word-object mappings all have assumed that the mapping to be learned is unambiguous: at each time, there is only one object and one word present from which to learn. While this simplification has been useful to further our understanding of lexical structure and the learning mechanisms involved, in the real world a word learning situation is often more ambiguous with several possible referents for a heard word (see Monaghan, Kalashnikova, and Mattock, this volume). While it has become clear that infants can track the co-occurrence probabilities between words and objects across learning situations and therefore resolve this ambiguity, there has been controversy about the mechanism underlying this ability.

One view argues that infants have implicit, relatively sophisticated *a priori* hypotheses about co-occurrence statistics and the probability that a word refers to a specific object, and that they test and confirm or reject these hypotheses based on some inference procedure, making a probabilistically optimal word-object mapping.

This mechanism has been implemented in probabilistic, Bayesian models. These models are based on prespecified probability distributions that determine the model's "decision-making" process; in this case, probabilities of words mapping to a particular referent. For example, Xu and Tenenbaum (2007) presented a Bayesian model which captured 4-year-old children's novel category label generalization in an empirical study which manipulated whether children themselves or the experimenter selected exemplar objects during training. The authors argued that the behavior seen in their empirical study cannot be accounted for by associative learning since their manipulation did not alter the statistical structure of the learning environment—and if all an associative learner does is to extract the statistics from the environment, this would not lead to different learning outcomes for these two conditions. Instead, they argued, their empirical results depended on a process of hypothesis testing. Specifically, the difference in training experience between the two groups (i.e., experimenter demonstration vs. independent choosing) had shaped children's hypotheses about the possible referents of the label, producing the contrasting generalization patterns seen at test. More generally, since the model was equipped with predetermined prior probabilities, this reflects a learning situation in which children have substantial prior knowledge, without, however, addressing where this prior knowledge may have come from.

An opposing view argues that correct word-object mappings (and the prior knowledge necessary to learn them) can be formed through associative learning. Yu (2008) presented a simple statistical associative learner that counted the co-occurrences of labels and their referents across learning events and calculated probabilities from these. The model received real linguistic input, consisting of a corpus of transcribed speech elicited from parents in a storybook narration task, and visual input, consisting of a list of the objects visible in the storybook at the time a given utterance was made. For each of these "scenes," the mapping between words and objects was ambiguous, and only around 5% of the co-occurrences were "correct." The model was tested by interrogating word-referent association probabilities calculated across the entire corpus. Like children, the model learned to associate words with their correct referents with a high degree of accuracy. Further, a second model, which could use its existing lexical knowledge to support the acquisition of new words, exhibited a vocabulary spurt. These models made important predictions about infants' word learning; in particular, that word learning is an incremental process, with word-object mappings starting out weak, but becoming stronger with experience. This "partial knowledge" account of word learning has recently been empirically tested and supported (Yurovsky et al., 2014), illustrating how models, with their explicit specification of mechanism, can shed light on real-world learning.

Taken together, these two models illustrate how modeling can force us to be absolutely clear what pre-existing knowledge and cognitive structures are necessary for learning. For example, on any given learning event both Yu's (2008) model and that of Xu and Tenenbaum (2007) make word-object mappings based on prior association probabilities. The critical difference is that in Bayesian models, those prior probabilities are determined *a priori* by the modeler, while in the associative model, prior probabilities are learned from naturalistic input. Thus, Yu's model relied on a probabilistic mechanism, but did not require the complex inferential processes or built-in knowledge central to Bayesian methods. More generally such differences between Bayesian and associative models once again speak to the core-versus-learned knowledge debate, with the former assuming native knowledge and the latter assuming that knowledge can be learned from the rich statistics of the environment. Models are therefore uniquely positioned to make important contributions to theory: modeling forces us to specify assumptions not only about the processing mechanisms but also about the representation and availability of data to the learner.

Timescales of language development

As described by Horst (this volume), from around 18 months, when infants are shown an array of two known and one novel object and are asked for a novel label (e.g., "Which one is the dax?") they often select the correct referent, i.e., the novel object. Traditionally this ability has been explained by intrinsic constraints such as mutual exclusivity (the knowledge that an object only has one name; e.g., Markman, 1991). McMurray et al. (2012) described a computational model in which referent selection arises from real-time competition between referents instead of such higher-level inferential processes. This model also addressed the finding that even when children select the correct referent, they often do not show long-term retention of the label-referent mapping (Horst & Samuelson, 2008). Specifically, the model demonstrated that while the mapping problem can be solved in the moment, this online association leads to only minimal strengthening of the word-object connection; to learn a robust word-object association takes many encounters of the same mapping. Thus, this model emphasizes the importance of cross-situational associative learning to capturing the real behavior demonstrated by infants in empirical studies of word learning.

Overall, by providing a mechanistic, low-level explanation of referent selection, McMurray et al. (2012) showed that observed behavior in children does not have to rely on high-level inferential processes (see also Twomey et al., 2016). As in Yu (2008) in this work, an apparently complex behavior can emerge from the interaction between two timescales of associative word learning: in-the-moment referent selection and cross-situational learning.

Conclusions

In this brief chapter it has been impossible to provide an exhaustive overview of computational models of word learning. First, a number of other neural network models not covered here have addressed different aspects of word learning (e.g., Colunga & Smith, 2000; Regier, 2005). Second, while we have mentioned two non-connectionist modeling approaches to word learning in Xu and Tenenbaum's (2007) Bayesian model and Yu's (2008) associative learner, there remain a range of other informative formal approaches to understanding word learning. One such approach consists in pure mathematical modeling. Notable here is McMurray's (2007) work on the vocabulary spurt, which demonstrates that the patterns of vocabulary acquisition commonly observed in children can be captured by a simple learning system situated in a structured learning environment without internal changes to the system that accelerate learning. Further, semantic network approaches have demonstrated that the age at which a word is acquired is influenced by the density of a word's semantic network and the diversity in the linguistic contexts in which this word typically occurs (Hills et al., 2010). Equally, Dynamic Neural Field models, a type of model related to the connectionist approach that focuses on how learning can occur on the basis of interactions between neural excitation and inhibition in large networks, have successfully captured a number of phenomena in early word learning (e.g., Samuelson et al., 2016; Samuelson et al., 2009; Samuelson et al., 2011).

Despite progress in these modeling approaches, currently neural network models have arguably made the strongest contribution to our understanding of the mechanisms of the development of word learning, providing explicit mechanistic accounts of often surprising phenomena and generating predictions that are subsequently captured in empirical studies with infants and children. Their strength lies in the ability to form complex associations (between words and objects, motor and auditory representations and so on) and to learn these multimodal representations from experience, thereby showing sensitivity to the statistical structure of their learning environment and the specific experiences to which they are exposed. In this way, these models have shown how the richness of the stimulus can overcome the need for innate learning biases and how specific learning trajectories can be explained by interactions between domain-general learning mechanisms and the precise structure of the learner's environment.

Acknowledgements

The writing of this chapter was supported by the International Centre for Language and Communicative Development (LuCiD; [ES/L008955/1]). The support of the Economic and Social Research Council is gratefully acknowledged. GW was further supported by a British Academy/Leverhulme Trust Senior Research Fellowship (SF150163), and KT by an ESRC Future Research Leaders fellowship [ES/N01703X/1].

References

Althaus, N., & Mareschal, D. (2013). Modeling cross-modal interactions in early word learning. *IEEE Transactions on Autonomous Mental Development, 5*(4), 288–297.

Althaus, N., & Westermann, G. (2016). Labels constructively shape object categories in 10-month-old infants. *Journal of Experimental Child Psychology, 151,* 5–17. https://doi.org/10.1016/j.jecp.2015.11.013

Aslin, R.N., Woodward, J.Z., LaMendola, N.P., & Bever, T.G. (2006). Models of word segmentation in fluent maternal speech to infants. In J. Morgan & K. Demuth (Eds.), *Signal to syntax: Bootstrapping from speech to grammar in early acquisition*. New York: Taylor & Francis.

Bladon, R.A.W., Henton, C.G., & Pickering, J.B. (1984). Towards an auditory theory of speaker normalization. *Language & Communication*, *4*(1), 59–69. https://doi.org/10.1016/0271-5309(84)90019-3

Chomsky, N. (1957). *Syntactic structures*. Mouton: The Hague.

Christiansen, M.H., Allen, J., & Seidenberg, M.S. (1998). Learning to segment speech using multiple cues: A connectionist model. *Language and Cognitive Processes*, *13*(2–3), 221–268.

Colunga, E., & Smith, L.B. (2000). Committing to an ontology: A connectionist account. *Proceedings of the Twenty-Second Annual Conference of the Cognitive Science Society*, 89–94, 1075.

Deng, W.S., & Sloutsky, V.M. (2015). Linguistic labels, dynamic visual features, and attention in infant category learning. *Journal of Experimental Child Psychology*, *134*, 62–77. http://doi.org/10.1016/j.jecp.2015.01.012

Elman, J.L. (1990). Finding structure in time. *Cognitive Science*, *14*(2), 179–211.

Fenson, L., Dale, P.S., Reznick, J.S., Thal, D., Bates, E., Hartung, J.P., ... Reilly, J.S. (1993). *The MacArthur Communicative Development Inventories: User's Guide and Technical Manual*. San Diego, CA: Singular Publishing Group.

Gliozzi, V., Mayor, J., Hu, J.F., & Plunkett, K. (2009). Labels as features (not names) for infant categorization: A neurocomputational approach. *Cognitive Science*, *33*(4), 709–738. https://doi.org/http://dx.doi.org/10.1111/j.1551-6709.2009.01026.x

Hills, T.T., Maouene, J., Riordan, B., & Smith, L.B. (2010). The associative structure of language: Contextual diversity in early word learning. *Journal of Memory and Language*, *63*(3), 259–273. https://doi.org/10.1016/j.jml.2010.06.002

Horst, J.S., & Samuelson, L.K. (2008). Fast mapping but poor retention by 24-month-old infants. *Infancy*, *13*(2), 128–157. https://doi.org/Doi 10.1080/15250000701795598

Kohonen, T. (1998). The self-organizing map, a possible model of brain maps. *Brain and Values*, 207–236, 568.

Li, P., Farkas, I., & MacWhinney, B. (2004). Early lexical development in a self-organizing neural network. *Neural Networks*, *17*(8), 1345–1362.

Li, P., Zhao, X., & MacWhinney, B. (2007). Dynamic self-organization and early lexical development in children. *Cognitive Science*, *31*(4), 581–612.

Lupyan, G., Rakison, D.H., & McClelland, J.L. (2007). Language is not just for talking - Redundant labels facilitate learning of novel categories. *Psychological Science*, *18*(12), 1077–1083. http://dx.doi.org/10.1111/j.1467-9280.2007.02028.x

Mareschal, D., & French, R. (2000). Mechanisms of categorization in infancy. *Infancy*, *1*(1), 59–76. https://doi.org/10.1207/S15327078IN0101_06

Mareschal, D., & Thomas, M.S.C. (2007). Computational modeling in developmental psychology., *IEEE Transactions on Evolutionary Computation*, *11*(2), 137–150.

Markman, E.M. (1991). The whole-object, taxonomic, and mutual exclusivity assumptions as initial constraints on word meanings. In S.A. Gelman & J.P. Brynes (Eds.), *Perspectives on language and thought: Interrelations in development*, 72–106. New York: Cambridge University Press.

Mayor, J., & Plunkett, K. (2010). A neurocomputational account of taxonomic responding and fast mapping in early word learning. *Psychological Review*, *117*(1), 1–31. https://doi.org/10.1037/a0018130

McMurray, B. (2007). Defusing the childhood vocabulary explosion. *Science*, *317*(5838), 631–631. https://doi.org/DOI 10.1126/science.1144073

McMurray, B., Horst, J.S., & Samuelson, L.K. (2012). Word learning emerges from the interaction of online referent selection and slow associative learning. *Psychological Review*, *119*(4), 831–877. https://doi.org/doi: 10.1037/a0029872

Miikkulainen, R. (1993). *Subsymbolic natural language processing: An integrated model of scripts, lexicon, and memory*. Cambridge, MA: MIT press.

Miikkulainen, R. (1997). Natural language processing with subsymbolic neural networks. *Neural Network Perspectives on Cognition and Adaptive Robotics*, 120–139.

Munakata, Y., & McClelland, J.L. (2003). Connectionist models of development. *Developmental Science*, *6*(4), 413–429.

Plunkett, K., Hu, J.F., & Cohen, L.B. (2008). Labels can override perceptual categories in early infancy. *Cognition*, *106*(2), 665–681. https://doi.org/10.1016/j.cognition.2007.04.003

Plunkett, K., Sinha, C., Møller, M.F., & Strandsby, O. (1992). Symbol grounding or the emergence of symbols? Vocabulary growth in children and a connectionist net. *Connection Science*, *4*(3), 293–312. doi: 10.1080/09540099208946620

Quinlan, P.T. (2003). *Connectionist models of development: Developmental processes in real and artificial neural networks*. Hove, UK: Taylor & Francis.

Räsänen, O. (2011). A computational model of word segmentation from continuous speech using transitional probabilities of atomic acoustic events. *Cognition*, *120*(2), 149–176. https://doi.org/10.1016/j.cognition.2011.04.001

Regier, T. (2005). The emergence of words: Attentional learning in form and meaning. *Cognitive Science*, *29*(6), 819–865. https://doi.org/10.1207/s15516709cog0000_31

Rogers, T.T., & McClelland, J.L. (2004). *Semantic cognition: A parallel distributed processing approach*. Cambridge, MA: MIT Press.

Rumelhart, D.E., Hinton, G.E., & Williams, R.J. (1986). Learning representations by back-propagating errors. *Nature*, *323*(6088), 533–536.

Samuelson, L.K., Kucker, S.C., & Spencer, J.P. (2016). Moving word learning to a novel space: A dynamic systems view of referent selection and retention. *Cognitive Science 41*(S1), 52–72.

Samuelson, L.K., Schutte, A.R., & Horst, J.S. (2009). The dynamic nature of knowledge: Insights from a dynamic field model of children's novel noun generalization. *Cognition*, *110*(3), 322–345. https://doi.org/10.1016/j.cognition.2008.10.017

Samuelson, L.K., Smith, L.B., Perry, L.K., & Spencer, J.P. (2011). Grounding word learning in space. *PloS One*, *6*(12), e28095.

Twomey, K.E., Morse, A., Cangelosi, A., & Horst, J. (2016). Children's referent selection and word learning: Insights from a developmental robotic system. *Interaction Studies 17*(1), 93–119. http://doi 10.1075/is.17.1.05two

Vihman, M.M. (1993). Variable paths to early word production. *Journal of Phonetics*, *21*(1–2), 61–82.

Warlaumont, A.S., Westermann, G., Buder, E.H., & Oller, D.K. (2013). Prespeech motor learning in a neural network using reinforcement. *Neural Networks*, *38*, 64–75. https://doi.org/10.1016/j.neunet.2012.11.012

Waxman, S.R., & Gelman, S.A. (2009). Early word-learning entails reference, not merely associations. *Trends in Cognitive Sciences*, *13*(6), 258–263. https://doi.org/10.1016/j.tics.2009.03.006

Westermann, G., & Mareschal, D. (2014). From perceptual to language-mediated categorization. *Philosophical Transactions of the Royal Society B: Biological Sciences*, *369*(1634).

Westermann, G., & Miranda, E.R. (2004). A new model of sensorimotor coupling in the development of speech. *Brain & Language*, *89*(2), 393–400.

Westermann, G., & Plunkett, K. (2007). Connectionist models of inflection processing. *Lingue E Linguaggio*, (2/2007). https://doi.org/10.1418/25655

Westermann, G., Ruh, N., & Plunkett, K. (2009). Connectionist approaches to language learning. *Linguistics*, *47*(2), 413–452. DOI: 10.1515/LING.2009.015

Xu, F., & Tenenbaum, J.B. (2007). Sensitivity to sampling in Bayesian word learning. *Developmental Science*, *10*(3), 288–297. http://doi.org/10.1111/j.1467-7687.2007.00590.x

Yoshikawa, Y., Asada, M., Hosoda, K., & Koga, J. (2003). A constructivist approach to infants' vowel acquisition through mother-infant interaction. *Connection Science*, *15*, 245–258.

Yu, C. (2008). A statistical associative account of vocabulary growth in early word learning. *Language Learning and Development*, *4*(1), 32–62. https://doi.org/10.1080/15475440701739353Yurovsky, D., Fricker, D.C., Yu, C., & Smith, L.B. (2014). The role of partial knowledge in statistical word learning. *Psychonomic Bulletin & Review*, *21*(1), 1–22.

Zhao, X., & Li, P. (2010). Bilingual lexical interactions in an unsupervised neural network model. *International Journal of Bilingual Education and Bilingualism*, *13*(5), 505–524, doi: 10.1080/13670050.2010.488284

Zorzi, M., Testolin, A., & Stoianov, I.P. (2013). Modeling language and cognition with deep unsupervised learning: A tutorial overview. *Frontiers in Psychology*, *4*. https://doi.org/10.3389/fpsyg.2013.00515

INDEX

Page numbers in *italics* refer to figures.

accents 83–84, 87–91
acoustic variability: accents 83–84, 87–91; asymmetric contrasts 8–9; bilingual word learning 114–115; bilingualism 119; infants'' word recognition 84–86; mispronunciations 83, 86–87; phoneme inventory acquisition 1–2, 7–9; vowel height and backness 7–8; vowels *vs.* consonants 5–7
acoustic-phonological processing 125–131
Acredolo, L.P. 37
adults: event-related potential indices 124–125; lexicon 57; words in meaningful contexts ERP studies 126–130
age *see* developmental time course
Akhtar, N. 47–48
alignment, structural 75, 76–77, 78
all-novel-object disambiguation trials 49–50
Altvater-Mackensen, N. 64, 144
American English 22, 25–26
amplitude and child-directed speech 36
animal research 2
Arias-Trejo, N. 61
articulation 5, 8
Articulatory Filter Hypothesis 3
artificial neural networks *141*, *142*, *143*; principles of 139–140; self-supervised learning 144; speech sound learning 144–145; supervised learning 141–143; word–object mapping 146–148
Aslin, R.N. 18, 89

association: computational modeling 148–151; cue combination 38–39; lexical networks 61; verb learning 75, 76, 78; word–object mapping 50
attention span and vocabulary size 101
attunement, perceptual 6–7
Au, T.K.F. 117–118
audio recordings 96–97
auditory system 2, 5
Australian accent 88

babbling 2–3, 6
backness in speech production 7–8
Baldwin, D.A. 37
Ballard, D.H. 33–34
Bayesian models 38, 149–150
behavioral measures of word learning 123–124
Benders, T. 144
Bertrand, J. 49
Best, C.T. 3
bi-accentual exposure 90–91
biases: intrinsic word-referent mapping constraints 31–33; noun bias 98; shape bias 45, 63–64, 65, 66; whole object bias 32, 37; word–object mapping 47
bi-dialectal exposure 91
bilabials 36
bilingual word learning: global estimates 110; lexical network 67; lexical processes 114–115; mutual exclusivity 32; vocabulary development 111–114; word

learning 115–118; word recognition 118–119; word segmentation 115
biological neural networks 3–4, 139, 140
birth order 100–101
book reading 105
Borovsky, A. 65
Bosch, L. 119
bottom-up approaches 20–22, 75–76
Boyer, T.W. 39
brain studies *see* event-related potential indices
Brown, C.A. 37
Brown, R. 97
Byers-Heinlein, K. 116, 117, 118

canonical babbling 2–3
Capirci, O. 36
Carpenter, M. 47–48
Caselli, M.C. 36
Cassidy, K.W. 36
categorization: internal biases 32; novel object categories 49; objects 45–46; semantic categories and lexical networks 63–64; speech perception 1–2, 6–7
category–word pairings 133–135, *134*
CHAT conventions 97
child-directed speech 35–36, 102–105
CHILDES system 97
Chinese 98
Christiansen, M.H. 36, 146
close set issue 61–62
co-distribution of cues 40
cognitive development 139–140
color as object category 63–64
components, ERP 124, 125–126, 131
comprehension *see* word comprehension
computational models *141, 142, 143*; artificial neural networks, principles of 139–140; phoneme acquisition 4; phonemes 140; self-supervised learning 144; speech segmentation 145–146; speech sound learning 144–145; statistical structure 140–141; supervised learning 141–143; word–object mapping 146–150
congruous words 127–128, *128*, 130
connectionist models *see* artificial neural networks
consonants 5–9
contextual cues 103
continuous speech and word segmentation *see* speech segmentation
contrast, principle of 47
contrasting sounds: categorical speech perception 2; labial and coronal consonants 8–9; native language attunement 4–5; vowel height and backness 7–8; vowels *vs.* consonants 5–7
conventional names 47
Conventionality, Principle of 47
conversation-eliciting speech 103
co-occurrences 33–34, 37–40
Core, C. 114, 118
coronal-to-labial change 8–9
corrective feedback, parents' 104
cross-situational learning 34–35, 74–78, 150
cues: co-occurring cues 37–40; extrinsic word learning cues 33–37; gesture use by parents 103; intrinsic word learning cues 31–33; parents" use of 103; segmenting words from speech 20–23; testing speech segmentation 18; verb learning 73–74; word–object mapping 47

Davies, R.A.I. 35
decontextualized language 104–105
deep learning models 142
developmental time course 62–63, 97–99, 150
DEVLEX models 146, 147
dialect 91
Diamond, A. 49
diary research 111–112
directives, parents' 103–104
disambiguation 34, 46, 49–50
distributional constraints 4, 34–35, 40
diversity, vocabulary 104
domain-general *vs.* domain-specific mechanisms 71, 78
dominant language and bilingual vocabulary 113
Dutch: bi-dialectal exposure 91; strong-weak word extraction 22
Dynamic Neural Field models 151
dynamic processing 58
dyslexia 129

early sound contrasts 7–9
electrophysiological studies: proto-word recognition and segmentation 23–25; speech segmentation 16, *17*, 18–20
Ellis, E.M. 65
Elman, J.L. 65, 145, 146
Emergentist Coalition Model 38
English: accents 87, 88–91; proto-lexicon 25–26; strong-weak word extraction 22; vocabulary acquisition 98; vowels *vs.* consonants in speech perception 6

English-French bilingualism 116
English-German bilingualism 112
English-Mandarin bilingualism 115, 117
English-Spanish bilingualism 112, 117–118
environmental factors in vocabulary size 101–102
ERP studies *see* event-related potential indices
errors, child 104
Evans, J.L. 65
event-related potential indices 123–125, *128*, *132*, *134*, 135–136; late comprehension negativity 126; lexical networks 60–62; N200–500 effect 125–126; retention of object–word mappings 131–135; testing segmentation of words from speech 16, *17*, 18–20, 23; words in meaningful contexts 126–130
expansion strategy and accent variability 89–90
explanations and child-directed speech 104–105
expressive vocabulary 98, 99
extra-linguistic cues *see* nonverbal cues
extrinsic cues 33–37, 37–40
eye-tracking studies 61–62

familiarity: effect on novel word learning 64–66; event-related potential indices 125–126, 127, 130; proto-word recognition and segmentation 23–25; speech segmentation 16, 18–20, 23; testing word–object mapping 51–52
fast mapping 39, 46, 50, 51
"feed-forward" supervised models 142–143
Fennell, C.T. 65, 116, 117
Fenson, L. 99, 100
Fernald, A. 35
Fernández, S.C. 112
first words 4–5, 96, 98
first-borns 100–101
Fisher, C. 77
Fitneva, S. 36
flexibility in verb use 104
Foong, J. 15
foreign language learning 31
French 6
French-English bilingualism 116
frequency 2, 7–9, 34
fricatives 2, 7
Fricker, D. 65
function as object category 63–64

gender and vocabulary size 100
generalization: and acoustic variability 85; computational models 149; overgeneralization errors 104; verb learning 73; word–object mapping 44, 49, 51
genetics and vocabulary size 99
genuine words 131–136, *132*, *134*, 135–136
German-English bilingualism 112
gestural cues 36–37
Gleitman, L. 72
Glusman, M. 117–118
Goodwyn, S.W. 37
grammar 36, 73
Gupta, P. 64

Halberda, J. 32
Hart, B. 96–97, 99, 102
Haryu, E. 75
head-turn preference method 16, *17*, 18–20, 23
Hebbian learning 143, *143*, 145, 146
heritability and vocabulary size 99
Hoff, E. 118
Horst, J.S. 39, 150
Huettig, F. 64
Huttenlocher, J. 100, 102
hypothesis testing 38–39, 75–79, 148–150

incongruous words 127–128, *128*, 130
incorrect association pruning 50
individual differences in word learning: birth order 100–101; early research methodology 96–97; environmental factors 101–102; gender 100; genetic factors 99; quantity and quality of child-directed speech 102–105; temperament 101
infant-directed speech 35–36, 102–105
input quantity and bilingual vocabulary size 112–113
intent as object category 63
Intersensory Redundancy Hypothesis 37–38
intonation and word-referent mapping 35
intrinsic constraints 31–33, 37–40
isolated word studies 125–126
Italian: vocabulary acquisition 98; vowels *vs.* consonants in speech perception 6
Iverson, J.M. 36

Jamaican accent 89
Johnson, E.K. 64, 89
joint focus and vocabulary acquisition 103
Jusczyk, P.W. 18

Kelly, M.H. 36
Korean 98
Kuhl, P.K. 3

labeling 148, 150
labial-to-coronal change 8–9
language-to-environment mappings 31–33, 31–37
late contrasts, early *vs.* 7–8
late negativity 126, 130
late-talking children 66
learning types and computational modeling 141–144
Leopold, W. 110, 111, 112
Lewedeg, V. 112
Lexical Gap Filling hypothesis 32
lexical networks: adult *vs.* children 57; developmental time course 62–63; familiarity and lexical acquisition 64–66; future research directions 66–67; perceptual overlap 63–64; phonological organization 59–60; semantic structure 60–61; structure, importance of 58–59
lexical processes and bilingual word learning 114–115
lexically irrelevant variability 84–85
lexicon *see* vocabulary acquisition and size
listening preferences 18
locational cues 48
Longobardi, E. 36
long-term memory 125, 126
low socioeconomic status 102

MacArthur-Bates Communicative Development Inventory 97–98, 99, 100, 101, 111, 146–147
MacWhinney, B. 33
Mandarin-English bilingualism 115, 117
Mani, N. 62, 64
mapping *see* word–object mapping
Marchman, V.A. 118
Mareschal, D. 147–148
mathematical modeling 151
Mattock, K. 34–35, 117
MCDI *see* MacArthur-Bates Communicative Development Inventory
McMurray, B. 39, 150, 151
McQueen, J.M. 64
mean length of utterance 104
memory: long-term memory 125, 126; perceptual memory 123–124; phonology 119; recent past and word–object mapping 47–49; retention of object–word mappings 131–136
Mervis, C.B. 49

methodology, research *see* research methodology
Mills, D.L. 125, 126
Miranda, E.R. 3, 144–145
mispronunciations 83, 86–87, 119
models, computational *see* computational models
Monaghan, P. 34–35, 36
motor experience 3
mutual exclusivity 32, 33, 47, 49, 117–118

N200–500 and N400 priming effects *see* event-related potential indices
narrative talk 104–105
native language: infants 2; speech perception 2, 3–5; speech segmentation 22–23
Native Language Magnet Theory 3
nativist stance 71, 78, 79
negativity, late 126, 130
Nelson, K. 98, 101
neural networks, artificial *see* artificial neural networks
neurobiology 3–4, 139, 140
Newman, R. 64
non-connectionism modeling 149–150
non-dominant language and bilingual vocabulary 113
non-nativist stance 71, 78, 79
non-rhotic accents 90–91
nonverbal cues 36, 47, 103
nonwords and event-related potential indices 125, 127, 130
noun bias 98
noun-to-object mapping *see* word–object mapping
Novel Name-Nameless Category principle 32
novel objects 49–52
novel words: familiar words, effects of 64–66; speech segmentation tests 16, 18, 19–20; transitional probability 21

object–word mapping *see* word–object mapping
object–word pairings *132*, 132–135, *134*
Oller, D.K. 112
online index of word recognition 19
other things present 49–50
overlapping words 59–60, 62, 113

"packaging problem" in verb learning 70, 78
parents: acoustic variability 90–91; computational models 145; extrinsic cues 33, 37, 39; quantity and quality of

speech 102–105; verb learning 70, 73–75; word–object mapping 47–50
Parra, M. 118
partial knowledge 149
partially mapped associations 65
past events, parents' descriptions of 105
Pearson, B.Z. 112, 113–114
perception, speech *see* speech perception
perceptual assimilation model 3
perceptual attunement 6–7
perceptual memory 123–124
Perry, L.K. 48
personality traits 101
phoneme inventory acquisition: artificial neural networks 140, 144–145; bilingual word learning 114–115; categorical speech perception 1–2; computational learning models 144–145; discussions and conclusions 9–10; labial and coronal consonants 8–9; N200–500 familiarity effect 130; pre-speech vocalizations 2–3; speech perception and early word learning 4–5; speech perception and production interplay 3–4; vowel height and backness 7–8; vowels *vs.* consonants 5–7
phonology: acoustic differences 83–84; bilingualism 117, 119; developmental time course 62–63; event-related potential indices 125–126; lexical networks 66; and lexical networks 59–60; memory skill 119; and vocabulary 58–59; word-referent mapping 35–36; *see also* acoustic-phonological processing
phonotactics: event-related potential indices 127, 130; lexical network building 64; word segmentation 20, 21–22, 145–146
picture priming paradigm 60–62; *see also* event-related potential indices
pitch 35, 85
plosives 7, 140
Plunkett, K. 61
pragmatic cues *see* socio-pragmatic cues
pre-speech vocalizations 2–3
priming 60–63; *see also* event-related potential indices
principle of contrast 47
Principle of Conventionality 47
prior retrieval of information 58
processing: accents 88; bilingualism 114–115, 118–119; event-related potential indices 125–131; lexicon structure 58; speed 84–85, 118; words in meaningful contexts ERP studies 126–131

productive vocabulary 98, 99
prohibitives, parents" 103–104
prosody and word-referent mapping 35–36
proto-lexicon: cues and speech segmentation 20–23; testing speech segmentation 16, 18–20
proto-words: event-related potential 135–136; future research 25–26; lexical acquisition facilitation 23–25
pruning incorrect associations 50
pseudowords 127, *128*, 130

quality and quantity of child-directed speech 102–105
questions and vocabulary acquisition 103, 105
Quine, W.V.O. 31

Rämä, P. 61
Ramon-Casas, M. 119
recall 105
recent past and word–object mapping 47–49
receptive vocabulary 97–98, 99
recordings, audio 96–97
recurrent models *142*, 142–143, 145
referential vocabularies 98
reliability of cues 39–40
repetition: proto-word recognition and segmentation 23–25; quantity and quality of child-directed speech 102–103; word–object mapping 48
research methodology: bilingual children's vocabularies 111–114; individual differences in word learning 96–97; testing segmentation of words from speech 16–20, *17*; word–object mapping 50–52; *see also* event-related potential indices
retention and word–object mapping 51, 131–135
rhotic accents 90
Risley, T. 96–97, 99, 102
Ronjat, J. 111, 112
Ross, E. 49

Saffron, J.R. 65
salience and phoneme inventory acquisition 2, 5, 7–9
Samuelson, L.K. 39, 48, 64
segmentation, speech *see* speech segmentation
self-organizing feature map 143, 144
self-supervised learning 144
semantic mapping 146–147

semantic memory 123–124
semantic priming *see* event-related potential indices
semantic structure: developmental time course 62–63; lexical networks 66; and lexical networks 60–61; novel word learning 65; vocabulary growth delays 58–59
Serres, J. 61
shape bias: lexical networks 66; novel word learning 65; object category names 45; semantic categories and lexical networks 63–64
short-term memory 126
simple recurrent network models *142*, 142–143, 145
Singh, L. 15
Sirri, L. 61
sleep and memory 125, 135
Smith, A.C. 35
Smith, L.B. 34, 39, 48, 65, 66
sociability 101
social cues *see* socio-pragmatic cues
socioeconomic status 99, 102
socio-pragmatic cues 32–33, 37, 38, 52, 73–74
sophistication, vocabulary 104
sound: categories of and phoneme acquisition 4; novel word learning 64; phonological overlap 59–60; *see also* acoustic variability
sound-symbolic properties of speech 30–31
Spanish accent 89
Spanish-Catalan bilingualism 119
Spanish-English bilingualism 112, 117–118
speaker normalization effect 145
spectogram *16*
speech, sound-symbolic properties of 30–31
speech perception: early word learning 4–5; infants 1–3; and production in infants 3–4; vowel height and backness 7–8; vowels *vs.* consonants 5–7
speech processing *see* processing
speech production: pre-speech vocalizations 2–3; and speech perception in infants 3–4; vowel height and backness 7–8; vowels *vs.* consonants 5–6; *see also* word production
speech segmentation 15–16; bilingualism 115; computational models 145–146; cues 20–23; proto-word segmentation 23–26; testing 16–20; testing methods 16–20

Spencer, J.P. 48
statistical learning: computational models 140–141, 145–146, 149, 151; extrinsic cues 33–34; phoneme acquisition 4; proto-lexicon 21; word–object mapping 47, 48
Storkel, H.L. 66
stress: accents 87; extrinsic word learning cues 35–36; mispronunciations 86; and pitch 85; speech segmentation 22, 146
structural alignment 75, 76, 78
super-novel objects 49
supervised learning *141*, 141–143, *142*
Swingley, D. 65
Switch task 116
symbol-grounding 30–31
syntactic bootstrapping theory 71–74, 75, 77, 79
syntax: diversity 104; lexicon structure 58

taxonomy and lexical networks 61
technology and research methodology 96–97
temperament 101
temporal context 47–49, 150
Tenenbaum, J.B. 149
testing methods *see* research methodology
thematic constraints and lexicon structure 58
Thiessen, E.D. 21
timescale, language development 62–63, 150
tokens and bilingualism 116–117
Tomasello, M. 47–48, 73, 77
tonal languages 85
top-down approaches 77–78
Torkildsen, J.V.K. 61
total conceptual vocabulary 113–114
transitional probability 21
translation equivalents 113, 114, 117, 118
twins studies 99

unfamiliar words *see* novel words
universal listeners 2
unsupervised learning *143*, 143–144

Van Heugten, M. 89
variability, acoustic *see* acoustic variability
variability, individual *see* individual differences in word learning
verb island theory 71–74, 75, 77, 79
verb learning 70–71, 78–79; association 75, 76; cross-situational statistics 35; flexibility in use 104; hypothesis testing 75, 77–78; structural alignment 75, 76–77; theories 71–74

Vihman, M.M. 3, 113, 115
visual similarities and word referents 65
vocabulary acquisition and size: acoustic variability and word comprehension 89, 91; bilingual children 111–114; bilingualism 118–119; birth order 100–101; computational models 147; environmental factors 101–102; familiarity and novel word learning 65–66; gender 100; heritability 99; individual differences, by age 97–99; lexical structure and growth of 63; mathematical modeling 151; quantity and quality of child-directed speech 102–105; and semantic structure 58–59; semantic structure and lexical networks 60–61; temperament 101
vocabulary spurt: bilinguals 112; computational models 139, 147, 149, 151; event-related potentials 123; lexical organization 66; word–object mapping 49
vocalizations: computational models 145; phoneme inventory acquisition 2–3; vowel height and backness 7–8
vowels 5–8

Walker-Andrews, A.S. 37
Welsh 115
Werker, J.F. 116, 118
Westermann, G. 3, 144–145, 147–148
White, K.S. 89
whole object bias 32, 37
Wilkinson, K.M. 49
Wojcik, E.H. 65
word comprehension: accents, effect of 89–90, 91; computational modeling 146–147; event-related potential indices 126, 127–134; mispronunciations, effect of 86–87; vocabulary size 97–98, 99; word–object mapping tests 51; *see also* word recognition

word order and vocabulary acquisition 98
word processing *see* processing
word production: computational models 147; expressive vocabulary 98, 99; testing word–object mapping 50–51; *see also* speech production
word recognition: accents, effect of 88; bilingualism 118–119; event-related potential indices 19; lexically irrelevant variability 84–86; *see also* word comprehension
word segmentation *see* speech segmentation
word stress *see* stress
word–object mapping 44; bilingualism 116; category names 45–46; closed set problem 62; computational modeling 146–150; computational models 150; cross-situational statistics 35; cue combinations 37–40; developmental time course 62–63; event-related potential indices 131–135, *132*; extrinsic cues 33–37; familiar words and novel word learning 64–66; fast mapping 46; intrinsic constraints 31–33; other things present 49–50; parental strategies to facilitate 103; phonological organization in the lexicon 59–60; semantic organization in the lexicon 60–61; semantic relationships 63–64; testing 50–52; *see also* verb learning
word-referent mapping *see* verb learning; word–object mapping

Xu, F. 149

Yu, C. 33–34, 39, 65, 76, 149–150
Yurovsky, D. 39, 65

Zipfian distribution 34

Taylor & Francis eBooks

Helping you to choose the right eBooks for your Library

Add Routledge titles to your library's digital collection today. Taylor and Francis ebooks contains over 50,000 titles in the Humanities, Social Sciences, Behavioural Sciences, Built Environment and Law.

Choose from a range of subject packages or create your own!

Benefits for you
- Free MARC records
- COUNTER-compliant usage statistics
- Flexible purchase and pricing options
- All titles DRM-free.

Benefits for your user
- Off-site, anytime access via Athens or referring URL
- Print or copy pages or chapters
- Full content search
- Bookmark, highlight and annotate text
- Access to thousands of pages of quality research at the click of a button.

REQUEST YOUR FREE INSTITUTIONAL TRIAL TODAY

Free Trials Available
We offer free trials to qualifying academic, corporate and government customers.

eCollections – Choose from over 30 subject eCollections, including:

Archaeology	Language Learning
Architecture	Law
Asian Studies	Literature
Business & Management	Media & Communication
Classical Studies	Middle East Studies
Construction	Music
Creative & Media Arts	Philosophy
Criminology & Criminal Justice	Planning
Economics	Politics
Education	Psychology & Mental Health
Energy	Religion
Engineering	Security
English Language & Linguistics	Social Work
Environment & Sustainability	Sociology
Geography	Sport
Health Studies	Theatre & Performance
History	Tourism, Hospitality & Events

For more information, pricing enquiries or to order a free trial, please contact your local sales team:
www.tandfebooks.com/page/sales

Routledge
Taylor & Francis Group

The home of Routledge books

www.tandfebooks.com